MOTHERHOOD DISCOUNTED

Care Work in America Before and After Roe

CAROLYN McCONNELL

SHE WRITES PRESS

Published in 2026 by
She Writes Press, an imprint of The Stable Book Group

1569 Solano Ave #546
Berkeley, CA 94707
https://shewritespress.com
Library of Congress Control Number: 2026904362
ISBN: 979-8-89636-314-9
eISBN: 979-8-89636-315-6

Interior Designer: Tabitha Lahr

Printed in the United States

In memory of Ann K. McConnell, who taught me that the world's ideas were mine for the thinking and whose dazzling mind I miss every day.

For Natalya and Tamar, who give me hope.

Contents

Introduction: Welcome to Motherhood!
You're Fired. vii
Chapter 1: Children as Pets 1
Chapter 2: The More Women, the More Witches 19
Chapter 3: Just So Stories. 39
Chapter 4: Family Values. 53
Chapter 5: The Grandmother Hypothesis 71
Chapter 6: The Girl Who Wouldn't Go Away. 85
Chapter 7: A Right Unknown 101
Chapter 8: No Fault of Her Own 123
Chapter 9: Faulty Vessels. 147
Chapter 10: The Prisoner's Dilemma 163
Chapter 11: Orphan Trains and Immigrant Cages 185
Conclusion: Crisis and Opportunity. 209
Notes 225
Acknowledgments. 269
About the Author 271

INTRODUCTION:

Welcome to Motherhood! You're Fired.

Self-reliant, self-made, independent—these are quintessential American compliments. To call someone a rugged individualist amounts to saying he's a real American. On the other hand, *dependent, co-dependent, needy* are not only insults but diagnoses of psychological defect. These values are so ingrained in our culture that most of the time we don't notice that they are symptoms of a toxic mythology that I call the "myth of autonomy." In this myth, independence is always good, and dependence always bad. Indeed, simply to be associated with dependency is to be tainted. Not coincidentally, the positive sides of these values are all manly virtues. Women are traditionally associated with dependency and assigned the work of caring for needy dependents, so denigration of dependency is fundamentally misogynistic. The autonomy myth has been deployed in different ways over time, but always in the service of power, especially power over women and their reproductive capacities.

My own family embraced the value of autonomy. I was raised to be independent, praised for my ability to take care of myself, entertain myself, think for myself. I was an only child and was expected to take responsibility for myself each day after school while my mother worked. I spent summers at our family's mountain cabin, roaming the woods and creeks unsupervised. As a young adult, I went to college thousands of miles from home, backpacked alone, drove across the country alone, and was fiercely insulted when a boyfriend tried to tell me I shouldn't do this. I considered independence my birthright.

But when I became a mother, I experienced a wrenching reversal of identity. I felt deep love, wonder, and joy at the remarkable being I had birthed, but I also felt cast out of the world of work and independence—exiled from the society of adults. Even while I was pregnant, I noticed some people's eyes slide quickly past my swollen form, as if they saw me only as an uninteresting and faintly grotesque container. I was awed by my new superpower, but the world processed only subtraction. I had added a new person to the world, yet somehow that meant I was no longer a full person.

Much of the day I was alone with a tiny, helpless, nonverbal, half-formed creature. Even as I experienced the deepest bond possible between myself and another human being, I was deeply isolated. I also felt kinship with every mother everywhere, each of us doing the work of making the human world go on. The dissonance between those feelings made me fiercely angry. At the moment that should have brought me into the center of society, I felt shunted to the margins.

With a totally dependent human intertwined with me—first *in* me, then literally hanging off my body—I was dependent on my spouse's assistance even to take a shower or go to the bathroom. My citizenship no longer computed. I had run smack into the autonomy myth, one aspect of which is that autonomy is a given and takes no work to achieve.

I have come to believe that the US's autonomy myth is the taproot linking the isolation I felt as a mother and the dysfunctions plaguing our politics. In this myth, the natural state for a person and the essential condition for full citizenship is autonomy, understood not only in its literal meaning of self-governance but also as self-sufficiency and lack of dependence on others. Therefore, the flip side of the autonomy myth is a dependency myth: If autonomy is the norm, then dependency must be either pushed out of sight or vilified as deviance. The thesis of this book is that this myth is both false and harmful as an ideal, warping US politics and stunting our country's ability to meet basic needs. Most especially this myth harms those who do the work of caring for dependents, including, and especially, mothers.

I didn't put it into words like this at first. I just knew that as much joy as motherhood brought me, it seemed a lot harder—and more unfair—than it had to be.

Before motherhood, I was almost comically naive. Our society is bizarrely segregated by life cycle; motherhood in the United States is a separate universe, of which those who are not parents can stay blissfully ignorant. I was white and middle class, but I was the child of a single mother, which should have given me some clue. My response to my exile from the world of adults was to want to get back in. When my maternity leave came to an end four months after my first child was born, I was delighted to return to paid work. But there was no going back. I was in for a rude awakening.

I had been warned. Other women had told me to keep my pregnancy a secret at work as long as possible. Many women get demoted or fired when their employers learn they are pregnant. When a friend of mine returned to work from maternity leave and refused to work more than full-time, she was told by her boss she was not being a team player and that she would have to wait for the promotion she had been expecting. There is no federal law forbidding discrimination against mothers, nor do most states bar it.

But I didn't work in the corporate world. I worked at a small, progressive nonprofit (I'll call it SPN). SPN was committed to social justice, community, supporting families, and walking our talk. After all, we had recycled carpet on the office floor and a worm bin out back where we composted our lunch scraps. We were all committed to the same idealistic project, and that brought kindness and warmth to the work. What I gave up in salary was more than made up for by the pleasure of working for a cause I believed in and the decency with which I was treated. I made more than the poverty rate for a single person, but less than what the local paper calculated would cover the basic costs of living for a person with a child in Seattle. Still, I knew that our executive director made only 17 percent more than I did. We were all in this together. So although the organization was too small to be covered by the Family and Medical Leave Act and had no maternity policies, I wasn't worried.

I requested a three-month unpaid maternity leave and to return to work half-time. My boss, S., said she would consider the request. There was silence for a month. Then S. said no to half-time. My coworkers got mad, marched as a group on the executive director. S. reversed herself, said I could come back half-time—as an "independent contractor." There was no room for bargaining. My choice was to take the job as a contractor or leave it. I didn't have the luxury of pondering the fact that the deal was manifestly illegal (there are clear criteria for independent contractor status, none of which my work fulfilled) or that there might be a reason my boss wanted to make me easy to dispose of.

As my spouse and I began puzzling out the problem of childcare, we learned that childcare is not like elementary school, where all you have to do is walk your child in the door. In the United States, you're on your own when it comes to childcare. There simply isn't enough quality care to fill all the need, so there are long waitlists for decent daycare centers. Full-time infant care typically costs several thousand dollars a month, easily as expensive as a mortgage, even in cities with expensive housing, such as Seattle. We decided to join forces with several friends and together hire a nanny, so that we could share the cost and be able to offer full-time work. But even so, for three days a week of care, the cost would be about the same as our monthly mortgage payment.

We would be paying more than half what I would be earning, before taxes. It was nearly irresistible to think this way, deducting the cost of childcare from my earnings alone, even though our daughter is as much my husband's child as mine. This is both because of the social assumption that childcare is the mother's responsibility and because of the structure of the US tax code, under which married couples file jointly. This means that the second earner's income is taxed at a higher rate than if she were single, and her income may very well push the family into a higher tax bracket. My spouse and I resisted this logic. We valued my having a career because it promoted equality in our relationship and brought me satisfaction. We also realized that proper financial accounting had to consider the future earnings I gained by keeping my career going. These factors are luxuries many families cannot afford.

When I returned to work, nobody pressured me to work extra hours. But somehow there was no longer a desk set aside for me. Where I once had an office with huge windows and a door that shut, now I shuttled between desks in cubicles as they were available. Even my voicemail seemed not to work consistently. I couldn't get our tech guy to make solving this problem a priority.

These were Very Bad Signs, but I was blithely unaware.

I was no longer included in most meetings, didn't get to help plan the organization's direction. I was no longer a full member of the team. Should it tell us something about the tilt of the playing field, that sports metaphors so dominate in our language about work?

I counted myself lucky to be allowed to play at all.

My contract was only six months long and was due to expire at the end of May. Since there was no suggestion that my work was no longer needed, I wasn't worried.

In early May, S. fired me.

She said my work had been unsatisfactory, mainly because I had been unavailable on the days I didn't work—though she never asked me to be available or to adjust my schedule. Because I was only an independent contractor and not an employee, she didn't technically fire me, didn't have to say or even think those words. Instead, she simply told me she was not renewing my contract.

When I applied for unemployment compensation, SPN contested my unemployment. The organization claimed that I hadn't been fired but instead had quit when I switched from full-time to half-time and became an independent contractor. I received an email from the operations manager of SPN:

> Just wanted you to know we received notice of your unemployment claim. On the form, they asked for the reason for separation. Given your desire to not return from maternity leave to your full-time staff position, the most accurate choice was "quit" rather than "discharge" or "lack of work" for example.
>
> In this process, I also learned that if you collect for even a couple of months, it would double our tax bill for four years, costing us $8,000 more in taxes. Since the decision to leave full-time, direct employment after your maternity leave was yours, SPN's unemployment tax rate shouldn't be increased.

> I don't think there's much either of us can do to influence their decision. We just fill out the forms they send us and the system will figure it out based on their policies.
>
> Take care.

I read this letter and sensed all its nuances of niceness and guilt-tripping and I wanted to throw up.

Soon after, I received six fat envelopes from the Employment Security Department. One letter read:

> You need to include an explanation for your failure to report the correct reason for your separation from this employer. Failure to report a material fact, in order to obtain benefits that you might not otherwise be entitled [*sic*], is considered misrepresentation (fraud) and carries an additional penalty . . .

It also asked when I began self-employment:

> What is your financial investment in this self-employment venture? What was your net income from self-employment during the last calendar year?

How long have you been beating your wife, Mr. Smith?

Another letter in the pile asked when I had decided to voluntarily quit and whether I quit because of a new job offer, relocation, domestic violence, unsafe working conditions, reduction of hours, illness, or disability.

Are pregnancy and childbirth disabilities? Pregnancy felt more like a heightened ability, my body suddenly displaying the capacity to build weird and miraculous alien life inside me.

And childbirth unleashed tremendous reserves of endurance and willpower. Yet it had disabled my ability to keep a job, apparently.

After an initial panic, I contested the claim that I had quit and that I had been an independent contractor. Eventually I won unemployment benefits. But that wasn't the end of the struggle.

After finally qualifying for unemployment, I received another letter from ESD, telling me that I had been "selected and scheduled" to participate in worker reemployment services that would assist me in my job search efforts. The class was three hours long, starting at 8:30 a.m. on Thursday, two days away. Attendance was mandatory. As if added as an afterthought, in a different font from the rest of the letter, the bottom of the page read:

> Our facility is not equipped for the safety of children. Please do not bring them to the workshops.

I pondered chickens and eggs. If I had enough money to pay for full-time childcare without a job, why would I need unemployment checks? Or a job, for that matter. I considered what the people who wrote the rules of unemployment insurance were thinking when they made these rules. The possibilities seemed to be one or more of the following: (a) they assumed workers had no children and that people sprang full-grown like mushrooms from the ground, just like the philosopher Thomas Hobbes said; (b) they assumed all workers had wives to take care of their children, a wife being a very nice thing and something I've always wanted for myself; or (c) the thought of how we all arrive on this planet and achieve the ability to hold a spoon, use a toilet, and say our names—never mind operate a forklift or a cash register or a computer—never crossed their minds.

Ninety percent of women become parents at some point in their lives. Given biology and our work culture, that will most likely happen smack in the middle of their working lives. But very few women have stay-at-home wives or house-husbands to care for their children. Lots of mothers will find themselves unemployed, yet the unemployment system is designed to exclude them. Among other things, if you're looking for part-time work, you're ineligible for benefits in most states. This matters not only because women need unemployment benefits but also because unemployment insurance helps to define what an ideal worker is, even who counts as a worker at all—who is an autonomous breadwinner and who is a needy dependent.

It seems to be all or nothing. You can stay at home or work full-time—or more than full-time. This is how the Mommy Wars between non-wage-earning and so-called working mothers was invented: Offer women a choice between two unhappy alternatives, then insist that their choices define their identities. And of course, divide them from each other. It was, as would eventually dawn on me, a classic autonomy myth trap.

As it happened, I was privileged enough to have childcare three days a week. But not at 8:30 a.m. on Thursdays. I called and rescheduled, but a few days later, I received a letter warning me that I had failed to report to a mandatory Job Hunter Orientation and demanding an explanation. Then a sweet-voiced investigator called to ask about my reason for not attending the Job Hunter Orientation. She asked me carefully if I lacked childcare just that one day or in general. I took the cue and said just that one day. Soon after, I received a bill to repay one day's worth of benefits: $37.

I went to the rescheduled Job Hunter Orientation and spent several hours waiting alongside women receiving TANF (welfare as we no longer know it) with their children in tow. We were eventually sorted into separate rooms, where we sat and waited. Finally I was called to see a counselor, who looked at my resume, tried to find a code to type in for "editor," and shook her head. "I'm getting nothing." She scanned further down my resume and saw I'd taught college courses, so she typed in a code for "teacher." Back came "Childcare Worker, $9/hour." That was the end of my orientation.

I eventually interviewed for a contract position with a major online news site. I did well in two rounds of interviews and was confident I was on my way to an offer. I casually asked if any of the work could be done from home. No, it couldn't, I was told, but the interviewer assured me that the department worked "banker's hours"—8:00 a.m. to 5:30 p.m. and only some Saturdays. I choked down a chortle as I realized how amnesiac our wired culture is. Once upon a time, banker's hours were 10:00 a.m. to 3:00 p.m., Monday through Friday.

My spouse and I conferred about childcare. We realized there was no way he could cover the days I would be at work, plus my commuting time. Even if there were a way to somehow line up additional childcare, I wouldn't want to spend twelve hours a day, five days a week, away from our daughter. It was only a temporary job, anyway.

I received an offer to teach part-time at a local community college. The classes ran five days a week. I asked about the childcare center on the campus, but the dean told me it had no affiliation with the college itself, so he couldn't help me get a slot. Still, I called the center. They didn't accept children under three.

I thought venomously about Linda Hirshman, the author of a much-ballyhooed article that garnered her appearances on *Good Morning America* and discussion in *New York Times* columns. She said women were choosing to drop out of the labor market. They had chosen badly, she scolded, and she dismissed the problem of lack of childcare. "Even with all the daycare in the world," women would have to make better choices.

"All the daycare in the world"—the phrase made me drool.

My husband and I decided that if I took the earliest teaching slot, from 7:00 a.m. to 9:00 a.m., and ran right home, he could just cover childcare for those times. Somehow we would find time for my course preparation. I turned down the well-paid, resume-building job with the major news site and accepted the modestly paid, dead-end, temporary teaching job. I also arranged to teach a night course at a local university extension program. I would be working full-time, without full-time childcare. I had made my choice, and I felt exhausted already.

In September, when my daughter was one year old, I started teaching. As if cued, my daughter woke each morning at 5:30 a.m., just before my alarm went off. I nursed her in the predawn dark, then slipped out of the bedroom, revving myself to liveliness as I drove toward the college.

I was frustrated and demoralized. I felt caught between impossible and contradictory demands. In the grip of the autonomy myth, our society has complementary assumptions about the nature of good workers and good mothers that make them mutually exclusive. A good mother—but not a good father—is someone who is available to respond to her child at any and every moment. On the other hand, a good worker is someone who is available for work at any and every moment. If a worker is not available at all hours, then she doesn't count as a good worker—or as a worker at all. In most state unemployment systems, you aren't entitled to unemployment benefits if you aren't available for any and all work hours in your field. As Evelyn Murphy and E. J. Graff say in *Getting Even*, their book on gender pay inequality, mothers in the workplace are often subjected to tests, to see if they choose family or work. They may be scheduled for extra-long hours or be asked to show up for meetings in the evenings or on weekends—but they weren't subjected to these demands before having children, and the men around them aren't subject to them regardless.

Eventually, I found my way out by earning a law degree, the badge of power and authority I needed in order to command a family-wage job. It gave me the chance to do battle with the likes of ESD and SPN on behalf of others. Going to law school while parenting small children was challenging, but while my classmates agonized over their class ranking, my babies kept me grounded with their smiles and first words and absolute needs.

My experience was peculiar to my race and social class, of course, and shaped by personal luck. My experience is not universal even among all American mothers. I don't know that many low-wage workers experience waged work as a source of independence, or that mothers in subcultures built on extended families feel as isolated as I did. But as I struggled to make sense of my experience, I believed it shared common causes with the experiences of every mother in this country, where the work of mothering doesn't count as work at all. This book is the product of my effort to understand those causes.

Although I have worked as a journalist, editor, and lawyer, I was also trained as a philosopher, and so this book is in part a search for the deep roots of the ideas that shape the culture of motherhood in the United States. To see women as fully human requires seeing dependency as an essential part of the human condition. This is the great unfinished business of feminism: As long as we devalue dependency work, women will never achieve equality.

The myth of autonomy is a major force contributing to the staggering rise in inequality in the United States in recent decades and our inability as a society to address it, let alone redress it. My focus is on mothers and motherhood and the puzzle of why this country so devalues mothers and makes motherhood, along with all forms of dependency work, a formidable barrier to equality.

Contrary to Hobbes, humans are not sprung like mushrooms from the earth. Our species is characterized by dependency. Unlike other species, our babies go through extended periods of helplessness and vulnerability. Whereas a giraffe baby, say, is up and running within hours of birth, human babies cannot even lift their own heads for months after birth and require years of intensive care if they are to survive. Humans need care at the other end of life as well, and many of us experience permanent or temporary disability at other points in our lives.

A full-grown healthy person, able to care for her own basic daily needs, is not the human norm. She is in fact a precarious achievement, made possible by infusions of work. Her ability to care for herself is a wonderful thing. To attack the myth of autonomy is not to deny that autonomy has value. It is rather to seek an ideal of autonomy that is not the opposite of dependency. For human beings, autonomy always arises from care work. It is always fragile, and it is never absolute.

In erasing the sources of autonomy, the myth of autonomy robs care providers of their autonomy and threatens the claim to full humanity of anyone who is dependent or even associated with dependency. This book seeks to place autonomy in its rightful context against a background of dependency, which must be understood as normal and not shameful. Another aim of this book is to demonstrate the profound derangement in the calls to "end dependency."

In the United States, the autonomy myth has apotheosized into privatism—that is, the notion that there is nothing higher or more transcendent than private property. This rests on an assumption that only waged work has value, and that a higher wage equals a higher value. This necessarily devalues those who provide care for dependents, overwhelmingly women who are typically unpaid or underpaid.

In our current political moment, when our social safety nets and public institutions are under attack and a toxic libertarianism is ascendant, this book's effort is urgent. The autonomy myth treats care work as a free natural resource, and, as a result, the United States has failed to sustain the labor that knits the fabric of our society together. That fabric is now dangerously frayed. The problematic concepts of debt and subsidy are also bound up with the myth of autonomy: Libertarians claim that hardworking grownups owe nothing to anyone and shouldn't have to subsidize anyone else. It's no coincidence that libertarianism tends toward a certain machismo. Reminding each libertarian that he had a mother who changed his diapers is to begin demonstrating the untenability of libertarianism.

Sections of the book explore the nature and sources of the myth of autonomy and the functions it serves. Then, across a range of issues, I use it to explain otherwise mystifying phenomena and opaque American debates. Throughout it all runs the deeper point that, until we confront and reject the myth of autonomy, we cannot achieve a just society in which women achieve full equality, in which women, too, can have autonomy.

Race is an inescapable element of the story, along with gender. Women and African Americans have, throughout America's history, been treated as twinned problems, raising related irritating questions about citizenship and democracy. Like women, African Americans have frequently been responsible for providing subsidies of reproductive labor for which they have not received recompense or even recognition. America's attitudes about gender are inescapably bound up with its attitudes about race. "African Americans" and "women" are not mutually exclusive categories, of course; misogyny and racism intersect. I have repeatedly found that satisfying explanations of puzzling facts emerge only when race is taken seriously. As a white woman, I cannot make sense of gender in the United States without accounting for race.

A note on terminology: Throughout the book, I have tried to avoid the term *caregiver*, in favor of *care provider* or *care worker*, in order to emphasize that care is work—and that it is not always freely given. Some authors writing on this subject, including the excellent Joan Williams, use the term "family work," but I don't find that phrase helpful. The word "family" tends to make my hackles rise, perhaps because I grew up in a unit—single mother and child—often smeared as "not a family." The word is too often used by the Right to label certain relationships legitimate and others illegitimate. The label also serves as a black box—or rose-blurred glasses—obscuring flows of labor and differentials of power within families. I find it more useful to consider dependency relationships between individuals, on the one hand, and the question of who benefits from a given system for the work of reproducing human beings and human society, on the other. The fundamental unit for discussing dependency and autonomy, as I see it, is care provider and care recipient. The most common instance of this unit is mother and child. The structure served by the autonomy myth is capitalism.

In general, I will refer to care providers as *women*, and use feminine pronouns for them. This is not to say that all—or only—women provide care. (I'm lucky enough to know some wonderfully caring men and nonbinary people.) But reproductive labor has long been socially coded as feminine and assigned to those gendered female. To paraphrase Silvia Federici, in capitalist society, "woman" is a work function—the function of reproducing the workforce—disguised as biological destiny. Therefore, it seems to me that avoiding feminine references would distort and obscure the power relations I aim to illuminate.

Capitalism profits both indirectly and directly from reproductive labor. Profit is extracted indirectly when one member of a family performs unpaid labor to create or restore another family member's ability to perform paid labor. Profit is extracted directly from waged or enslaved reproductive labor. The line between the indirect and direct extraction of profit from reproductive labor is drawn along class and racial boundaries, and both types have existed throughout the history of capitalism. To describe paid work in terms of care as emotion tends to obscure the hard, underpaid labor involved, as if it is done for love rather than money. This justifies its low pay.

For that matter, this same trick of calling it "love" rather than "work" applies to unpaid care work, justifying both its lack of support and women's consignment to it. Whether this work is paid or unpaid, as historian Premilla Nadasen has pointed out, whatever emotion the worker does or does not feel, care work is simply work that must be done to reproduce human life and society.[1] Therefore, the most precise and demystifying term for the work I discuss throughout this book is *reproductive labor*. But I will also use the term *care work*, because *care* is a short and familiar word, whereas *reproductive labor* is multisyllabic and unfamiliar to many. Furthermore, humans need to give as well as receive tender loving care.

I am a middle-class, cisgender, heterosexual, healthy, and nondisabled white woman. My insights come from my own experience, and no doubt I have blind spots and limitations, but I trust that I gesture at the full picture and inspire others to fill it in. This is a personal story as well as an analytical and journalistic one. I want to understand what I experienced when I was mothered, when I became a mother, and when I began caring for my aging mother. What will my daughters experience? How are these experiences shaped by those of my mother, grandmother, and foremothers stretching back beyond memory? How did we come to this particular, impossible moment in American history, and how can we get beyond it?

CHAPTER 1:

Children as Pets

When my children were small, during the phase when I was struggling to cobble together bits of freelance work, I wrote an article for a local news website about efforts to create a modest paid parental leave program in Washington state. The proposal was extremely modest: up to a couple hundred dollars a week for up to five weeks. By comparison, our neighbor to the north provides about a year of paid family leave. Most European countries are at least that generous, and Estonia provides more than a year and a half of paid parental leave.[1,2] (Estonia!) Or compare it with the US unemployment compensation system, which pays up to half a worker's wages for up to twenty-six weeks (more during economic crises, such as the COVID pandemic).

You might have thought there wouldn't be much opposition to this little bill. You'd be wrong. Republican legislators named the bill one of the top two worst bills of the year and the business lobby worked to kill it. But the blame can't stop there—Democrats controlled the state house, senate, and governorship, and they failed to fight for the program. While these forces didn't quite succeed in killing the law, they put it in a coma. The law did not receive any funding, and for ten years there was still no paid leave program in Washington. Progress has been similar in other states. As of 2017, a total of four states offered paid parental leave, but none provided more than six weeks' leave.[3] Meanwhile, nationwide, the United States remains one of only a few countries in the world that offer no paid parental leave, in company with Papua New Guinea and several tiny island nations.[4] In 2017, after years of effort by activists, the Washington legislature finally provided funding for family leave and increased the benefit to 90 percent of the worker's salary for up to twelve weeks. The first claimants began receiving benefits in 2020.[5] By 2025, the number of states offering paid leave had increased to thirteen, and in late 2020, the federal government finally began offering paid parental leave to its own employees.[6] But there is still no nationwide leave.

This struggle over a small state benefit provides a window into the autonomy myth and its importance in the smooth functioning of American capitalism. To begin to understand why creating a family leave program was so hard, I start with the comments on my article. There were a lot of them, and two-thirds expressed the same feeling: The legislation is "a token for the irresponsible," a "confiscation of my tax dollars" for "social parasites." One reader even called the legislation morally depraved. "Time off is good. All of that is fine, but just don't expect someone else to pay for it." "People should set priorities: By what right do these leave-takers confiscate my tax dollars to further their 'have it all' personal agenda?" "It's OK, Seattle, the government state will be your lifelong surrogate parent!"

These weren't mere trolls spewing the usual vitriol. There were no attacks on me personally, no profanity. By internet standards, the comments were high-minded and coherent. In fact, they reveal a whole philosophy: Start with the charges of irresponsibility and parasitism and getting someone else to pay for you to "have it all." To claim that a parent who receives social assistance for childrearing is irresponsible is to claim that childrearing is the responsibility of the parents alone. Having children is a personal agenda, and the "time off" (that is, from paid employment) to do it is a luxury for which one should expect no handout from the rest of society. Money taken in taxes and given to support childrearing is confiscation that in turn fosters, in the recipients, dependency on the state ("life-long" dependency, no less). Independence is good and normal; dependence is depraved and abnormal. Indeed, the goal should be to end dependency.

Presidential candidate Ben Carson said as much in a 2015 speech to the Conservative Political Action Conference. "I'm interested in getting rid of dependency."[7] US Senator Jim DeMint has written, "America must end its addiction to . . . subsidies . . . that lead to debt and dependency."[8] The House Ways and Means Committee declared that the major goal of the 1996 welfare reform act was to "attack dependency." Nor is this antipathy to dependence limited to the Right; as great a liberal lion as Eleanor Holmes Norton advocated for "weaning from public assistance" and stated that welfare is problematic because it "deepens dependence." Indeed, FDR himself said in his 1935 State of the Union address to Congress, "the government must and shall quit this business of relief."[9] The roots of this attitude go further back still, to the abolition of slavery and the end of the Civil War. One of the arguments against providing any assistance to the newly freed was that it would breed dependence. Even in the face of terrible epidemics among freed people in the war-ravaged South, and the danger that disease would spread to the white population, Congress refused to properly fund the medical division of the Freedmen's Bureau, let alone provide the promised forty acres and a mule. The argument went that assistance would only prolong the inevitable extinction of the inferior race.[10]

The commenters on my article were not expressing weird or fringe ideas; they were espousing a foundational, pervasive

American philosophy. It's so pervasive that it goes all the way down to pets and children. In Seattle, where I live, there are a lot of dogs. There are more dogs than children, actually, a fact that says a lot about this town. I do not have a dog, but I do have cats, so I get that people love their pets. Still, there are limits. Although I think pets should largely fend for themselves, on rare occasions I will take a cat to the vet, and when I do, the staff inevitably refer to me as the cat's "mother," sometimes when my actual human child is present. I find this to be both bizarre and telling.

Apparently, many people confuse children and pets. You might be tempted to think this is just Seattle-specific weirdness, but I got this idea from the economist Nancy Folbre, a proud Texan. If you think of children as pets, you will naturally be annoyed by demands that society provide support to parents, much as I am annoyed by the imposition of dogs and their turds in public space. The thinking goes like this: Parents acquire children because they want love and companionship. They want to lavish love on small, cute creatures, and in turn receive the adoration of said small cute creatures. (Sadly, children don't stay small and cute, and they don't always provide unalloyed adoration.) That's understandable, and perhaps it's more charming to get such pleasure from acquiring warm-blooded children or fuzzy poodles than from, say, purchasing statuary or playing massively multiuser video games. But who's to say who gets the most pleasure from their hobby: the pet owner, the parent, or the gamer? Either way, clean up the poop yourself, keep the critters quiet, and don't expect the rest of us to help pay the costs. In this mindset, children are like any other consumer good: a matter of individual preference and responsibility, to which only those who can afford the purchase are entitled.

This is exactly what the US Board of Tax Appeals stated in 1939, when it held that childcare expenses are not deductible as work-related expenses and instead that having children (while working) is merely a form of consumption that one person may happen to prefer. The board refused to consider childcare anything "other than a personal concern."[11] These are the basic assumptions underlying a refusal to provide social supports for childrearing, and in fact of libertarian politics more broadly.

As Folbre points out, however, the analogy quickly breaks down. While poodles will never become productive members of human society, human babies will—the flip side of their not staying small and cute. They will eventually become workers and taxpayers, contributing to Social Security, among other things. While it is a politically useful fiction that each of us pays for our own Social Security funds, in fact current benefits are paid by taxes on current wage earners. Those who are babies now will become the taxpayers who pay for the Social Security benefits of the current generation of wage earners when those wage earners in turn grow old. Of course they don't just "become" productive members of society; they are reared into grownups through the hard work of care providers. (Also, children are a terrible consumer good. In my experience, raising children is not particularly *fun*. If you were to set out to make a massively expensive purchase with the goal of maximizing your enjoyment, you'd be insane to pick a child.)

One of the most striking things about human beings that makes us different from other creatures is our long periods of dependency. First there is the nine-month gestation, one of the longer incubation periods among animals. Then comes birth, which is more difficult and perilous for humans than for other creatures, owing to our large brains and the narrow hips required for walking upright. Just getting a human born into the world requires a lot of work.

But that is only the beginning of the work required to get a human being to independent adulthood. A human baby is unable to lift its head for at least a month after birth, unable to eat solid food for six months, unable to walk until about a year.

Human children are typically dependent for twelve years or more, depending on the cultural context. Childrearing requires tremendous labor over a long period of time. To get each one of us from infancy to adulthood, someone had to change about six thousand diapers, make at least sixteen thousand meals, carry us for hundreds of miles, patch hundreds of wounds, clean up snot and vomit and urine and feces, bathe and dress and scrub—never mind rock, hold, comfort, say, "I love you." Each of us started as a parasite on a parent's labor, and many of us end our lives similarly dependent. Perhaps the idea is that this repugnant state shouldn't be allowed to spread beyond the helpless. But it can't help doing so, because someone has to provide care. To do the work of care, the care provider must curtail other, wage-earning work. She therefore becomes dependent on some other source of support. If parenting is the responsibility of the parent alone, it is puzzling how she could ever fulfill it.

Law professor Martha Fineman coined the phrase *autonomy myth*, and I draw heavily on her work. Fineman explains that there are two basic types of dependency. One is the basic helplessness in which all humans begin their lives and many end it. That helplessness includes raw physical need and also social neediness. Children must be taught how to behave appropriately and succeed as members of a social species, training that takes decades. This in turn generates the second form of dependency: To undertake care work, whether meeting the dependent's basic physical needs or teaching the social skills a child needs to survive, diverts care workers' efforts from working on their own behalf, which makes them dependent on support from some other source. Fineman calls this *derivative dependency*.[12]

With dependency built into human reproduction, perhaps no one should have children— which is a tenable position only if you prefer the human race to end. Even so, each of us arrives in a state of debt. Far from being pathological, dependency is universal and inevitable. Once you acknowledge this basic human fact, the goal of ending dependency is revealed as truly bizarre.

One of the commenters on my article wrote, "I for one am not planning on being a social parasite in my dotage." Perhaps he meant that he would off himself the moment he retired. If not, he was ignoring the question of who would be paying for his Social Security or Medicare benefits, let alone who would wipe his bottom in the nursing home in which he might find himself. That person would likely be a low-paid woman of color or immigrant. The comment betrays the seductive fantasy that, as human beings, we can escape indebtedness —"neither a borrower nor a lender be"—and owe nothing to anyone, free to reject the pleas for help of whinging, lesser beings. In Ayn Rand's novel *The Fountainhead,* a kind of bible of libertarianism, protagonist Howard Roark puts it this way: "I do not recognize anyone's right to one minute of my life . . . No matter who makes the claim, how large their number, or how great their need." Donald Trump, during his 2016 run for president, said he identifies with Roark.[13]

The autonomy myth makes visible only certain types of dependency and renders other types invisible, distorting questions of who owes what to whom, which is to say, allowing some people to profit from the work of others. It is a twisted notion of autonomy that has grown out of control, to the exclusion of other values and the distortion of a true understanding of human autonomy. The autonomy myth treats autonomy as a fact, a given, when it is actually a capacity created through the provision of care. This myth has deep roots in America's foundational ideas, but in embracing it, we have taken certain turns that were in no way historically inevitable and that have caused us to abandon other American ideals, among them equality.

One of the annoying features of reproductive labor in the United States is the tendency for it to become invisible. A clean house, well-prepared meals regularly on the table, and flourishing children are hardly ever noticed; it is their absence that disturbs. Sociologist Kari Wærness describes witnessing an incident in a home childcare facility that encapsulated the invisibility of good care: A child spilled a glass of milk at lunch. The childcare worker calmly said, "Uh oh, that's why we have plastic on the table," fetched a cloth, cleaned up most of the spill, then handed the cloth to the child to finish the job. He was immediately happy again, and the moment passed, with no one but Wærness noticing the skill involved—the care in preparing a child-proof environment, the "everyone-makes-mistakes acceptance of a small child's natural clumsiness; the avoidance of blame; the efficient, can-do solving of a problem; the child's assumption that he was part of the solution, expected to clean up a mess that he had made and presumed to have the competence to do it."[14] Anyone who has done childcare wishes for such skill.

Another annoying feature of reproductive labor is that its rewards bleed out and benefit those who didn't do the work. It is very difficult for a care provider to recoup all or even a fair fraction of the added value her labor created. I raise a child, who through my lavishing of care becomes a highly successful member of society. That child may care for me in my old age or may move continents away and cut all contact. I can't ensure that I receive the full return on my investment. It is also easy for the recipients of care work to ignore their indebtedness, at least in a culture that devalues care work.

This problem has arisen not just because we happen to have a large proportion of jerks among us but also because it is built into the structure of dependency work by the logic of individualized negotiation. A mother, or other dependency worker, needs the cooperation of others to obtain the necessary resources to care for her charge. If she is negotiating alone with another individual, this puts her at a disadvantage, because she is in a worse position than the other person if negotiation breaks down. The other person can walk away, but because of the vulnerability of her charge—whether it is a tiny infant, a disabled relative, or an ailing elder—the care provider cannot. Negotiation theorists speak of a BATNA, or Best Alternative to a Negotiated Agreement, otherwise known as your walkaway point, the moment when you say "forget it" to the rug seller or used car dealer because you know you're better off with no deal. It is the only standard that can protect you from accepting unfavorable terms. A family care provider negotiating individually has no BATNA. The absolute need of her charge means she can never walk away. This makes her inherently vulnerable to exploitation.

This dynamic most obviously affects unpaid care workers trying to provide care to their family members. Paid care workers, on the other hand, can walk away, at least in theory. But they, too, are placed at a disadvantage by the needs of their charges, whether those they are paid to care for or their own family members who are dependent on their wage. Furthermore, if their workplace is the home, where much reproductive labor takes place, they are as isolated as unpaid family care workers and thereby disempowered in their negotiations. Often bosses pretend that paid care workers are "just like family," to obscure power imbalances and justify low wages, long hours, poor working conditions, and lack of boundaries on the work. Furthermore, while the work of mothers and other providers of care work within families may be taken for granted, paid care workers are often erased entirely, with the boss taking credit for the clean house, delicious meal, or well-groomed children. If a care worker is undocumented or enslaved, she faces great barriers to walking away, the more so if she has children of her own.

The most plausible just so story I've ever heard about why women everywhere are oppressed by men and not the other way around lies in this structural vulnerability of care workers. The average lone man might be stronger than the average lone woman, but not that much stronger—and anyway, she can just walk away. She has a BATNA. But the average woman who has just had a baby cannot simply walk away. So she will make a bad deal. She will make bad deals again and again and again, from the dawn of history down to the present, to the point where we get foot-binding and femme couverte and the English system of primogeniture and disenfranchisement of women and clitoridectomy and domestic violence and the gender wage gap and on and depressingly on. This is so not because women are stupider or weaker than men, but, paradoxically, because we have a capacity that men lack, namely, the capacity to give birth.

This story explains why there is a general tendency for men to wield power over women. But it does not explain why we in the United States have the particular gender power structure we do. As I write above, it is easy for recipients of care work *in this culture* to ignore their indebtedness. But that begs the question at issue: Why should it be a downside for the benefits of care to flow out and benefit others? In many imaginable societies, that would make care workers highly valued. It is a downside specifically in a society in which only value that can be captured by an individual in the form of money counts—namely, a capitalist society.

We must be more specific in describing the cast of characters in our mythical negotiation if we want to accurately diagnose where we, in America, are today. The negotiation is built on a set of four relationships—dependent, care provider, wage earner, and wage payer—that are ultimately unequal. The dependent's capacity to care for herself is unequal to that of either care provider or wage earner, and the power of both dependent and care provider is unequal to the wage earner's, whose power in turn is unequal to the wage payer's. When the care provider is paid, the roles of care provider and wage earner collapse into one. In that case the paid care worker is typically low-paid as well as disadvantaged because no one else provides her with care to help sustain her waged work. The care provider supplies labor that the dependent needs, and which cumulatively will transform the dependent into a wage earner with skills that some wage payer in the future will need, and that in a larger sense the human race needs in order to continue. But the dependent usually cannot pay her. And the dependent's absolute need creates a moral obligation for the care provider to continue providing care. Furthermore, although society and the whole human race need reproductive labor to be done, that need is generalized, whereas the need of a dependent for care and of a care worker for support is concrete, immediate, and urgent. Thus these relationships are asymmetrical.

It's worth pausing to emphasize that the wage worker, too, is dependent, because in modern capitalist societies we have a strange blind spot when it comes to that form of dependency. The wage worker is dependent on an employer for wages, without which the worker cannot survive, and is vulnerable and indeed subordinate in relation to the employer. Thus, work for a wage was once denigrated as *wage slavery*. Nowadays we typically view wage earning as conferring (manly) independence. It wasn't always so. As political theorist Nancy Fraser points out, to reinterpret wage labor so as to divest it of dependency required shifting focus from the experience and means of labor—who controls the tools or land, who organizes the work and how—to the remuneration of work, that is, the freedom to spend the wage earned from work as you choose.[15] But this is a sleight of hand, obscuring the actual dependency in laboring for a wage and rhetorically shifting all dependency onto those who do not earn wages.

My favorite cartoon ever, by Emily Flake, shows a man sitting at a kitchen table and a woman holding a baby. The caption, perhaps spoken sarcastically by the woman, reads, "Maybe the unseen hand of the market will change the diaper." The joke is that market forces will never provide for dependency needs. This is so for a multitude of reasons. First, dependency does not involve arm's-length exchanges among self-interested equals. Furthermore, as I note above, the fruits of care work have a special tendency to spill out and benefit the wider society. Economists term this *positive spillover*, which boosts the economy but makes it very hard for a care worker to capture and monetize the value created by her labor. It is hard even to measure the results of any individual's caring labor, because its results are often intangible—decreased pain for an elder, greater happiness for a child, more independence for a disabled person—and long-term, in the form of increased human capability. Finally, this work has a special moral quality: To do caring labor well, you must care. Doing care work successfully requires empathy and individualized attention to its recipient. Anyone who has ever been in the hospital knows the difference a kind, attentive nurse makes. Successful care work requires intrinsic motivation and is sustained through interpersonal relationships, which are hard to measure and price and make it hard for care workers to even consider withholding their labor. Capitalist markets fundamentally depend on reproductive labor; indeed, they are parasitic on it. Yet they fail to fully compensate it. One of the ways capitalism accomplishes this is by rendering it invisible.

The US Tax Board, in 1939, not only characterized childcare as a merely personal concern but also stated that no income flows from it. In most families of the time, this was plausible, since most mothers were not wage earners and no money changed hands in compensation for their care work. But in the case before the Tax Board, Mrs. Smith actually was a wage earner, which is exactly why the case made it to the board—and why she needed to pay for childcare. But because "the wife's services as custodian of the home and protector of its children are ordinarily rendered without monetary compensation," even when rendered *with* monetary compensation, "no taxable income results."[16] Childcare is simply valueless. It and all other forms of reproductive labor are not work. Instead, they are love, instinct, destiny, identity. The flip side of the wage earner's alienation from his labor through the wage is the identification of the unpaid care worker with her labor through her lack of wage.

This blindness persists. As late as the 1995 edition, the best-selling economics textbook by Paul Samelson and William D. Nordhaus made no mention of unpaid care work except to note that some key contributors to well-being are not included in the gross domestic product, including "do-it-yourself work at home," such as "cooking meals, growing tomatoes, or educating the children." It listed these activities under the heading "Leisure Time."[17] It's leisure time, I suppose, if you're not the one doing it, in which case it isn't really do-it-yourself but do-it-your-wife. Care providers themselves fall for this erasure. When the California Work and Family Coalition held roundtables to publicize California's paid family leave program, many participants reported performing family care work but did not describe themselves as care providers. "They said, 'I'm just a daughter, a mother, fill in the blank,'" said Coalition director Jenya Cassidy.[18]

In an effort to make this invisible work economically visible, in 2023 the National Partnership for Women and Families issued a study of the hours women and men devote to unpaid care work, finding that women give away at least $627 billion worth of free care work each year while men give half that. Even this number underestimates the care penalty, because the study assumed a low rate of pay ($14.55 an hour), whereas a care worker could earn much more than that if she devoted the time to other work—investment banking, selling real estate, or even waiting tables, say. That low pay was a reasonable approximation of the market rate for care work—but that rate is discounted precisely because so much reproductive labor can be gotten for free. It's a feedback loop to ensure that our society gets reproductive labor done on the cheap.

The market keeps finding new methods for doing so. In the last few decades, with healthcare costs spiraling upwards, US hospitals began enacting policies to discharge patients much more quickly. In 1980, the average hospital stay in the United States was 7.3 days. By 2016, it fell to 4.5 days, where it remains.[19] Government policy encouraged this transition when Medicare in the early 1980s moved from paying per day of hospitalization to paying a predetermined rate tied to a given diagnosis. This shifted the burden of long hospitalizations onto hospitals, giving them an incentive to discharge patients quickly.[20] But this also shifted the burden onto family members to provide care at home, for free, that once would have been done by paid, skilled healthcare workers in the hospital. This cost-cutting—really, cost-shifting—seems to have worked. Medicare's runaway spending per person, for years predicted to bankrupt the entire US budget, has flattened startlingly in recent years, to the tune of shaving $3.9 trillion (yes, with a *T*) from the US budget.[21] While the full causes of these savings are unclear, they coincided with the shift of care to unpaid care providers in the home, which clearly played a role. Meanwhile, private entities extracted profits from the need created by this shift. The home-health and hospice-care industries boomed.

The autonomy myth's function, then, is to justify an economic system that divorces production from reproduction and compensates only production. By reproduction I mean both biological reproduction—birthing babies—and, more broadly, social reproduction, the perpetuation of a society. This split between production and reproduction enables employers to offload the cost of reproducing labor and pocket the difference.

Again and again, employers receive the value of labor power without having to pay the costs of reproducing it. And they get away with this because the autonomy myth serves to obscure the debt, by devaluing care for dependents, indeed, rendering care invisible as not-work and treating those who are dependent in either the primary or derivative sense as less than fully human.

The economic system I am referring to is, of course, capitalism. However, as Nancy Fraser points out, capitalism is not just an economic system but a whole social system. The economic system, which is based on private property, market exchange, wage labor, and production for profit, depends on a whole backdrop of supports that are defined as noneconomic. These background supports include care work and social bonds, as well as nature as a source of resources and sink for waste disposal and subject peoples from whom wealth—in the form of both raw material and enslaved or coerced labor—can be stolen. This splitting of economy from background supports is essential to capitalism.

The United States is the most advanced capitalist economy in the world and, not coincidentally, the place where resistance to social support for reproductive labor has been greatest. Although other countries established robust social welfare programs to remove some basic needs from capitalist markets and support care work, in the United States we never created more than limited social programs. And in 1996, President Clinton and Congress ended welfare as we knew it, shifting from a system of guaranteed (if modest) payments to poor mothers to grants states could use, if they chose, to offer time-limited and conditional assistance to poor families. Unfortunately, some states chose to use the grants to balance their budgets in other ways. Many states put tremendous barriers in the way of getting any cash assistance at all. If you somehow got welfare, as of 2023, no state's cash benefits for a family of three would put you at any more than 60 percent of the poverty line, and nineteen states' grant levels amount to less than 20 percent of the poverty level. Twelve states set time limits even shorter than the national requirement, with five states limiting lifetime benefits to two and a half years or less.[22] Dependency was even erased from the name of the program: Aid to Families with Dependent Children (AFDC) became Temporary Aid to Needy Families (TANF). As if we aren't all needy.

From the debate leading up to passage of welfare reform, and the enacted law itself, two basic points emerge. Most important, dependency must be reduced by getting poor women to contribute to society by working—that is, working for pay. The corollary is that unpaid caring for one's family members is not work and does not contribute to society. (Much as taking care of your own poodle does not contribute to society and is not something anyone else will pay you to do.) To qualify for any assistance under TANF, the recipient must "engage in work," and the list of what counts as work includes paid employment, training for paid employment, education "directly related to employment," and even providing childcare services to others.[23] But it does not include caring for one's own children or elders. This is astounding. It announces that mothering has no social value.

The second point is that getting mothers to get married is the solution to the "crisis in our Nation." TANF opens with 1,200 words on how important marriage is and how bad unwed motherhood is. This, too, is astounding, given that, as noted in the law when it was passed, out-of-wedlock births were on track to become a majority of all US births, and, as of this writing, are about 40 percent of births. And pushing women to get married tends to increase, not decrease, dependency. You want women to get married so that they can be provided for by a man.

Welfare reformers didn't really seek to end dependency; they sought only to reduce a certain type of dependency on the government, while increasing women's dependency on markets and individual men. You can see this in one of the comments on my article: The commenter expressed anger at the idea of parents taking leave at his expense and in the next breath raged at parents who didn't take leave and instead sent their children to daycare. It was contradictory on one level, of course. But on a deeper level the contradiction can be resolved as a rejection of any social support for childcare, instead pushing women to be supported privately by a husband. The family should be autonomous, and women should be dependent on individual men.

Despite the refusal to provide social support for dependency and the asserted goal of ending dependency, dependency hasn't ended. Like every culture, ours has structures for dealing with dependency. In America, we assign support for dependency to families. In particular, we privatize dependency within nuclear families. In the recent past, that meant a breadwinner earning the wages to support the care provided by a non-wage-earner, roles typically filled according to gender, with the care provider gaining a right to those wages through marriage. Our tax system, through such means as joint filing and the provision of health insurance and other benefits through employment, still inscribes these roles by encouraging one parent in a two-parent household to specialize in wage earning and the other in care work.

In such a model, the irresponsibility of a parent in need of paid leave is not so much in becoming dependent as in failing to make herself successfully dependent on an individual breadwinner. For the commenters, the problem with paid leave is therefore not so much dependence as independence: Socializing support for care work would liberate care workers from some of their dependence on individual breadwinners. This suggests something about the real goal of those who claim to seek to end dependency.

This is our national mythology about autonomy. The next question is how we came to embrace these strange beliefs.

CHAPTER 2:

The More Women, the More Witches

The origins of the autonomy myth lie in witchcraft. Or, rather, in witch-hunting. There is a through line between demonizing welfare recipients, denying social support for mothering, denigrating dependency, and witch-hunting. Don't take my word for it—take Reverend Pat Robertson's. In 1992, when Robertson was running for president, he railed against a feminist movement "that encourages women to leave their husbands, kill their children, practice witchcraft, destroy capitalism, and become lesbians."[1] His unhinged ravings reveal genuine connections between the ways women's reproductive powers have been coerced and why, since the US's beginnings and before. For these powers to be taken for granted in the autonomy myth, first they had to be brought under control. That was accomplished through witch hunts, the dark, nearly forgotten prequel to the autonomy myth.

In describing this prequel, I will necessarily paint with broad strokes, summarizing features relevant to the development of the autonomy myth during the approximately three centuries leading to the founding of the United States. This is a long sweep of time in which a lot happened and I clearly can't tell the whole story of these centuries. I will focus on what these centuries meant for women, through the story of the witch hunts.

In grade school, I was taught a mostly upbeat version of the United States' founding: The Pilgrims came to the New World to find freedom and worship God in peace. But things in Europe must have been ghastly, for so many to have willingly boarded small wooden ships and travelled perilously across the Atlantic to try to carve new lives from a hostile alien continent (not to mention from its original inhabitants).

Even after the end of the Black Death pandemic that killed about a third of Europe in the fourteenth century, the plague repeatedly broke out again in parts of Europe. There were also numerous famines, and, in the era just before and during the colonization of North America, there were seemingly unending wars—wars of succession (Polish, Portuguese, English, Spanish), civil wars (English, French) and international religious wars (the Schmalkaldic War, Eighty Years' War, Thirty Years' War)—that killed millions. Some of my ancestors fled to the New World to escape conscription into these wars. One ancestor, the wonderfully named Ulalia, born in England in the early seventeenth century, is said to have sickened, seemingly died, and been placed in her coffin, but then woken up at her own funeral. She then went to Massachusetts. (After nearly being buried alive, perhaps she found the old country claustrophobic.) She and her husband, Henry Burt, and several children left old England for the new sometime in the 1630s, when England was building to its civil war, in which hundreds of thousands would die, including King Charles I, beheaded for treason in 1649. Ulalia and Henry's exit was well-timed.

The Pilgrims sought to create the new Jerusalem in the colonies, yet they were also escaping from horrors. But they brought some of the Old World's darkness with them.

The basic institutions and technologies of the modern world, from the printing press to maps to nation-states, developed in the centuries just before and during European settlers' arrival in the New World. In this era, Europe began the transition from feudalism to capitalism, and medieval scholasticism was gradually replaced by scientific empiricism. It was also a time when hundreds of thousands of people, mostly women, were accused, tortured, and executed for witchcraft. The witch hunt was not a feature of the superstitious "Dark Ages," but rather an invention of the early modern era, as much a part of the development of modern Europe as the printing press—indeed, witchcraft trials and the printing press debuted around the same time, the second half of the fifteenth century.[2]

In Europe in the fifteenth through seventeenth centuries, common lands were privatized and production-for-market replaced production-for-use. As the working classes were kicked off the land and forced to work solely for wages to produce commodities for export, prices rose while wages fell. Starvation spread, and the population of Europe declined. At the time of Ulalia and Henry's migration, both land and money in England were tight. Measured in the number of kilograms of grain a day's labor would buy, by 1650, wages in England, for example, fell to one-third what they had been in 1450 and did not return to their late-medieval level for centuries.[3]

With wages so low, every family member had to work for wages all the time. Everyone in the family was "slaving away by day and night," in the words of a worker in Nuremberg in 1524, so as not to starve. There was no time for housekeeping. Nor was there much house to keep in huts inhabited by both people and animals, with little furniture, utensils, or clothing. At the same time the commons, where much communal life once had taken place, by the sixteenth century had been enclosed or privatized, leaving no place but home for social reproduction. Conditions were so wretched that the population of Europe declined significantly in the fifteenth and sixteenth centuries.[4] As would be true of capitalist economies ever since,

Silvia Federici writes, "the exploitation of labor put in jeopardy the reproduction of the workforce."[5]

In response, workers initiated violent struggles for food. These riots were often led by women, demanding bread for their starving children. Federici describes numerous riots that included or were led by women in the early seventeenth century, in response to British Enclosure Acts: In 1607, in Yorkshire, England, a "Captain Dorothy" led thirty-seven women in an attack on coal miners who were digging up what had been the village commons. In 1608 a similar group of women joined to tear down fences and hedges enclosing formerly common land in Lincolnshire. In 1609 a group of women gathered at night to dig up hedges and fill up ditches forming an enclosure in Warwickshire. Similarly, the food riots—assaults on granaries and bakeries by starving crowds—that occurred repeatedly in European cities and towns in the sixteenth and seventeenth centuries were typically led by women.[6] For example, in 1629, a crowd of women and children led by a "Captain Ann Carter" boarded ships at Maldon, England, to prevent grain from being shipped away for sale on the international market.[7] Federici speculates that the notion of the witch's cabal or witch's Sabbath may have come from subversive nighttime meetings of peasants planning resistance; the first descriptions of the witch's Sabbath date from the mid-fifteenth century, the same time frame as the peasants' revolts.

With the labor force threatening to die off or revolt, European states responded by creating the first systems of public assistance. The assistance was stingy and always came with stigma and control. In France, recipients were required to parade through the streets annually, and in England you could get aid only by being incarcerated in the parish poor house and performing forced labor.[8] The English Poor Law of 1601 codified restrictions on movement of paupers and distinctions between the deserving and undeserving poor. Then as now, the question was how to provide aid to stop absolute starvation without removing the imperative to work for low wages.

Around the same time, severe penalties were introduced to punish women for reproductive transgressions. Contraception, abortion, and infanticide were newly criminalized. For example, a 1532 law issued by Emperor Charles V, who ruled both the Holy Roman Empire and Spain, made both abortion and birth control newly illegal in the large fraction of Europe under his rule, and it prescribed death by drowning for women who used birth control or caused abortions on themselves. The new laws inscribed the assumption that women were murderers. A French royal edict issued in 1556 required women to register every pregnancy and punished with death any woman whose baby died before baptism, if she had failed to register the pregnancy. Under a 1624 English law, any woman found to have concealed the death of a bastard baby was to be executed, unless she could get a witness to the child's having been born dead. Scotland passed a similar law in 1690.[9] English midwives were newly required to be licensed by the state and had to swear an oath not to provide contraceptives or abortifacients.[10]

Although it is difficult to know how effective (or safe) traditional methods of contraception and abortion were, clearly there were such methods, communicated among women through oral lore and family recipe books. Herbs such as savin (juniper), ergot of rye, pennyroyal, and rue were known to cause abortion. Other herbs, such as myrtle and myrrh, were used as oral contraceptives and in vaginal pessaries with honey or acacia gum to block sperm. Medical historian John Riddle, who compiled references to these herbs and then cross-referenced them with modern laboratory tests of the chemicals in the herbs, has argued that women used herbs effectively for thousands of years to control their fertility.[11]

In *Hamlet,* after Ophelia has been seduced and abandoned by the hero, she gives a strange speech about flowers: "There's fennel for you, and columbines. There's rue for you, and here's some for me; we may call it herb of grace o'Sundays. You must wear your rue with a difference."

Each of these flowers has a traditional symbolic meaning: Fennel stands for flattery, columbine for betrayal, and rue to this day means regret. But they have other meanings as well: Riddle and others argue that knowledge of abortifacient herbs was so common in Shakespeare's time that contemporary audiences would have easily understood that Ophelia was also reciting the recipe for an abortion.[12] Rue was mentioned widely in Greek and Roman texts as an abortifacient, while fennel contains plant estrogens, which in large quantities can cause uterine contractions, and columbine contains toxic substances that could cause abortion.[13] Because these substances are toxic in large amounts, perhaps Shakespeare's intent was to hint that Ophelia died from a botched abortion attempt. Modern readers have more trouble decoding this passage, because this knowledge was lost—that is, suppressed—in Europe between the fifteenth and seventeenth centuries. Riddle found that after the era when witches were hunted and birth control and abortion newly criminalized, references to contraceptive herbs largely disappeared from the written record. Europe's population, after centuries of stasis, began dramatically increasing. Ulalia Burt, for example, birthed at least twelve children.

The new criminalization and surveillance of reproduction seem to have been an effort to boost population and control the reproduction of labor, and part and parcel of it were waves of witch hunts. The very first systematic witchcraft trials in Europe began in Switzerland in 1428. Although both heresy and inflicting harm on others by magical means had long been prosecuted, in the middle of the fifteenth century, *being* a witch was newly defined as a capital crime. Twenty-eight treatises on witchcraft were written between 1435 and 1487. In 1486, the pope issued an edict on the subject of witchcraft, newly labelling it the highest crime against God and the state. Witchcraft was first codified as punishable by death in 1532 by Charles V. The first English law against witchcraft was enacted in 1542, and in 1604, England established the death penalty for witchcraft even in the absence of any harm to persons or property.[14 15]

But it took more than codification to whip up a witch hunt. It was only after authorities began instructing communities to look for witches in their midst and threatening to punish anyone who harbored a witch that witch trials erupted. In Scotland, from which some of my ancestors fled, the Presbyterian Church in 1603 ordered ministers to interrogate their parishioners as to whether they suspected any neighbor of being a witch, threaten to punish anyone who assisted or hid a witch, and install boxes in churches to encourage parishioners to denounce their neighbors anonymously.[16] Bishops of the Anglican church regularly issued "inquiries" as to whether anyone was aware of any witches in their midst. Given that under the English witchcraft law of 1604 not only witches but "Ayders Abettors and Counselors" of witches could be put to death, it was best to respond to these inquiries by pointing fingers. Judge Matthew Hale, who would later become England's chief justice, instructed the jury in a 1662 witch trial that whether witchcraft was real was not up for discussion. "[T]he wisdom of all nations had provided laws against such persons [witches], which is an argument of their confidence of such a crime." Hale later created the doctrine, applied in both England and the United States until the late twentieth century, that a husband could not be convicted of raping his wife.[17]

Witch hunts were a useful way of putting women down, for a witch was dangerous yet did not come by her fearsome powers naturally—she got them from the devil. The witch hunts focused on women's control over reproduction, both biological and social. The *Malleus Mallificarum*, or *Hammer of Witches*, the foremost European guidebook for hunting witches, written in 1484, listed seven methods employed by witches, including "destroying the generative force in women" and "procuring abortion." All seven methods involved sexuality, and all except practicing fornication and adultery involved reproduction and women's control of it. According to the 1484 Bull of Pope Innocent VIII on witchcraft, witches "destroy the offspring of women" and "hinder men from generating and women from conceiving." The *Malleus Mallificarum* described women in general as "necessary evils," while King James I of England succinctly said, "The more women, the more witches." In both Europe and colonial America, women made up about 80 percent of executed witches. Poor women were particularly vulnerable to accusation, as were midwives, who, according to the *Malleus Mallificarum*, "surpass all others in wickedness." For example, the Bishop of London's inquiries of 1577 and 1586 instructed the community to look for witches especially among "midwyes in the time of womens travayl of childe."[18] Midwifery constituted a body of autonomous women's knowledge, and midwives supported the autonomy of the women they served. Therefore, they were dangerous.

In an inversion of women's association with the birthing and nurturing of children, accusations of witchcraft often centered around women harming children. Witches were believed to especially target children and drink the blood of babies as part of their satanic rites. For example, in the trial Matthew Hale presided over in 1662, witnesses testified that widows Amy Duney and Rose Cullender had threatened the health of their children, who then went into fits and vomited pins and nails. The children testified that they had visions of Cullender appearing at the feet of their beds and trying to lure them out of the house. Based on this evidence, Duney and Cullender were both convicted and then hanged.[19]

Accused witches were subjected to gruesome torture and public humiliation, and thousands of women were burned alive. Terror was precisely the point. The French lawyer and witch hunter Jean Bodin wrote, "We must spread terror among some by punishing many." Even in England and America, where witches were typically hanged rather than burned to death and torture was less prevalent and less extreme than in European witch trials, accused women were nevertheless typically stripped and beaten and their bodies searched for the witch's mark or witch's teat.[20]

It is difficult to reach an accurate accounting of how many women were accused or killed, but historians who have studied the witch hunt archives estimate that at least a hundred thousand women were executed throughout Europe, and perhaps as many as half a million.[21] In 1585 in Trier, Germany, two villages were left with only one female inhabitant each after executions of witches. In the Torsåker region of Sweden, one-fifth of the female population were executed as witches in 1674 and 1675 (the Swedish witch trials would give colonial New England the idea that witches fly on broomsticks).[22] The witch trials served as an appalling, vivid lesson to women of the price of maintaining traditional knowledge about birth, birth control, and abortion, and of resistance to the new order. Henceforth, women in England, Europe, and their colonies would have no option but to submit their reproductive capacities to producing a workforce.

Old women, midwives or not, were especially targeted. Postmenopausal women were at once dangerous and useless: no longer a source of more workers, but still a potential source of reproductive knowledge and rebellion. Old women seem to have been targeted in part for their insistence on traditional rights, such as the right to use the commons for subsistence, the right of widows to receive support, or even merely for begging for help. Frequently mentioned in both European and American witch trials is an accusation that an old woman demanded charity from a neighbor or took something like a bit of food and then became angry when the neighbor refused the request or accused her of theft—this was evidence she was a likely witch. In Salem in 1692, one of the first three people to be accused was Sarah Good, a destitute woman who was accused of witchcraft shortly after begging at the minister's house.

It was at this moment in history when the notion of breeding dependency as a pathology first arose: Almsgiving had previously been praiseworthy, but under the new Protestant ethic it was considered pointless or even dangerous for providing an alternative to hard work. The witch hunts created a metaphysical justification for refusing aid. English Puritan Thomas Cooper instructed readers in 1617 that, to avoid witchcraft, we must:

> be wise in our Liberalitie, and Almesdeedes, not distributing to each sort of poore, because many times Witches go under the habite . . . especially take heed if any such suspected seeke unto us; . . . not to relieve them with morsels.[23]

Old women in Europe during these centuries were both more in need of assistance than before—because of peasants' ouster from access to land—and less likely to get it.

Witch hunts closely correlated with privatization of formerly common lands. Most of the witch trials in England occurred in Essex, where the majority of the land had by the sixteenth century been enclosed. Notably, Essex was also a hotbed of Puritanism, the sect of Protestantism from which America's Pilgrims came.[24] Essex was the original home of William Pynchon, the founder of Springfield, Massachusetts, who in 1651 would lead one of the first North American witch hunts.[25] In the Scottish Lowlands, which were highly privatized by this time, 4,000 to 6,000 witches—more than 1 percent of the female population—were tried, and about 1,500 were executed.[26] By contrast, in Ireland and the Scottish Highlands, where the land was still largely used collectively, very few witch trials occurred.[27] Once witchcraft trials got going, they became a regular part of village life. In Essex, only trials for theft were more common.[28]

Modern-day observers, looking back at the Salem witch hunts in isolation, have seen a sudden, brief outbreak of collective madness in need of explanation. Some historians blame mass hysteria started by bored teenagers freaking themselves out with a fortune-telling game, while the tidiest proposed culprit is a hallucinogenic fungus in the villagers' rye.[29] But witch accusations and trials were a commonplace and well-rooted practice, so to search for an isolated cause is wrong-headed. The more pertinent question is why there were so few witch trials in colonial America, at first.

When North America was colonized beginning in the early seventeenth century, witch trials were on the wane in Europe. Accusations of witchcraft were initially rare in the colonies, and no one was prosecuted there for witchcraft until 1647.

In part, this was because women, especially old women, were at first in short supply in the colonies— the first generation of colonists was heavily male.[30] With few women, there was little to fear from women as a class. Women's contraceptive lore, already under suppression in Europe, was further disrupted by colonists' settlement in a new world with unfamiliar plants. Too, with resources abundant and colonists few in the New World, there was little need to subdue any impoverished masses. But within a few generations, as the coastal colonies became settled and Native American resistance kept colonists pinned in a limited land area, resources grew tighter. The gender imbalance also righted itself, in part because the birthrate was so high (Ulalia Burt's twelve babies were unusual but not unheard of). By the late seventeenth century, women became a majority in some established colonies as younger sons struck out for less-settled places.

According to historian Carol Karlsen, in the first years of New England colonization, widows commonly inherited not only the traditional one-third use-right share of an estate but even received property in their own right, and while oldest sons received double portions, daughters inherited equal shares with younger sons. But as land grew scarcer, widows and daughters more rarely inherited. Meanwhile even sons were facing shrinking inheritances or receiving them from their fathers late in life. Based on close analysis of records of the New England witch hunts, Karlsen found that accused witches were typically women who had inherited—or stood to inherit or control—some level of resources in their own right because their husbands had no direct male heirs. They therefore had a level of autonomy that women in their society rarely gained. They were also resented, within a situation of scarcity, for interfering with the normal transfer of wealth from one generation of men to the next. There was tension between fathers and sons, too, but this could not be expressed within a patriarchal society. Older women became scapegoats for generational tensions.

Events in England provided a trigger; in 1645, Matthew Hopkins, England's self-proclaimed Witchfinder General, initiated a renewed witch hunt. The New England colonists were well aware of Hopkins's efforts, as they began in Essex, from where many Puritans had emigrated, and occurred during the English Civil War, in which 20 percent of New England's population returned to England to fight.[31] Massachusetts Bay Colony Governor John Winthrop's brother-in-law likely brought news of the witch hunt with him when he returned to Salem from London in 1645.[32]

New England's first major witch hunt began two years later, prompting a wave of witch trials that lasted until 1663. Sixty people were accused, resulting in executions of ten women and one man.[33] New England's last witch hunt, the infamous Salem trials, in which fifty-eight were indicted, was modelled on England's 1662 Bury St. Edmund witch trial, which was presided over by the eminent judge Matthew Hale and widely written about.[34] But New England one-upped the mother country; Hale sentenced only two witches (both elderly women) to die in Bury St. Edmund, whereas the Salem trials ended in 1693 with the hanging of fourteen women and five men, plus one man pressed to death by stones.

The American witch hunts largely followed the European model: Usually, men were the accusers, and they accused postmenopausal women. As in Europe, the few men accused were secondary targets who got caught in the snare because they were related to an accused witch.[35] True to the European form, the first woman to be accused in the 1647 craze was Margaret Jones, a midwife and old "cunning woman," and in the Salem witch hunts at least twenty-two of the two hundred accused witches were midwives or healers.[36][37] Even before the first prosecution, New England's most famous woman leader, Anne Hutchinson, was, along with one of her women supporters, Jane Hawkins, informally accused of being a witch. Both of them were midwives.[38]

My ancestors, Ulalia and Henry Burt, witnessed one of the first witch prosecutions, in Springfield, Massachusetts. After their first New World home in Roxbury, Massachusetts (now part of Boston) burned down, they journeyed another hundred miles west to what was then the farthest edge of colonial settlement. They arrived in Springfield in 1638, just two years after its founding by William Pynchon.[39] As historian William Gaskill describes, for the settlers, Springfield lay just on the border between civility and barbarism. In 1637, the Springfield settlement nearly failed due to a bad harvest and outbreak of war with the indigenous Pequots.[40] As stories circulated of people carried off into the dark by Indians, most of the settlers fled, leaving only twelve households.[41] New England, and especially frontier settlements like Springfield, "for all its hopeful beginnings, meant . . . the skin-prickle of being watched, the twisting grip of a curse and the terrors of the dark," according to Gaskill.[42]

At this point, Springfield founder Pynchon would have been glad to have the Burts as new settlers, and they apparently settled in. Henry Burt became an exhorter, or lay preacher, in the Puritan church, responsible for exhorting the flock to avoid sin, of which the worst were idleness, murder, and witchcraft.[43] His son Jonathan became a town selectman.[44] With labor in short supply, wages were double what they were in England, paid by the day, but workdays were ten hours long during the spring and summer, and costs of goods were high. For example, one pane of window glass in Pynchon's company store cost a day's wages.[45] Springfield's fortunes turned, and by 1641, it had grown to forty-five households.[46] Some settlers, including its cutthroat entrepreneur-founder Pynchon, were extracting great wealth from the area, both from the abundance of the wilderness in the form of furs and from the settlers themselves. Pynchon ran Springfield as a company town, where the currency of most transactions among villagers was credit or debt in the only store, owned by him. In this way, Springfield was partly a subsistence economy, with villagers growing and making much of what they consumed, and partly a capitalist venture. The Puritan settlers on the one hand saw wealth as a sign of God's favor, yet, on the other, resented those who put profits above community.[47] Neighbors depended on each other, but for this very reason relations could easily curdle if someone, instead of being *toward*, was perceived as *froward*—selfish, facing away from the community.[48]

In 1651, Henry and Ulalia's neighbor Mary Parsons, who seemed to have suffered from postpartum depression and psychosis following the deaths of two of her three children, accused a neighbor of being a witch. Soon Mary Parsons was herself accused by another neighbor of being a witch. Then

Mary's husband, Hugh, was also accused—by Mary, among others. Although it was unusual for a man to be accused, Hugh was abusive to his wife, perpetually angry, greedy, envious, and widely disliked. He was also considered unable to control his wife, a crucial failure of his patriarchal duties. He was arrested after he requested some milk as partial repayment of a debt and the neighbor refused; the neighbor then accused him of bewitching her cow. Nearly the entire town—including the Parsonses' next-door neighbor, Ulalia's son Jonathan—turned on the Parsons.[49]

But the witch hunt did not spread beyond them. Had it spread, Ulalia, who had given birth to her last child in 1647, might have been a target, because she was in the suspicious postmenopausal demographic. Instead, the witch hunt fizzled out after Mary and Hugh Parsons were sent off to Boston for trial. Few of the accusers made the difficult, hundred-mile journey to testify. Instead, their accusations, in the form of signed affidavits, were read aloud by Boston judges, thereby losing much of their power. The jury acquitted both Mary and Hugh Parsons of the charge of bewitching their neighbors, for lack of evidence. But then matters took a strange turn: Mary suddenly confessed to causing the death of her child. She was sentenced to death, but before the sentence could be carried out, she died in prison. Hugh Parsons left Springfield with his surviving daughter.[50] Despite the not-guilty verdict, his land was appropriated by Pynchon and quickly bought by my ancestor Jonathan Burt, who moved into the Parsonses' house.[51] For Springfield and my ancestors, the witch hunt was over when the troublesome couple had been expunged. In Salem, however, forty years later, there would be no such fizzling.

In the colonial American witch trials, there were a few striking innovations. First, the crime of witchcraft was redefined in contractual terms: The early New England statutes defined a witch as one who made a compact with the devil.[52] In the land of wheeling and dealing, where Manhattan Island was wangled off the original inhabitants for a few beads, and the land for Springfield acquired from the local Agawam tribe for the price of a few coats, hatchets, knives, and strands of wampum, the colonists well knew how destructive a contract could be when one party was devious and dramatically more powerful.[53] At the time of the Salem witch hunts, the New England colonies had within memory made the transition from a subsistence economy to a market-based one in which some were getting wealthy while others were struggling. The shift to a contractual notion of witchcraft was most visible in Salem, where, prompted by leading questions from the magistrate, the accusers repeatedly claimed the accused had tried to force them to sign the devil's book.

The second innovation seems related: In colonial America, the devil was an Indian—the very "savages" from whom the continent was being wrested and who, at the time of the New England witchcraft outbreaks, were violently resisting. Most of the accusers in Salem were survivors of attacks by Native Americans against English settlements in Maine. Satan, as the accusers described him, was "tawny." One of the Salem accusers, Abigail Hobbes, in what appears to be a kind of survivor's guilt, confessed to having entered a pact with Satan weeks before the attacks by Indians that killed her family and destroyed her Maine community. Indian raids had brought a wave of impoverished refugees from Maine to Salem, a burden the townspeople resented.

Third, in Salem, for the first time, most of the accusers were not men but girls and young women, accusing mostly older women (although one five-year-old girl and a few men were also accused). Most of these younger women were orphans whose families had been killed in the raids in Maine; thus, they were not only traumatized but impoverished, facing dismal prospects within a society that subjugated and circumscribed all women's lives. Several who had grown up in reasonable comfort had been forced to become servants in Salem after their parents were massacred and their homes destroyed. They were also mostly adolescents, on the cusp of a womanhood that stretched grimly before them. They found, in witchcraft possession and accusation, the only socially permissible way to express resentment of their situation. Indeed, it was the only way for a woman to make her voice heard in a theocracy that barred women from speaking in church. Within the ritual of possession, they could speak the unspeakable and command the attention of the entire community.

It began in the minister's household, when first the minister's eleven-year-old niece and then his nine-year-old daughter began complaining of bites and pinches by "invisible agents." They shuddered, whirled, howled, went limp and then rigid. They interrupted family prayer and ceased doing the spinning, baking, candle-making, and sewing normally expected of them. Neighbors flocked to the parsonage to see the girls' wildness themselves. Soon such scenes spread to other households and then to other villages.[54]

Yet the possessed women and girls did not initially make any accusations against anyone. That took a push from men in power, the ministers and magistrates who forcefully demanded that the girls name the witch or witches responsible for their torments. When the girls began naming names, the authorities gave immediate credence to the accusations. When one of the early accusers, Sarah Churchill, tried to recant, the authorities refused to believe her.[55] When the accused were interrogated, the interrogators did not ask whether they had engaged in witchcraft, but how and with whom: The first question magistrate John Hathorne asked Sarah Good was, "What evil spirit have you familiarity with?"[56] In this society, it was assumed that Satan was perpetually at war with their City on a Hill.

In this context, the young women's behavior was disruptive and shocking, yet supported the assumptions of powerful men. These young women commanded New England's public sphere for over a year with their tales of "a conspiracy of Indians and grandmothers," as historian John Murrin puts it. Supported by the authorities, the crisis grew until the accusations spread from marginalized old women to the well-to-do and powerful. This soured the powerful on the whole idea of witches, especially in a context in which the witch hunt was fading away in Europe and skepticism of witchcraft was rising. However, before 1692 you couldn't read any texts skeptical of witchcraft in New England, given the theocracy's tight control on the press.[57] Witch hunts in America ended, but so did the power of women to take center stage in American court rooms. According to Murrin, after Salem women were essentially barred from legal processes except to be humiliated for sexual transgressions, while men ceased to be convicted of sexual crimes against women or required to take responsibility for children born to them out of wedlock.[58] The result of the witch trials, as in Europe, was to put women firmly in their place. They would be enclosed within their families and kept firmly under the control of their male relatives.

The witch trials also inscribed in the American subconscious division among women as an elemental condition. In Salem, daughters turned on their mothers, accusing them of practicing witchcraft against them or forcing them into witchcraft. Sons turned on their mothers and husbands on their wives. Sarah Good, for example, was sent to prison after her husband testified to having seen a witch's mark on her shoulder. But fathers and sons did not turn on each other; not a single son accused his father or father his son during the colonial witch trials.[59] Just as in Europe, old women were disposable, the scapegoats for cultural tensions. In Europe these tensions cut between classes, but in America the witch trials sliced between generations, most especially between generations of women. A cultural phenomenon rooted in terror of the power in female solidarity became a ritual demonstration of division among women.

In 1692 during the Salem proceedings, Cotton Mather had trumpeted them with a quickly churned-out promotional book called *Wonders of the Invisible World.* But in 1693, the trials simply ended in silence. The accused who had not yet been executed were released from prison, but their seized estates were not returned, and their jailers kept the fees charged for their imprisonment. Women returned to their homes, to live intimately among the people who had accused them and sent their sisters, mothers, and daughters to their deaths.

Witchcraft as a nightmare of female power still fascinates to this day, and witch-hunting persists in new forms. Pat Robertson's 1992 diatribe about witches and lesbians points to the terrifying prospect of women's reproductive powers being out of (men's) control. More recently, Pizzagate and QAnon—conspiracy theories centered on the ritual abuse and killing of children—are witchcraft tales. Their adherents would gladly execute Hilary Clinton as a witch. The push on the Right to require examinations of the genitals of female athletes they suspect of being transgender also grotesquely echoes the Puritans' examination of women's bodies for the devil's mark or witch's teat. Like the witch hunters, anti-trans activists claim they are protecting children.[60] Activists pushing for a ban on abortion pills in Texas in 2025 described their opponents as "pro-abortion witches" who dared to laugh at the claim that "We are all drinking other people's abortions in the wastewater."[61] And in 2022, when state legislators unleashed by the US Supreme Court introduced bills to punish both abortion doctors and aborting women with the death penalty, they were taking pages directly from Charles V's book. [62]

The Salem witch hunt was terrible PR for the Puritan theocracy and likely hastened the end of its grip on power. Around the time of the Salem witch trials, the British crown refused to grant the New England colonies a renewed charter to run their own affairs, and it imposed religious tolerance—of all Christian sects—on the colonies. Eventually a secular, rationalist revolution based on the consent of the people would triumph in America. Yet what "consent" means and whose consent matters remains an unsettled question. And America's dark impulse to demonize women's reproductive powers repeatedly erupts whenever the contradictions between the imperatives of wealth and our need to reproduce ourselves grow too great.

CHAPTER 3:

Just So Stories

Before his nomination to the Supreme Court, Clarence Thomas liked to tell the story of how his sister was a welfare queen. "She gets mad when the mailman is late with her welfare check. That's how dependent she is," he sneered. In fact, when reporters for the *Chicago Tribune* tracked her down in Pin Point, Georgia, in 1991, Emma Mae Martin was working as a cook at a hospital, often reporting to work at 3:00 a.m. Nor was she new to hard work: She worked two minimum-wage jobs while her brother attended law school but had to quit those jobs to take care of an elderly aunt who had suffered a stroke. That led to four or five years on welfare, trying to make it on $169 a month while caring for the aunt and her own four children as a single mother (her husband had abandoned her years before).[1] She cared for the aunt until the aunt died and raised her children to become equally hardworking: one a baker, another a carpenter, another a soldier, the other a student at the time of the article.

When Emma Mae and Clarence were children, and their mother was struggling to raise her children cleaning houses (one of the only jobs available to a Black woman in the South), Clarence and his brother were sent to live with his well-off grandfather while his sister remained with their mother. His grandfather not only made sure that Clarence, unlike Emma Mae, was well-fed but encouraged him to become the first in his family to go to college. Thomas got far out of Pin Point, to college and then law school. Free of family responsibilities, he focused fiercely on school, studying hard while facing down racism. Thomas's story about his sister the welfare queen helped catch the eye of Ronald Reagan, another teller of tales about welfare queens, and landed him an appointment as head of the Equal Employment Opportunity Commission, which in turn led to his appointment to the Supreme Court.

When I was a child, there was a photo of the Supreme Court justices above our toilet. It amused my mother, who taught constitutional law among other things, to place them there. This made the justices familiar characters to me—not exactly family, but homey, the way photos of the pope or JFK function in Catholic homes. Maybe that's why I followed the story of Thomas and his sister, why it bothered me so much. Thomas's biography is an impressive one. But so is Emma Mae's. The reason hers is less triumphant than his, it seems to me, is less about her own dependency than about her failure (refusal?) to disavow herself of others' dependency on her. This is unfair, and that unfairness is foundational.

Since Thomas became a Supreme Court justice, he has been the fiercest originalist on the court, seeking to identify the intent of the Founders when they wrote the US Constitution. I think he's right to try to understand our foundations, so bear with me for a brief excursion into philosophy and political theory, and into why we tell the stories we do. In particular, I want to consider the stories the Founders relied on in crafting the Constitution.

The word *autonomy* means self-rule, freedom of will and action, not being controlled by or beholden to another. These days, in the United States it is often paired with responsibility, understood narrowly: responsibility only for oneself and those directly and properly dependent on oneself. Those who have autonomy are believed to deserve both freedom from government interference and government protection from the interference of others. Because they are self-governing, they do not need outside regulation. Only those who are autonomous can be full citizens in a democracy. That is, only they deserve freedom from subjection.

Prior to the rise of modern democracy, the norm was for people to be subjects rather than citizens. Dependence was typical—most people were subordinate—whereas independence was a rare privilege. An old meaning of *independence* captures its link to money: To have an independence was to have sufficient income to live on, without the need to work. This meaning survives in the phrases *independently wealthy* and *a person of independent means*. As some began to challenge their subjection to kings, initially only those with such financial independence were deemed eligible for political rights. Eventually, though, revolutionaries began to demand citizenship for the masses. This required a claim of independence by workers, which in turn required an inversion, from associating wage labor with dependence (wage slavery) to associating it with manly independence.

These ideas are closely related to the concept of the social contract, a thought experiment designed to solve the puzzle of how government could ever be legitimate. Even at this first threshold step the experiment is revolutionary; why should government need any justification? Once upon a time, hierarchy was taken as a given. That some should rule and others follow was natural, part of a divine order. Beginning in about the seventeenth century, however, some in Europe began to question this assumption. Such questioning brought England to the point of civil war, execution of the king, and revolution. Around the same time, Europeans began settling North

America, creating new communities from scratch and coming into contact with people who lived in radically different ways and without governmental structures that were recognizable to the Europeans. So the question of whether orderly government could be justified was not merely academic. Some theorists began to posit the notion that every human being is free and equal. But if that's the case, how could anyone be ruled by anyone else?

Some thinkers thought their way to justifying government with a just so story called "the social contract." In this story, we are to imagine ourselves prior to the formation of government, in what social contract theorists call "the state of nature," without any rules, and then think through what sort of rules we would consent to. What you imagine the state of nature to be determines what you think is worth agreeing to in order to get out of it.

Thomas Hobbes thought life in the state of nature was a war of all against all in which life was "nasty, brutish, and short," so he thought it was worth it to give unconstrained power to a sovereign in return for peace and safety. You weren't free in the state of nature in any meaningful sense, what with doing nothing but fighting viciously for your life, so even under the thumb of a powerful ruler you were not only safer but freer. As evidence of the state of nature's awfulness, first he cited the English Civil War between the monarchy and the Puritans, and second "the savage people in many places of America." His use of Native Americans as evidence of the awfulness of the state of nature was dubious on two grounds: The "savage people" of America in fact had structures of community and governance, and they probably experienced less violence than the Europeans of Hobbes's era.

The liberal John Locke, on the other hand, thought the state of nature was nicer. You were free and independent, and if you wanted to hang on to that freedom, you could just set up some predictable rules to protect it and allow you to reliably accrue property and hang on to it. It wasn't so much that humans are naturally bad, but that they have a hard time judging their own cases. This leads to "inconveniences," in Locke's words. Like Hobbes, he also uses the supposed miserableness of Native Americans as evidence. So humans agree to turn over their natural right to rule over themselves to political representatives who will act as umpires between conflicting interests.

In Locke's version of the story, what makes government necessary is the creation of money. Locke believed that it was the process of mixing one's labor with nature's raw materials that created property rights. Initially, no one can accumulate any more stuff than can be consumed before it rots. So there isn't a lot of conflict, nor any need for complex rules. But when money is invented, value can be stockpiled and inequalities accumulated, and therefore fights over possession erupt. So you need rules. You need a process for choosing representatives who will be neutral arbiters of property rights. In Locke's story, at the moment of creating a political community, you give up your natural political right to judge and punish, handing over political life to representatives, who will protect your right to go on about private life peaceably.

The language theorists use, from Hobbes to Locke to Jean-Jacques Rousseau, is telling: Those who enter the social contract "give birth" to a new society. In Hobbes, the new entity is the "Artificial Man, we call a Commonwealth;" in Rousseau, it is an "artificial and collective body;" and in Locke, the "Body Politick."

An odd feature of all of these social contract stories is that we are supposed to imagine ourselves as fully formed, autonomous, free-floating individuals choosing to come together to form social and governmental bonds. The protagonist of the story is an unaffiliated grown man, roaming alone through the forest, occasionally running into others like himself. Hobbes is explicit: In imagining the state of nature, we consider ourselves like mushrooms, sprung fully formed from the ground. Of course he knows that's not true, but he and other social contract theorists tell the tale as if it might as well be true. Locke acknowledges that children are not born able to govern themselves and explains that the sense in which humans are each born free and equal is that each has the capacity to grow into independence. It is not that Locke and Hobbes do not recognize that humans come into the world as babies and must be nurtured into self-governing adults; it's that they do not think any of that has anything to do with politics.

For Hobbes, Locke, and other contract theorists, the crucial move that allows them to reject the divine right of kings and justify governmental authority is to distinguish political authority from familial authority. Defenders of the rights of kings, such as Sir Robert Filmer (now completely forgotten except as the foil for Locke's takedown), derived this right ultimately from Adam's right as a father and husband: His power to bring sons into existence gives him the right to rule over them, and he thus becomes the first king. You might notice that this skips a step: It's not Adam who gives birth but Eve. Adam must first gain power over Eve's procreative powers, which then gives him the authority to rule over the children she births. His authority over her reproductive powers allows him to birth a political order. In any case, political authority and familial authority are the same thing, and both are natural. All authority arises naturally from basic biology, underwritten by God's will. This story is tidy, intuitive, and clear, and fits the facts people saw all around them: From birth, everywhere, some people ruled over others.

The contractarians, on the other hand, insisted that family authority and political authority were completely different. Locke even points out that children are equally subject to their fathers' and mothers' rule while they are children, using this point as a *reductio ad absurdum* of equating paternal rule and political rule. Of course, it would be ridiculous to equate a mother's power to spank a toddler with a king's authority to send people to war; they just can't be the same sort of thing at all. Locke explains that a father's authority over his children and wife is natural, as is a mother's authority over her children, but political authority is not; it is based on consent. From here, we get the basic liberal division between public and private. Sometimes the contrast is between government (public) and civil society/economic markets (private), and sometimes between economic markets (public) and family (private), but always the family is private. And always women are relegated to the family and the private sphere.

The political theorist Carole Pateman describes this story as the replacement of rule by the father with rule by brothers, her point being that, because of this essential division between the familial and the political, liberal social contract theory is permeated to its heart with patriarchy.[2] Locke, for example, writes that, unlike political obligation, a wife's subjection to her husband "had a Foundation in Nature" and his will should "take place before that of his wife." This is another way of saying that women were not among the free and equal individuals taking part in social contracting.

You might be tempted to think this is an easily jettisoned, archaic mistake, but theorists are still working with these ideas. When I was in college and graduate school in the 1990s, I studied the new writings of John Rawls, the most famous modern liberal contractarian. He states that we should assume that those in the imaginary state of nature who agree on rules for justice are heads of households, consenting to government on behalf of their families. But is this consistent with justice? Why should only heads of household get to decide? These are not new worries. From the first, feminists have asked the contract theorists, in the words of Mary Astell in 1706, "If all men are born free, why are all women born slaves?"

The problem, for contractarianism, is fundamental. In a later version of his theory, Rawls dumped the heads of family assumption. But that doesn't solve the problem. Contractarianism assumes that social order derives from the voluntary association of equally situated individuals. The construct is that a just society is one that would be chosen by reasonable and rational persons. Rawls claims he can get to a theory of a just society without assuming anything about the dealmakers except rationality. As with any contract, they give as much as they get, and this reciprocity is what makes the agreement just, as well as determining who gets to partake in the dealmaking, which is to say who counts as a free and equal citizen. But what about those unable to reciprocate—infants, the disabled, and the frail elderly—that is, dependents? Are they to be excluded from the dealmaking? Perhaps the idea is that others will represent their interests. However, mere rationality won't assure this. Even if the dealmakers know the basic and inescapable fact that humans spend a major fraction of their lives in states of dependency, they may not imagine themselves as doing any of the work to care for those who are dependent. They may imagine that others will be into that, just as some are into keeping pets. The problem, though, is that the work of caring for dependents is not just any work: It is the work necessary for there to be a society at all. Bare rationality gets you agreement among those who are free and equal, but how do you ensure that the work to get them to that state is done fairly? Contract theory begs the question because it excludes from politics a fundamental fact about humanity.

The American founders were steeped in social contract theory. As Thomas Jefferson writes in the Declaration of Independence, government derives its just powers from the consent of the governed. The American founders were particularly influenced by Locke, picking up Locke's phrase "life, liberty, and property" in the Declaration of Independence, although, crucially, Jefferson turned it into "life, liberty, and the pursuit of happiness." The just authority of government is limited by the "unalienable" rights of individuals, regardless of their ownership of property. The Founders fundamentally differed from Locke, not to mention Hobbes, in believing that, by constituting a government, the people did not turn over their sovereignty to rulers but retained it. The US Constitution speaks in the voice of "We the people," and the people's ongoing authority to revise it is baked into its provisions for amendment. The Founders even understood the people as retaining the final right of interpreting the Constitution. James Madison writes in Federalist 49 that constitutional disputes cannot be resolved "without an appeal to the people themselves, who, as grantors of the commission, can alone declare its true meaning and enforce its observance."[3]

This implies little about how people attain the ability to effectively exercise their rights, or what government affirmatively ought to do. But it does posit the individual as a given, prior to politics, making it tempting to forget how individuals come into being or to dismiss this process as pre- or nonpolitical. As I explain above, the separation of politics from private life, in which human reproduction occurs, was crucial to the liberal social contract theory that influenced the American founders. The switch from property to "pursuit of happiness" suggests a broadening of the notion of the political, but the founders took for granted that only some people had the autonomy necessary to participate in governance. Jefferson writes in 1816 that of course even in a pure democracy three categories of persons would be excluded from participation: children, slaves, and women.[4] He bases women's and slaves' exclusion not on some innate defect in their natures but on social necessity. Women could not be permitted to participate in political meetings with men "to prevent depravation of morals, and ambiguity of issue"—that is, wanton sex outside of marriage and children of unknown paternity—scrambling the orderly passage of property from one generation of men to the next. Slaves, on the other hand, could not participate because "the unfortunate state of things with us takes away the rights of will and of property," which coyly avoids the question of why this "unfortunate state of things" is with us. It also suggests that these rights of will and property float away by some inevitable natural process rather than being taken away from certain people by certain other people, such as slaveholders like Jefferson.

Jefferson and others, finding this unfortunate state of things profitable, managed to ignore the fact that it is incompatible with democracy. Democracy depends on the consent of the governed, and no one can agree to be enslaved forever. It took a bloody civil war to establish this point, a revelation that ought to have led to a deeper consideration of consent. Instead, the Thirteenth Amendment that outlawed slavery has only ever been interpreted narrowly, becoming an ancient artifact whose work is done. It is never cited by sane lawyers in live cases. (However, during the 2018–19 US government shutdown, when thousands of government workers were forced to work without paychecks, there were murmurings about the amendment.)

Consider why slavery is inconsistent with democracy. One could argue that freedom of contract means you could make a contract to enter slavery. The first problem is that refusal of the deal has to be possible, which it never was for actual slaves. The second, broader-reaching problem is that any normal contract is one you can break; you may have to pay a penalty, but you can back out. In legal jargon, the term for not being able to back out is *specific performance*, and courts are reluctant to order specific performance of a contract except in rare circumstances, precisely because it looks like slavery. A contract for slavery is one you can't ever get out of.

In contracting for slavery, you agree never to have a chance to refuse to agree to anything, ever again. To view agreeing to give up all freedom as an exercise of freedom is contradictory. A free person can make promises and keep them, but can also revisit and reconsider them as circumstances change. No free, rational person would ever willingly agree to enslavement. But if this is so, then the sort of consent necessary for democracy must be something broader and deeper than the single moment of turning over our political right that Locke imagined. The kind of consent that justifies government and makes it democratic has to be ongoing.

Locke's ties to the political formation of America were not merely theoretical. He actually drafted the 1669 Constitutions of the Carolinas, establishing a governing framework for these colonies, with slavery at its heart. The Constitutions granted slaveholders absolute power of life and death over their negro slaves and specified that negro slaves' conversion to Christianity could not alter their status. While the Constitutions were suspended by 1690 and replaced, they helped deepen and racialize the divide that would haunt America's political ideals from then on, between those free men whose consent to government legitimized it and those others whose consent was irrelevant. Even in Locke's later, more liberal works that inspired the Founders, he justifies chattel slavery as originating in "just war." He does not explain how the capture of slaves in Africa or the purchase of slaves from traffickers count as just war.

Like that of slaves, women's consent has always been problematic. Marriage was traditionally understood as a contract, but, like a contract for slavery, it was a contract to give up your right to any freedom going forward. It was also what lawyers call a *contract of adhesion*. This sounded to me at first, in law school, like a derogatory term that could be used to invalidate unfair contracts but turned out to cover most contracts the average person typically encounters, from cell phones to software updates to car loans. Contract law mystified me, as it seemed to rest on faulty premises. (Needless to say, it was not my best subject.) Historically, the contract was *for* a wife, not *with* one. The earliest English laws treated marriage as a private contract between men for the purchase of a wife.[5] Over time, the bride eventually became a party to the deal, but it was a take-it-or-leave-it contract; all you got to choose was which man—maybe. All the rest of the terms were set. Once you were married, your money, your labor, your person, and your will belonged to your husband. The beauty part was that this raw deal was then used to prove that women deserved it: No free, rational being would agree to such a contract, but most women do, so naturally women must not be free, rational beings. This is exquisitely circular logic. But if you step outside of the circle, the strange case of women prompts deeper thought about consent.

Jefferson's three exclusions point the way to a circular problem in contract theory: Consent is crucial to democracy because it protects freedom and equality, but freedom and equality are also necessary preconditions for consent. With that, the outlines of a theory of democracy as demanding attention to the preconditions and context of meaningful consent begin to emerge. Because care work is the central condition for creating the sort of being who can engage in rational consent, care work must be at the heart of this theory. How a society provides for the rearing of children is a profoundly political question. It establishes who is viewed as a full citizen, who is indebted to whom, and how those debts are paid. The debts owed to those who do the crucial work of caring for dependents cannot be paid by the dependents receiving the care. Furthermore, the benefits created by care work flow beyond these dependents and beyond the care workers, out to society more broadly. Therefore, a just society must be one in which all members contribute to supporting care work.

Which brings us back to the story of Emma Mae. I am not African American, so Emma Mae's story is not mine and, as we all know, the term "welfare queen" does not mean white women. But my mother went on welfare briefly after I was born. Occasionally, when I've heard people spouting off about the evils of welfare, I've mentioned this fact. It always stops them dead in their tracks—for a moment. Then they dismiss her as an exception. They focus on the brevity of her time on welfare. Yes, she had resources of class, family, and race that got her off the dole before long. My mother was queen for only a day. But I refuse to be let off the hook. The welfare benefits she received for less than a year were crucial to her life and mine; they enabled her to decide freely to keep me. By letting "welfare queen" be a shameful smear on Black women, we smear all women, shaming ourselves into thinking that the work of care has no value. And we deny all women their full freedom.

What would it take for us to place Emma Mae, and for that matter her ailing aunt and her four children, at the heart of our political theory? Her brother Clarence thought she was a parasite and a shirker. I believe he had it precisely backward.

CHAPTER 4:

Family Values

What I remember most vividly from when my children were small is being alone with them. Admittedly, it's mostly a sleep-deprived blur. Of course, I wasn't really alone all the time. My husband took a relatively long parental leave after our first was born and was (still is) a deeply involved father. For that matter, he was alone with our babies a lot, while I worked for pay. I also had friends and outings. But my baby and I were alone a lot. I remember hours of breastfeeding, then hours spooning tiny portions of mush into her reluctant mouth, hours sitting on the floor next to rubber mats decorated with the alphabet while she banged small plastic toys together, hours carrying her back and forth across the living room, trying to soothe her out of fussing and into sleep. I remember days in empty, rain-soaked parks receiving gift after gift of dandelions solemnly presented to me one after another. I remember hearing my daughter's first laugh on a swing in an empty playground. It was sometimes beautiful, but it was also often excruciatingly boring and intensely lonely.

It seemed wrong at the time to be so alone as I did the work of socializing a child. Now it seems to me to encapsulate facts about our historical moment and the modern American family.

The myth of autonomy depends partly on a myth about the family. It is a myth of the autonomous or private family as the ideal, "natural" family. The autonomous family contains dependency. That is, it provides for dependents, and it keeps dependency contained within the bounds of the private family. With that function comes a structure: the nuclear family of wage-earning husband, housewife, and 2.5 children—Ozzie and Harriet's family. This is the family the American Right extols and demands a return to, as if it were the natural, primordial form of family. In recent years, even those demanding a modernized, egalitarian family take for granted the basic structure: All people, regardless of gender and sexual preference, should be free to form nuclear families. This has the advantage of taking those who extol the nuclear family at their word, taking an unassailable moral high ground within the terms already set. But it does not question the basic structure of the nuclear family and its central role in privatizing dependency.

In fact, the nuclear family is a historical anomaly. It has not been the norm even in American history. For example, only beginning in the 1920s did the majority of children in the US live in families in which the man was the primary wage earner, the wife was not involved in full-time labor for wages outside the house or alongside her husband, and the children were in school instead of in the labor force.[1]

Historian Stephanie Coontz defines family as a mechanism for sanctioning relations between biological and social reproduction, that is, between procreation and the perpetuation of human society. How wealth is created and passed down is a central element of every human society, so family type is always linked to the mode of production within a society.

The first type of family in North America was the kinship system of the original inhabitants, characterized by networks of kin and marital alliances, and in many cases was matrilineal. This type was replaced and destroyed by the characteristic family in the American colonies and early postrevolutionary United States: the household-family system. In the colonies, the center of production was the household. It was where food, clothing, and other goods were made for consumption and sale. Households grew crops, then cut and threshed the crops to become food or fibers for cloth that they spun into fabric and in turn sewed into clothes. Therefore, the first type of family to arise among the white settlers in the American colonies was the household family. It was characterized by a lack of boundaries between economic transactions and personal relations, and between public institutions and family ones. Individuals within families and households within community were all governed by patriarchy—older white men ruled. But as Coontz explains, not all white men ruled, and men did not rule only over women. Property-owning men ruled, including over lower-status men. The father in a household had paramount authority over those within the household, including wife, children, apprentices, and servants (male or female). But he could be punished for not maintaining proper order within his household. Furthermore, the mistress of a household ruled over children and servants, and servants were considered part of the family. The family was not defined in biological terms. Vertical relations were crucial; it was inequality all the way down, accepted as the natural way of things.

A typical household might contain children from the current marriage, children from a previous marriage to a deceased spouse, servants, apprentices, and perhaps a cousin. Children were frequently orphaned and for this reason might grow up in households other than that of their parents. In addition, children were often sent to live in households other than their parents' in order to learn a trade by the age of eleven or twelve. The lower classes frequently did not have their own households, instead living in the households of their employers throughout their lives.

Colonial authorities tried to ensure that everyone was part of a family, even fining single men. But the family was not understood as qualitatively distinct from the rest of the world as we now see the family. The notion of family as a refuge is part and parcel of the movement of economic production out of the household and into the factory that occurred with the rise of capitalism. Until then, household production was the basis of the economy, and the household was the basis of the political order. It was not viewed as an emotional refuge from the economic or political world. The household family was a little commonwealth, defined by hierarchy, obedience, and production.

Women were subordinate, but then all relationships were seen as hierarchical, so that didn't make women special. Women were thought quantitatively weaker, but, according to Coontz, there was little sense of qualitative differences between the sexes. Women's subordination was less about gender than simply a social necessity, along with other forms of subordination. Recall that Jefferson's exclusion of women and slaves from democratic participation was justified by necessity, not inherent difference. Order required that each person be placed in a hierarchy, owing obedience to those above and commanding it from those below. To be dependent was to be situated as an inferior within a hierarchy, but such a status was the norm for all genders. Most people were dependent. There was no personal shame in being dependent, and those who were dependent were not seen as economically nonproductive. Women's productive labor in the household was understood as economically important. A wife was an economic necessity, not a decoration, and spouses were called *yoke mates*.

The American Revolution called all hierarchy into question. Political order was now to be based on consent. Equality, not hierarchy, became the norm in human relationships. This, for the first time, made the subordination of certain categories of people into anomalies that required explanation. If social order no longer required hierarchy, then how could women's subordination be justified? The same was true of slaves. The new answer was "nature." For the subordination of women and slaves to be just, they must be qualitatively different from men and nonslaves. Women's subordination was newly gendered, and slavery racialized. While the new ideas professed the naturalness of independence, they were also a prescription: Only those who were independent could be full citizens, and those who were dependent—women, children, servants, slaves—could not. As Coontz puts it, colonial society saw the family as a little commonwealth that modeled the hierarchical relations binding all of society, whereas in postrevolutionary America, egalitarian society was made up of households whose independence formed the basis of social liberty.[2]

Intriguingly, some women voted in the colonies and early Republic. To be sure, in most colonies and later the states, only property owners of any gender could vote, so there was less at stake. Married women could not vote, because they owned no property: Upon marriage everything that belonged to a woman became her husband's. So it was a very small proportion of women who were ever allowed to vote. Nevertheless, the division between those entitled to full citizenship and those not entitled did not cut clearly along gendered lines. But soon after the Revolution, one state after another began explicitly gendering the right to vote, denying it to women. The last state to allow women to vote was New Jersey, which revoked it in 1807.[3]

Racialized slavery, too, solidified and spread after the Revolution, and with it the enslaved family form, which was characterized not by autonomy but by its vulnerability to rending. W. E. B. Du Bois wrote that the threat that children could be taken away from their mothers and kin and sold away was one of the essential features of US slavery and made it fundamentally different from other types of unfree labor, such as indentured servitude. Slave narratives—the stories written by formerly enslaved people about their ordeals—and abolitionist tracts both put the taking of children from their enslaved mothers at the center. "I have borne thirteen children and seen almost all sold off into slavery, and when I cried out with a mother's grief, none but Jesus heard," wrote Sojourner Truth. Frederick Douglass's autobiography begins with his separation from his mother, which was foundational to his becoming aware of himself as a slave.[4] Depicting the horrors of ripping children from their mothers' arms was a particularly effective tool in stirring the nation's conscience against slavery. We all instinctively know that a mother's care is essential to being human. Taking children from their mothers is dehumanizing—which was the point, its function in the system of slavery. Historian Laura Briggs writes, "By such means, enslaved children and their mothers were instructed that they were not to be treated as people, the subject of the care and work that passes cultures down from one generation to another, but instead were bodies, flesh, cultivated for the labor they could do."[5] The terror of losing a child was so acute that the mere threat of it was an effective tool of coercion to make enslaved people compliant. Although the outright selling of children away from their mothers ended with the abolition of slavery, the taking of children as a tool of control would be used again and again throughout the US's history.

Meanwhile, with the rise of capitalism came what has been called the *cult of domesticity*, the notion that home is a sacred haven from the impersonal, grasping world of the market. Capitalism conceptually splits work into waged work outside of the home and unwaged work within the home, which is to say between men's labor and women's. Capitalism depends on the reproductive labor that keeps the current workforce fed, clothed, clean, and healthy and creates the next generation of labor, but it doesn't pay for this labor. This is one way—indeed the first, foundational way—that capitalism extracts surplus value. It achieves this by separating reproductive labor from waged labor and rendering it invisible, allowing it to be uncompensated.

Along with the cult of domesticity came the notion of the *family wage*, a wage sufficient for a man to support a non-wage-earning wife and family. The family wage was a complicated historical development, at once a demand that forced concessions from capital and a capitulation to it. By demanding a family wage, working men used it as a method for demanding higher wages. Through this demand, they insisted on the value of their families and the need for space in their lives that was independent of wage labor. Workers claimed their labor as a source of pride and, therefore, a basis for power. As I mention in Chapter 1, they reversed the traditional association of wage earning with dependence and turned it into a source of independence. But the family wage also served to yoke men thoroughly to wage work: If your family depends absolutely on the wage you earn, you will submit to nearly anything in order not to lose it.

The rhetorical split between work and home also distorts historical realities. Industrialization is typically thought of as a move of production out of the home and into the factory. But historian Joan Wallach Scott points out that before industrialization many women, especially young women, worked outside of their own homes, often as servants. With the rise of factories, the shift was not from working in one's home to working outside it but from one type of nonhome workplace to another. Furthermore, in many cases, capitalism caused an *increase* in production within the home, in the form of piecework or outwork, often performed by women or whole families. This wasn't just a feature of early, primitive industrialization. According to Scott, in Europe piecework did not peak until the turn of the twentieth century (and it is now having a resurgence in America, with the rise of Uber, Lyft, and Mechanical Turk, and delivery services like Amazon Flex, Caviar, and DoorDash).

The cult of domesticity was full of ironies. Catharine Beecher was one of the chief American propagandists of domesticity in the nineteenth century, celebrating in her handbooks on domestic economy women's special role in the private sphere, while supporting herself in the public sphere with her books and speeches extolling domesticity.[6] Born in 1800, Beecher herself grew up in a household that included her seven brothers and sisters, three half-siblings, one orphan cousin, two bound servants, several students boarding from nearby Litchfield Law School and Litchfield Female Academy, an aunt and uncle and grandmother who visited for extended periods, plus numerous eminent visitors coming to see her father, the Reverend Lyman Beecher. This was hardly the peaceful haven from the public world that Beecher extolled in her handbooks.

Domesticity has to be seen as prescription, not mere description. It is better understood not as a split between the work world and the home but as linking work and home. "Home is the center from which men go forth to business, and business is the field from which they go home with the spoils," writes Coontz. Or, as a New England pastor put it in 1827:

> It is at home, where man . . . seeks a refuge from the vexations and embarrassments of business, an enchanting repose from exertion, a relaxation of care by the interchange of affection; where some of his finest sympathies, tastes, moral and religious feelings are formed and nourished; where is the treasury of pure disinterested love, such as is seldom found in the busy walks of a selfish and calculating world.[7]

In Charles Dickens's *Great Expectations,* the protagonist Pip works in an office next to his fellow clerk, Wemmick. In one chapter, Wemmick takes Pip on a visit to his idyllic home. This being Dickens, the scene is exaggerated to the point of satire: The clerk has created a tiny castle, complete with moat and drawbridge, within a slum. Inside the moat is a perfect cottage with lovely gardens and an Aged Parent on whom the clerk dotes. Wemmick asks Pip not to mention this home at the office. "The office is one thing and private life is another. When I go into the office, I leave the Castle behind me, and when I come into the Castle, I leave the office behind me." As Pip and Wemmick left the cottage to return to the office, "Wemmick got drier and harder as we went along, and his mouth tightened into a post-office again." The passage beautifully illustrates the cult of domesticity, first developed during the industrial revolution and raised to an art form by the Victorians.

Dickens was wildly popular in America, and it was Americans who embraced the cult most of all. Alexis de Tocqueville, reporting on American democracy in the early nineteenth century, writes of the "extreme dependence" of American women "confined within the narrow circle of domestic life." In contrast to French women, American women never managed "outward concerns" of a family, conducted business, or took part in politics, as Americans have never "supposed that one consequence of democratic principles is the subversion of marital power."[8]

The ideology of domesticity was a response to the growth of capitalism and anxiety over the rise of competitive markets. Early modern European philosophers were intensely concerned with the problems raised by emergent capitalism—how to simultaneously justify, indeed glorify, individual pursuit of maximum gain within the market while maintaining the strong constraints against uninhibited selfishness on which functioning markets themselves depend. Domesticity's gendered solution was to divide the world into men's and women's spheres. Part of the humor of the scene from *Great Expectations* is that Wemmick has created his idyllic home without a woman, for his elderly father—although of course there is a female servant. Men could pursue profit and self-interest ruthlessly, safe in the knowledge that women were keeping the home a haven from the market, a place where love and selflessness ruled. With production gone from the home, wives lost their status as straightforward economic assets and instead became decorative and moral assets.

In *The Wealth of Nations*, published the same year as the Declaration of Independence, Adam Smith famously writes that "It is not from the benevolence of the butcher, the brewer, or the baker that we expect our dinner but from regard to their self-interest." Nancy Folbre points out that Smith ignored how dinner actually arrived at the table—through the domestic labor of wives, mothers, cooks, maids, and slaves. Earlier economists listed in their tallies of economically valuable production "taylors and their wives," "millers and their wives," "farmers and their wives," and even the economic contribution of children.[9] Smith, on the other hand, believed that only production of material things produced the surplus needed for growth. Services might be necessary but didn't produce economic growth. And he completely excluded domestic labor from productive work.

In America, this shift can be traced through the census. As Ann Crittenden describes in *The Price of Motherhood*, when the US census first began measuring economic activity in 1820, its unit for this purpose was families, not individuals, thus reflecting the assumption that all members of the family contributed to economic production. Families, not individuals, were labelled by occupation. But by 1850, the census recorded the occupations of individuals. In 1860, women were asked their occupations, with most answering "housekeeper." But in 1870, economist and Civil War veteran Francis Walker became head of the Census Bureau, and he dismissed the idea that women's household work had any economic value. "We may assume that speaking broadly [a wife] does not produce as much as she consumes." (Perhaps he assumed that wives regularly consumed the children they bore, instead of raising them into productive citizens.) He decreed that only housekeeping work for wages would be counted as an occupation; women's work for their own families was merely "keeping house," thus defined as nonproductive. This small inversion of words worked the miracle of rendering most women's toil—birthing, cleaning, canning, gardening, sewing, mending, nursing, and teaching, of producing the next generation of productive workers, maintaining the current generation, and caring for the prior generation—completely invisible and irrelevant to the economy. Walker even erased most of women's wage-earning labor, because he instructed his census workers to ignore money earned by women from taking in boarders or doing piecework in the home.[10]

Women didn't allow their labor to be disappeared without a protest. In 1878, the Association for the Advancement of Women issued a letter to Congress, signed by many of America's most highly educated women, decrying Walker's census for overlooking the labor of twelve million women. They suggested that the Census Bureau hire women to collect statistics on women and children, a sly commentary on the potential for the census to both observe and shape economic life.[11] The suggestion was ignored. Instead, by 1900 women without wage-earning jobs outside the home were officially labelled "dependents." As Crittenden puts it, "the notion that women at home were 'dependents' had acquired the status of scientific fact. The idea that money income was the only measure of human productivity had triumphed. With official blessing, husbands could consider wives not as economic assets but as liabilities. The theft was breathtaking."[12]

Because it is the wage that supports the family, the wage-earning man becomes responsible for all labor, productive and reproductive. As a result, marriage demonstrates a man's willingness to accept the responsibilities of steady work to support non-wage-earning dependents. Thus, not only can a married man claim the need for a "family wage" but, by being married, he signals that he deserves a good wage and will work hard to keep it. Conversely, marriage suggests a woman is only tenuously tied to the labor market. This still echoes today in the motherhood wage penalty: What is often loosely described as a gender wage gap is, in fact, mainly a gap between mothers and others. Setting aside part-time work, women who are not mothers make nearly as much as men, ninety cents to a man's dollar. But full-time wage-earning mothers in 2024 made seventy-one cents to a man's dollar, and single mothers fifty-six to sixty-six cents to a man's dollar. These numbers haven't budged for years.[13] To top it off, mothers are much less likely to be hired in the first place. Meanwhile, fatherhood actually boosts men's earnings.[14]

The assumption that women should be home and out of the wage market was never extended to all women. It didn't apply to Black women, both because Black men were not granted a real "family wage" and because Black women's labor was in demand outside the family (at low wages, of course). Because the cult of domesticity didn't apply to Black women, they didn't fall for it in the same way. For example, while white reformers often made claims of rights based on the romantic rhetoric of moral motherhood, Black women's organizations stressed the value of women's work in and out of the home. "Black suffragists were . . . demanding votes for women on the basis of their work as—rather than their mere being—mothers," writes historian Eileen Boris. The National Association of Wage Earners, founded in 1921 to elevate working conditions for Black women, always welcomed housewives as members.[15] With so many Black women employed in domestic service, the distinction was not between work and not-work, but between work for someone else's family and work for your own.

One must be precise. The conflict between care work and waged work is typically treated as an inevitable result of industrialization's physical split between home and work and as the cause for women's segregation into low-paid fields. But as described above, for many women home and work were split before industrialization, and waged work was frequently done in the home after industrialization. Instead, the supposed modern split between home and work was rhetoric that served to keep women's wages down and, by keeping women's wages down, to push all wages down. Women's poor fit with the wage market, and supposed lower need for wages, justified paying women less. Then women were crowded into sex-segregated fields that were supposedly a natural fit for women, which had the effect of pushing their wages still lower. Then the existence of these sex-segregated fields was used as proof of a natural sexual division of labor. Joan Wallach Scott notes that, where employers hired women, it meant that they were trying to save money. There was nothing inevitable about it, just people making choices that served their interests.

This played out in America in the field of public education. Universal public education was achieved early in America relative to other countries, but it was done on the cheap, by hiring women as schoolteachers. This goes a good way toward explaining the low status of teaching and the skimpy funding for public education in America to this day. Until the mid-nineteenth century, most schoolteachers in America were men. Often they served as schoolteachers only in the offseason of their usual work, or they were ambitious young men using teaching as a stepping stone to careers in the church or the law. Teaching offered opportunities for making valuable connections with influential people. But in the mid-nineteenth century, the "common school," a precursor to today's public schools, arose. These schools were open to all, free, and established and funded by local taxes. This meant that many more teachers were needed, but towns didn't want to raise taxes to pay higher salaries, which would be necessary to attract more teachers. There weren't enough men willing to take these jobs at the wages small school districts were willing to pay. The solution to this problem was women. "God seems to have made woman peculiarly suited to guide and develop the infant mind, and it seems . . . very poor policy to pay a man 20 or 22 dollars a month, for teaching children the ABCs, when a female could do the work more successfully at one-third of the price," wrote the Littleton, Massachusetts, School Committee in 1849.[16] This statement exemplifies the use of naturalized gender roles to justify keeping wages down.

Nothing in history is really linear. Even after this shift, men still sometimes took teaching jobs, and schools were delighted to land a male teacher when they could get one. My great-grandmother, who grew up in Butte, Montana, was valedictorian of her high school class and then was permitted by her family to go to college at Stanford because there was a sick aunt in California whom she could care for while at college. After graduating in 1906 (the year of the earthquake), she came back to Butte and got a job teaching school, the only job for a woman of her class in that time and place. Soon, a man showed up to join the high school teaching faculty. That man would successfully parlay connections he made while teaching into a career at Anaconda Copper, eventually rising to vice president. This was my great-grandfather. When they got married, my great-grandmother was fired, because married women were barred from teaching. I imagine that for my great-grandmother, home and work felt both separated and linked: She was exiled from waged work by marriage, but marriage gave her a higher economic and social position. She used to say to her children that her husband stole her job.

The domestic family united all men by virtue of their not being women. While the open use of violence to enforce hierarchy was no longer as acceptable as it had been in previous eras, in its place came woman's oppression by her own biology. As described in Barbara Ehrenreich and Deirdre English's *For Her Own Good*, in the nineteenth century the medical profession began to churn out theories about women's biological incapacities, both physical and mental.

The domestic family united men as a class, but it also united women with each other and women with their children. Intense expressions of friendship among women were common. As late as the 1908 publication of *Anne of Green Gables*, Anne's attachment to her friend Diana is depicted more swooningly than her relationship to Gilbert. Just as intense were women's connections to their children. Plenty of nineteenth-century novels depicted romance between men and women culminating in marriage, but few had any interest in the couple within marriage. In the nineteenth century, the axis of the family was not the adult male-female couple but the parent-child relationship.

It was also in this era that the notion that a family should be self-sufficient arose. Where once the household family was embedded in both obligations and supports from the wider society, the domestic family was supposed to be immune from interference. Paradoxically, with the decline of broader, informal connections that could support families in need, the self-sufficient family required the development of formal institutions to support families when self-sufficiency faltered. The task of maintaining the self-sufficiency of the family by caring for inevitable dependencies within the family (children, elders, the sick) was pushed onto women—especially mothers—within the family. But if the flow of wages from the family's breadwinner failed, there had to be institutions to allow the mother to keep doing this care work so that, among other things, this work didn't get pushed out of the family and onto state institutions such as orphanages. Thus, institutions such as mother's pensions arose. At this point, institutional supports were acceptable because they were seen as protections of capitalism and the self-sufficient family, rather than socialist threats to it. They were, of course, available only to those families that met the racial and sexual requirements; rarely were non-white, unmarried, or divorced mothers granted mother's pensions. If you conformed to the ideal of the domestic family in every way except lacking an inhabitant of the wage-earner role, the state would step in and fill that role.

As the nineteenth century progressed, the use of mass-produced clothing, preserved food, and medicine increased. Housewives' production within the home contracted, but non-productive tasks, such as transportation of people and goods, expanded. Not only were some things once made within the home now mass-produced for purchase, but a lot of goods and services that were once delivered to the home—such as milk, ice, and knife sharpening—now had to be procured from stores. (The internet-enabled rise of home delivery in the twenty-first century is thus less futuristic than retro.) This marked a shift in the family type from production to consumption, from the domestic family to the consumer family, as Coontz puts it.

With universal public grammar school established, next came public high schools and kindergartens, increasing the amount of time spent in formal education outside of the home. Thus, childrearing, too, was increasingly mass-produced.

Perhaps because so many functions were emptying out of it, the family also shrank. Formerly, those who did not breed had vital roles to play within families—as aunts, uncles, cousins. These roles withered in importance as the nuclear family took over. Once upon a time, everyone simply found themselves in families, perhaps eventually extending them by producing children; by the mid-twentieth century, all were commanded to "start" families.

As mothers were spending less time on childrearing, the axis of the family shifted from the parent-child relationship to the couple relation. Marriage also grew to take up a larger fraction of more people's lives. In earlier eras, people had often married late and many not at all, but during the first three decades of the twentieth century, the average age of marriage and the proportion of the population that was unmarried both declined. That shift didn't stop until the early 1960s, when the rate of marriage was higher than it had ever been before (or has been since).[17] In the 1920s, for the first time in US history, the majority of children lived in families in which the man was the primary wage earner, the wife was not involved in full-time labor for wages outside the house or alongside her husband, and the children were in school instead of in the labor force.[18] It wasn't until the 1950s, for the first time ever, that the majority of all marriages consisted of a male breadwinner and a female housewife.

It is worth pausing over this remarkable fact. The American Right has extolled what it calls "the five-thousand-year history of traditional marriage."[19] Writers across the political spectrum who disagree on whether the type of marriage where "he brings home the bacon, she cooks it," is good or bad, obsolete or ripe for revival, unthinkingly agree that this is "traditional marriage."[20] But this type of marriage didn't flourish for five thousand years across countries worldwide. In America, it was more like twenty years. The conservative thinker and presidential candidate Patrick Buchanan identifies "the golden age of marriage" as lasting from 1945 to 1965, "when the average age of first marriages fell to record lows for both men and women and the proportion of adults who were married reached an astronomical 95 percent," and married women with children stayed out of the wage market.[21] "Traditional marriage" was an anomalous, brief historical phenomenon.

That modern creation, the self-sufficient nuclear family, was at mid-twentieth century ascendant—just in time to show its cracks and fragility as well as the price paid to maintain it. That price would be paid by women.

CHAPTER 5:

The Grandmother Hypothesis

In 1929, my maternal grandmother's idyllic childhood in a small Minnesota town was cut short by the Wall Street crash and then the grinding misery of the Depression. Her father's real estate business collapsed. He kept it limping along by accepting payment partly in eggs and produce. Across America, there was plenty of work to be done, but the market to pay for it had broken down. People were hungry, and farmers were still growing food, but nobody had the money to buy it. In that way, my great grandfather was lucky to live in a small town surrounded by farms; he and the farmers could match each other's needs without the intermediary of money. My grandfather's father was not so lucky—he lost his bank job in the crash and never found it again.

My grandmother was able to go to college by landing a scholarship, but once there, she was so broke that she didn't get enough to eat and went on dates so boys would buy her cups of hot chocolate. (My mother rolled her eyes at this story. "My mother was a cocoa whore.") My grandmother finally dropped out after two years. She had to make a living at one of the three careers open to women—marriage, teaching, or nursing—so she went to nursing school and eventually got her bachelor's degree by trading nursing services at a college for tuition. Meanwhile, her parents were struggling back home in Minnesota, including caring for my great-great-grandfather, who died in 1935. They were relatively privileged, to be in a position to provide this care. Many elders' life savings were wiped out, leaving them destitute as their children lost their jobs and even their homes. Various charities sprang up around the country to offer assistance, but they were woefully inadequate. This was a crisis of capitalism, and a crisis of care.

It was in this context that Congress enacted the first national social insurance. In 1935, the Social Security Act created a system of old-age benefits for workers. It also included benefits for victims of industrial accidents, unemployment insurance for temporarily unemployed workers, and aid for mothers and children, blind persons, and persons with disabilities. But the pension system was the centerpiece. Today, when we speak of Social Security, we mean pensions for the elderly.

As calls for a national pension system built, there were questions about how to structure it. In private pension systems, there is a direct relationship between what participants pay in and what they get out: The number of years you spend paying in and at what rate determines the size of your payout. That wasn't going to work so well when Social Security was established, because it wouldn't have helped those who were already elderly. The crucial insight embodied in Social Security, and other national pension systems as they developed in the early twentieth century, was that current workers could contribute to a government fund to be distributed to former workers, with current workers seeing themselves as providing for their own future security. This structure of one generation supporting the preceding one is not new. Social Security shares that structure with human life itself.[1]

In recent decades, anthropologists and biologists have theorized that grandmothers are central to the story of how humans became human. The theory begins from the puzzle of why human females, unlike most primates, live long after their fertility ends. Human beings live much longer than apes, but a woman's reproductive years are only a bit longer than an ape's. A third of the average woman's life span is postmenopause. At Darwinian first glance, this would seem like a waste (and postmenopausal women often are treated that way). However, what has become known as the Grandmother Hypothesis posits that if a grandmother provides care for older children, a mother can give birth to more children, closely spaced, without thereby endangering the survival of the children she already has. While mother is tied up nursing a newborn, grandmother can forage to feed still helpless but weaned older grandchildren, watch over them to make sure they don't drown or get eaten by lions, and teach survival skills. Living long enough to provide all this care, at a time when she is not burdened with infants of her own, tends to increase the number of descendants a grandmother has, and therefore this postfertility longevity is selected for. This theory seems to be correct; it has been confirmed by numerous anthropological studies as well as by mathematical modelling.[2] It seems to hold even in relatively modern societies. For example, an analysis of Finnish church birth and death records for the years 1731–1890 showed that having a maternal grandmother close by while a grandchild was five years old or younger increased the odds of the child's survival past weaning. The effect disappeared for grandmothers older than seventy-five years of age, possibly because they may not have been able to help with child rearing and required care themselves, and it was much more pronounced for maternal than paternal grandmothers. A grandmother's presence also reduced mothers' likelihood of dying, which itself helped their babies survive.[3]

The theory is interwoven with the fact of human infants' extended helplessness. Other species' babies can survive with a relatively brief period of care, so they don't need grandmothers. It is in a species characterized by extended dependency that support from others besides a mother is selected for. Furthermore, the theory suggests a connection between postreproductive longevity and the development of culture as a distinctive human survival strategy: Long-lived grandmothers and other elders are available not only to feed grandchildren, but also to teach them lessons learned in a long life. They pass on stories.

Even though my mother and grandmother had a difficult relationship, they never broke ties, and my grandmother played a large role in raising me. My mother sent me to spend each summer with my grandparents. This enabled her to work full-time during the summers when she went to law school, boosting her income and career, and to have respites from single-parenting. Because they were retired, my grandparents could provide time and attention to me during those summers. One summer, my grandfather covered the keys on an ancient manual typewriter with tape and taught me to type. Another summer he taught me the names of all the local wildflowers. My grandmother took me with her when she gathered signatures on a petition to remove Secretary of the Interior James Watt from office. She turned it into an opportunity for socializing, thereby teaching me that political activism could be fun. She also taught me to make bread, always pairing the slow work of mixing and kneading with stories. She told me tales from her youth, tales of my ancestors (including the resurrected Ulalia), and tales of our community.

As I describe in Chapter 2, grandmothers are often the keepers of tribal memory and traditions. As a result, they can be forces of resistance in the face of oppression and social disruption, but also targets of reaction, such as during the witch hunts. Division among generations leaves a society fragile, because generational reciprocity is a crucial human survival mechanism. In any society, the economic production of the currently working generation feeds and houses those not currently working, including those too old to work anymore and those too young to work yet. Traditionally, this meant able-bodied adults supporting their parents—who once supported them—and their children—who will one day support them when they grow too old to work. In the United States these days, however, this generational solidarity is frayed.

In this on-your-own society, we are often encouraged to save for retirement. Certainly, we can save up money. But what we mostly need in old age is others' labor. We have the illusion, in an advanced economy, that we can save up labor, because we can save money with which to command labor. But someone has to actually do the labor, of growing food, serving it, and cleaning up after it, cleaning up those who eat it, and so on. Labor is not something that can be saved up. Actual workers have to do work in the here and now.

There is one way we do save up labor to spend later: child-rearing. We invest tremendous amounts of labor in keeping fragile babies alive, teaching them to read, write, hold a spoon, use the internet, and behave socially appropriately, to rear them into adults who can work hard enough to support themselves and dependents. Viewed one way, the labor invested in their rearing renders them autonomous—but, viewed in another, renders them indebted to their parents, who may call that debt by seeking to be supported in their dotage. Traditionally, children were the old-age pension system. But this was a risky proposition, because children might die, might fail to earn enough to help their parents, might move away, or simply be ingrates who decline to help. Or, if conditions were right, they might accuse their mother of being a witch.

Communitarian critics of modern American individualism often hearken back to the tight bonds of traditional society with nostalgia, recalling the ties within families and groups that ensured people who needed care received it. The first problem is that getting your needs met depended on the ability, good luck, and good will of the particular individuals in your family or group. Second, those bonds were often oppressive and hierarchical. If you followed the rules for the social role you were born into and showed the appropriate level of deference and submission, you might receive support. For example, as recounted in Laurel Thatcher Ulrich's *A Midwife's Tale*, at the turn of the eighteenth century, Massachusetts midwife Martha Ballard was forced to live under her son's thumb to survive near the end of her life when her husband was imprisoned for debt. It was no picnic, although she was taken care of. On the other hand, if you broke any of the rules, you might find yourself an outcast—or, during the witch trial era, dead. Just ask Hester Prynne or Jude Fawley.

This is where Social Security, or any other social safety net program, can be transformative. Social Security spreads out the risk and burden of caring for elders, from individual families to the entire society, thereby rendering the elderly and their families secure. Further, because of the myth that elders have earned their Social Security payments, and the consequence that Social Security is structured as a genuine entitlement, elders are further freed from a sense of dependency, indebtedness, or shame. This is true autonomy. It comes from social support.

In selling Social Security to the nation, Franklin D. Roosevelt pitched it soothingly as a mere modernization of family and community supports:

> Security was attained in the earlier days through the interdependence of members of families upon each other and of the families within a small community upon each other. The complexities of great communities and of organized industry make less real these simple means of security. Therefore, we are compelled to employ the active interest of the Nation as a whole through government in order

> to encourage a greater security for each individual who composes it. . . . This seeking for a greater measure of welfare and happiness does not indicate a change in values. It is rather a return to values lost in the course of our economic development and expansion.[4]

Even so, opponents fought hard against the bill, decrying it as a socialist invasion of the private realm.[5] A representative of an Illinois manufacturers' association testified that if Social Security was passed it would undermine America by "destroying initiative, discouraging thrift, and stifling individual responsibility."[6] A third of Republican legislators voted against the bill, saying it sent America down the road to socialism. Alf Landon decried it as imposing "the largest tax bill in history," and made repeal a centerpiece of his presidential campaign in 1936.[7] To assuage such opposition, supporters framed the program in individualistic terms.

Social Security might have been framed as simple social reciprocity—members of a society together support those in need and can expect support in turn when they are in need. Instead, in a subtle but fateful slide, Social Security's benefits were depicted as earned by individuals through their wage work. Roosevelt was adamant that old-age pensions be funded through individual contributions to a dedicated fund, maintaining the notional connection between individual work and payout.[8] This framing shaped the program's development.

Social Security could have been structured like private pension systems, with payout based on what each worker has paid in. As noted above, that wouldn't have helped those who were then already elderly. An alternative would have been to abandon any pretense of delivering benefits to individuals according to what they paid in and simply grant each retiree an equal monthly stipend, funded by taxes. This would have supported the social reciprocity conception. In fact, that alternative was proposed by Dr. Francis Everett Townsend, and it was popular. At the Townsend movement's peak in the 1930s, there were 3,400 Townsend Clubs around the country, with five million members—but it was opposed by employers and the wealthy.[9] [10] Many have argued that the pressure of Townsend's movement caused Congress to create Social Security. Had America embraced Townsend's expansive vision, we all would have enjoyed a more comfortable old age, and women in particular would have been far less likely to be impoverished as elders. Today the average monthly Social Security benefit is $1,900, not nearly enough to live on, and of course not everyone qualifies for that much, or anything at all.[11] In comparison, Townsend proposed a $200 monthly check to every elder; that would be $4,600 in 2025 dollars.

Another alternative would have been to provide a reward for work that the market failed to compensate—most importantly, care work. Indeed, Townsend's plan accommodated this idea by delivering equal benefits to all, without regard to earlier earnings. Townsend said that he got the idea after looking out his window one morning to see two old women dressed in once fine, now ragged clothes, picking through his garbage in search of food. Perhaps he saw that they may never have earned high wages but made a contribution to society nonetheless, and designed a system that wouldn't leave them out.

Instead, Social Security represents a conflicted compromise that supports the autonomous family. Payouts are notionally tied to payments in, in that checks are generally larger for those who earn more. Initially, only wage earners were granted retiree benefits; non-wage-earning wives got nothing. Widows and orphans were provided for under another program created by the Social Security Act, Aid to Dependent Children (ADC), colloquially known as mothers' pensions or welfare. But this system provided no reward to men for taking on the burden of supporting families; husbands and fathers got no greater retirement benefits than single men. So in 1939, Congress passed major amendments to Social Security. The amendments increased a married man's retirement benefits by 50 percent once his wife reached age sixty-five. That is, a married man could claim benefits based on 150 percent of his earnings, whereas single people could claim benefits based on only 100 percent of their earnings. A married woman who worked for wages would pay taxes on her earnings, but, except in the unlikely event that she earned as much or nearly as much as her husband, would receive no more benefit than one who did not engage in work for pay. Policy makers recognized that this meant single men and all female workers were being overtaxed to subsidize married couples. But this was seen as good thing, because it increased a man's incentive to marry and decreased married women's incentive to work for wages. To really tilt the scales, librarians, school teachers, social workers, nurses, and hospital employees were excluded from the program, with the intended result that about half of women, even if they worked for wages, couldn't qualify.[12] If a woman wanted a pension, she had better get married, and to a good breadwinner.

The 1939 amendments also extended retiree benefits to wage earners' widows. To qualify, you had to be married and living with the retiree when he died. If you were divorced, if you ran away from an abusive husband, or if he abandoned you, you got nothing. Social Security survivors' benefits were, and still are as of this writing, relatively generous and given automatically, without stigma and without means testing. They are a genuine entitlement based on the survivor's dependence on the deceased man, and, in turn, on the fiction that he had paid for the benefits with taxes on his earnings. This meant that widowed mothers who had been in durable marriages to men who qualified for Social Security received survivors' benefits, while ADC was left to divorced mothers, never-married mothers, or those who had married the wrong men. The result, as Gwendolyn Mink and Rickie Solinger put it, was that the stigma of welfare began to congeal, although the process took many years. This separation into two programs served to draw a line between two forms of welfare: one for citizens and one for subjects. "The critical difference between these two forms of welfare lies in their relation to individuals' autonomy. While welfare for citizens enables them to be self-ruling persons, welfare for subjects enables the government to rule them," writes Dorothy Roberts.[13]

The refusal to treat African Americans as full citizens also played a role in the design of Social Security. Under the original act, Social Security old-age pensions were designed to exclude about three-fifths of African Americans, mostly by excluding agricultural and domestic laborers.[14] Even as African Americans moved into jobs that were included in the Social Security system, they still got short shrift. As Jill Quadagno explains in *The Color of Welfare,* Social Security transferred money from African Americans and wage-earning women to whites and homemakers, and to a lesser degree it still does.[15] Partly this is because African Americans had (and still have) lower life expectancy than whites; thus, they had fewer years in which to claim retirement benefits. They also earned less, and because benefits were tied to past earnings, the benefits African Americans received were smaller. Furthermore, there was (and still is) an earnings cap on Social Security taxes.[16] That is, Social Security taxes are deducted from wages only up to a certain amount (set at $176,100 in 2025). Earnings above that amount are untaxed. With African Americans and single women typically earning below that amount, most of their earnings are taxed for Social Security, whereas higher-earning white men get more of their wages tax-free.[17]

Furthermore, Social Security was designed to reward a certain kind of family structure, rather than a particular kind of work. Wives of wage earners will receive benefits whether they themselves earned wages (and therefore paid Social Security taxes), or provided care, or not. This means that a wife who works full-time for wages, has no children, and pays a full share of taxes gets the same benefit as a wife who doesn't work for wages but cares full-time for children, and the same benefit as a wife who neither works for wages nor has any responsibility to care for children or elders.

Edward McCaffery, in his book *Taxing Women*, explains that there is another tax subsidy these breadwinner-homemaker families receive under the Social Security system: The value of the work in the home that homemakers provide is untaxed.

"Of course it isn't taxed," you might say. "No wages are paid, so there is nothing to tax."

But the work does have monetary value that becomes visible as soon as you have to hire someone to do it, and economists have a standard method for measuring the value of things that don't happen to be bought and sold. The price you would have to pay in the market for these services is their "imputed value." Mothers who work for wages have to pay for services such as housecleaning or childcare out of the taxed wages they earn, but families in which someone (typically a wife) provides these services without wages receive their imputed value tax-free. This issue is compounded by joint tax filing, in which a married couple's earnings are summed together for tax purposes. With joint filing, the lower-earning spouse's income is, in effect, added on top of the higher-earning spouse's income, which could push the couple into a higher tax bracket. As I describe in my introduction, the couple is faced with the choice of having the lower-earning spouse either stay home to provide untaxed care work or work for wages that are taxed at a high marginal rate and will likely be eaten away by the cost of necessary services, such as childcare and housecleaning. To be clear, my point is not that taxing unpaid care work would help care workers, but rather that US tax structures reward family units that fit into gendered breadwinner-housewife norms.

McCaffery explains that the history of Social Security, as it has been reformed since 1935, should be understood as a decision to give homemaker spouses credit for that imputed income on which they were never taxed. He describes it as a benefit to these wives, but, because they get the credit based on their marital status, it is better understood as a benefit for married men, who get benefits based on 150 percent of their taxes instead of merely the 100 percent that unmarried people get—or the 0 percent return that wage-earning married women get. This means, as described above, that a wife who earns less than her husband will pay taxes on her earnings but not receive any more in Social Security benefits than if she hadn't worked for wages at all. These incentives and penalties were well understood and intentional, when Social Security was established. The aim was to discourage married women from working and to reward men for marrying.

There is yet another way that Social Security is structured to benefit breadwinners at the expense of care providers. To qualify for Social Security, you have to have earned wages for at least forty quarters (ten years), but the benefit checks you get are based on averaging your earnings over thirty-five years. If you had earnings for more than thirty-five years, your lowest earning years are dropped, but with fewer years, the calculations will include low-earning years, which will lower your benefits.[18] This method assumes a breadwinner's typical life cycle—always earning wages, except for maybe a few brief spells of unemployment or underemployment. A care provider who drops out of the wage market for extended periods will be penalized later with reduced Social Security checks (unless she is married to a breadwinner). Social Security could, but doesn't, provide any credit for the time providing care—except indirectly and imprecisely, in the form of benefits for spouses (whether or not they provided any care), and thus not to single mothers.

After the establishment of Social Security, women moved into the wage market in spite of the incentives. This helped prop up Social Security, because wage-earning women were paying more in taxes despite getting no extra benefit out. This is part of what enabled the expansion of the Social Security program, in the form of Medicare, in the 1960s. (Later, undocumented immigrants would also help prop up Social Security and Medicare by paying taxes in without getting benefits out.) Also, because Social Security goes to elders who earned wages and their spouses—rather than just to those who had previously provided care for the young—it effectively redistributes resources from parents to nonparents. Furthermore, by socializing transfers from the young to the old but leaving transfers from parents to children private, it renders old age secure while leaving care for children insecure. It also violates the principle of reciprocity, because the elderly are "repaid" by the next generation not for their work rearing that generation but for their waged work—or marriage to a waged worker.

At the time Social Security was established, most people had children and raised them within marriages, so the flawed solution it represented was papered over. But many people now have no children, and many women are raising children outside of marriage. This is fracturing the pretense of reciprocity and threatening what fragmentary social insurance we have. Social Security has been immensely successful at reducing poverty among elders. But its flaws limit the possibilities for building on it.

My grandmother was an indomitable force. She was diagnosed with emphysema in her sixties but lived on a small fraction of lung capacity for another fifteen years. During the last ten years of her life, she was able to stay in her own home thanks to home health aides who fed her, cleaned her, and talked to her. She told tales to the end, although they grew more and more fantastical over time.

At the end of her life, my grandmother presided like a queen over this cadre of care workers, on whom she was dependent. Yet at the same time she was autonomous because she had the resources to command all this labor. While our society does not offer home care as a social benefit, a net of public programs created the wealth that enabled her to afford home care. From the GI bill that helped fund my grandfather's education, to Social Security and Medicare, to a public pension from my grandfather's work for the University of California, public support made my grandparents independent in old age. These public programs made my grandmother's old age more comfortable than her parents', or that of any previous generation.

My grandmother was cared for first, as a child, by her mother. She in turn provided care to my mother and me, and finally in old age received care in her turn. However, it was not the care she had once given, nor simply her humanity, that entitled her to dignified care in her old age. Her entitlement came from her affiliation with my grandfather's high-status wage work. She had fitted herself into the family form that public safety net programs were designed to bolster, and it paid off. Those who did not fit into this form would be less fortunate.

CHAPTER 6:

The Girl Who Wouldn't Go Away

I want to tell a tale about what happens to families when the myth of autonomy comes to full flower.[1] This is a personal story. It is, among other things, a story about me and my mother.

In the summer of 1971, my mother, age twenty-four and many months pregnant, came to Seattle. I don't know how she got there, but she had little money, so she must have hitchhiked or taken a Greyhound. She didn't have a place to stay, so she went to Seward Park in southeast Seattle, where there were other young people camping out, and she slept under a weeping willow along the shore of Lake Washington. Sometime that night, the police swept through, booting people out of the park. But they let my mother be.

Perhaps she was hidden by the willow's drape, or the police saw her belly and chose to ignore her. She liked to think it was the latter, that they honored her pregnancy. It seems just as likely that seeing a pregnant woman sleeping in the park horrified them, but my mother had a powerful ability to hold her own vision of things. This made all the difference.

My mother was unmarried. If she had been like so many other young, single, and pregnant women circa 1971, she would have gone to one of the many homes for unwed mothers in Seattle, to birth and then give up her baby. She could have walked from Seward Park to the Seattle Florence Crittenton Home, where that year more than a hundred young single women and girls lived while they waited for the births of their children and then, within a few days of giving birth, gave them up to strangers.

Like my mother, most of the women at the Seattle Crittenton Home were from out of town. Families wanted their unmarried pregnant daughters hidden from sight, often sending them to homes in other towns where no one would recognize them. A brochure from a Montana Crittenton society illustrates this impulse: Although there were enough unwed mothers in Great Falls, Montana, to prompt Crittenton supporters to request that a home be established there in 1903, the Crittenton society refused, on the theory that families wanted their unwed pregnant daughters elsewhere, not in their own small hometown.

When Meredith Hall, in 1965, got pregnant in high school from a first and only sexual encounter that resembled a rape, her small town shunned her, and her mother sent her away to live with her father and his new wife. She describes in her memoir that she was forbidden to leave their house during daylight, for fear someone would see her in her embarrassing state. During dinner parties, she was instructed to hide in her room and stay still, lest her footsteps betray her presence. Eventually, she was banished altogether to a home for unwed mothers, where she gave birth and then was made to give up her baby. She was never allowed to return to school in her hometown and never really readmitted to her family, her bond with her mother forever broken by the act of separating her from her baby.

She was, in the evocative phrasing of Ann Fessler's book title, a "girl who went away." Fessler interviewed hundreds of these women, who in fact felt thrown away. Nearly every high school class had one. Nearly everyone knew some girl who had mysteriously left school to visit an aunt or recover from an illness. People knew in some sense what had really happened, yet at the same time no one spoke of it openly, least of all the girl to whom it happened. So it was secret, known and not known—an unspoken threat of the consequences of misbehavior, all the more frightening for being shadowy and hidden.

Hannah Arendt describes the central but paradoxical role of secrecy in totalitarian regimes. On the one hand, the point of concentration camps, disappearances, and other punishments is to enforce obedience through fear, so people must know about them on some level. Yet a degree of secrecy is necessary because it impedes rebellion and any clear, articulated understanding of the thing feared. Just so, knowing that disappearance would be their fate if they got pregnant induced sufficient terror to keep most girls in line.

It never occurred to me until I was grown up and read Fessler's book that my mother could have been one of these girls who went away, she from me and I from her forever. Once I understood this, it became a disturbing puzzle to me—how could we in America have done this, so recently, and why?

A part of the answer is that it was a fruit of the autonomy myth, ripening and then rotting.

My mother wouldn't have been so easy to send away. She had been out of her parents' house for nearly eight years. Four years earlier, she had been featured in an *Esquire* article on the shocking new phenomenon of unmarried couples shacking up. While single motherhood still "wasn't done," some people were beginning to do things that weren't done.

Yet in one of those paradoxes of history, in which opposing forces act at the same time, the imperative to give up babies was just peaking. In 1971, 169,000 American babies were given up for adoption in the US, 90,000 of them to unrelated strangers. As it turned out, that year, the year of my birth, a tide began to turn. American adoptions peaked in 1970 at 170,000 and then began to drop, falling to half that number by 1975.[2] In 2014, only 18,000 children under the age of two were placed for adoption in the US.[3]

Many, if not most, of these 170,000 babies adopted in 1970 were born to single women, because in that era women were not supposed to be single and pregnant. That was nothing new. It had also long been true that single women got pregnant anyway (look at the plots of nineteenth-century novels). But hundreds of thousands of American women giving up their babies was a new thing. Adoption in the US surged after World War II, hitting 50,000 for the first time in 1944, passing 100,000 in 1959. In the early postwar years, 80 percent more children were adopted than before and during the war.[4] In this era, unwed motherhood was a problem to which adoption became the solution.

Part of the reason was that, contrary to popular belief, the sexual revolution started long before the 1960 arrival of the Pill. By the 1950s, 39 percent of unmarried women had "gone all the way" by the time they were twenty years old. By 1973 that figure had risen to 68 percent.[5] For a range of reasons, including the rise of the automobile, in the 1920s courtship began to shift away from the watchful eye of family—from the porch to the car—and young people made use of their freedom. They began creating their own norms of dating and sexual behavior. Mostly, the code was, "nice girls do but don't tell." Of course, if you were caught—by getting pregnant—you were no longer a nice girl. Yet contraception was largely illegal and unavailable.

At the same time, as historian Leslie J. Reagan has documented, the 1940s saw a shift in social policy regarding abortion. Until then, abortion had been quietly tolerated except in cases in which patients died, and most towns had an experienced, competent abortionist who practiced only barely under cover. Safe abortion was available, if not always easily so. In the 1930s, growing demand for abortion had pushed it from private homes and offices into clinics and hospitals. Abortion was tolerated because capitalism's crisis had created an excess of workers. Families clearly could not support more children. But this shift made abortion more visible, and therefore more vulnerable to crackdown. Then, beginning in the 1940s, there was a reaction against women's changing roles, including their movement into wage work during World War II. With the war's end, the pressure was on for women to go home and make babies. Authorities began hunting down and prosecuting abortionists. This was paired with a more general attack on deviance and subversiveness. While leftists were hauled before the House Un-American Activities Committee (HUAC), everyday women in large numbers were forced to testify in trials of their abortionists. These witnesses were equally on trial, forced to reveal their most intimate secrets in open court. Meanwhile, the crackdown pushed competent providers out of the work and abortion deeper underground.

Thus, abortion was suddenly unavailable to the growing numbers of pregnant, unmarried women.[6] The predictable result was that a lot of women got and stayed pregnant. Many got married. But many didn't. An estimated 200,000 to 300,000 American women and girls who got pregnant out of wedlock in an average postwar year didn't marry or abort.[7] So there were simply more out-of-wedlock births than there had been. Nonmarital births spiked sharply during World War II and didn't drop off afterward. In 1940, there were 89,500 nonmarital births, or 3.8 percent of births in the US. By 1965, 291,200—or almost 10 percent of all births—were out of wedlock.[8]

Until the mid-twentieth century, a single, pregnant white woman was considered "ruined," forever outcast. But hundreds of thousands of women is a lot of outcasts to ignore. Society was maintaining increasingly unrealistic standards for the sexual purity of women, so it needed a safety valve.

Meanwhile, the mid-twentieth century command for all to "start" families created a problem for the infertile. In the postwar era, when marrying and having 2.5 children was defined as normal, to be infertile was to fail to achieve normalcy. These two new problems—rising nonmarital births and the infertile being unable to obey the imperative to start nuclear families—were potential solutions to each other. But other pieces of the puzzle were required.

"Bastards" had traditionally been considered forever tainted by their origins: tethered to the ruined women who birthed them and carrying the bad blood that had led to the sin. It was said that women who got pregnant out of wedlock were, as a result of being low-class, biologically incapable of resisting seduction. Studies found a high correlation between "mental defect and illegitimacy."[9] No one else wanted these children. But in the twentieth century, a psychoanalytic notion of deviance gained currency in place of the older theories of tainted blood. Children were now viewed through the lens of autonomy, as separate from their mothers—a notion that would have far-reaching consequences.

It was a newly women-centered theory. The older moralistic framework had placed the causal origin of sinful out-of-wedlock sex on the man. Of course, since men were simply obeying their natural urges, women had always borne the brunt of the blame, for failing to successfully resist men. The difference in the new theory was that it entirely blamed the woman's abnormal psyche for her condition. It psychologized the problem. Once upon a time, "he ruined her," but in postwar America, "she got herself in trouble." In fact, in the literature on single motherhood from that time, men are weirdly absent. It is as if single women impregnated themselves by pure force of disordered thinking, producing babies Zeus-like from their heads.

For example, by mid-century the Seattle Crittenton Home employed a staff psychiatrist as well as trained caseworkers. Its

1954 newsletter insisted that "treatment not punishment was the answer." Single pregnant women must be viewed:

> in light of current psychiatric thinking and see it was not by "chance" a girl became pregnant out of wedlock. As we review the girl's life, we see that she slowly moved toward this pregnancy out of wedlock with almost the finality of a Greek tragedy. . . . We see casework service as an opportunity of exploring with her the forces in herself and her environment which brought her into this conflict with society.[10]

The newsletter described one client, whose "pregnancy was undoubtedly an attack at the mother and not only was she desiring to punish the mother but also was attempting to make up to her and 'give' her this child." The newsletter approvingly noted that eventually she was brought to "substitute for giving the child to the mother giving the child to the caseworker," that is, giving the baby up for adoption by a stranger. My grandmother, who was a public health nurse, childcare worker, and social researcher, spoke in just these terms. She said to me once that my mother exhibited the Electra complex.

There were many other homes for unwed mothers besides Crittenton, but Crittenton was the largest network of such institutions, its shifting aims and methods representative of the wider culture's norms. The Crittenton Society was started in the late nineteenth century by the wealthy New Yorker Charles Crittenton. After his four-year-old daughter died of scarlet fever, he fell into a depression, emerging from it with a religious awakening. He ventured into New York City's slums to evangelize and was appalled by the misery of the prostitutes he met there. He decided to found homes for "lost and fallen women and wayward girls." By 1897, he had established forty-six homes across the country. He founded the Seattle Crittenton Home in 1899.[11]

In the early days, the homes were not only for pregnant women but for any of those vulnerable to sin. Crittenton said at the opening of the Seattle home, "It should not be supposed that it is necessarily a refuge only for fallen women. It is intended as much for girls who are homeless and ill or are otherwise in danger of going to the bad."[12]

In the first decades, the Crittenton homes encouraged women to keep their babies. Indeed, until the 1940s, Crittenton homes *required* mothers to keep their babies for at least six months.[13] Women often stayed for years. The homes provided training to women, to prepare them to support themselves and their children through menial work. The job of maternity homes was to help the sinning woman spiritually redeem herself through hard work and dutifully rearing her child, who itself was part of her punishment, a scarlet letter announcing her sin to the world. She could find moral redemption but not rehabilitation.

In the 1940s, the Crittenton mission, and those of other maternity homes, began to change, shifting definitively after World War II. Its staff shifted from religious to secular. In the 1940s, the Crittenton Society reversed its position from requiring women to keep their babies to insisting they give them up. The Society adopted the views of social reformers, that adoption was the answer to unwed pregnancy. In 1960, the Seattle Crittenton home instituted a rule of not accepting anyone who had decided to keep her baby.[14]

In confluence with the new nuclear model of the family, the new psychological framework had the convenient implication that if taken away from their birth mothers, the babies would be unstained. The disorder was limited to the mother's mind and thus was not communicated to the child. If married couples started families from scratch, then it was possible to imagine babies as raw ingredients that could be acquired without any reference to family roots. It was convenient, that is, in the context of a demand for babies as commodities.

This solution required a strange new inversion: Mother and child would seem to be the *ur* form of the family, the irreducible conceptual core from which more expansive definitions radiate and against which borderline instances are measured. In the past, an unwed mother might be an improper mother, but she was unquestionably a mother. But if families were started only by married couples, an unwed woman and child could not be a family. In the new psychological framework, as historian Rickie Solinger explains, an unwed mother was redefined as "not a mother." Surrendering her child to a real mother—that is, a married woman—was the price she paid to mend her conflict with society, readying her to become a real mother someday by marrying a man. Girls absorbed these lessons. One woman in Fessler's book described her reaction when she got pregnant as a teenager: "I was throwing up and one of my friends said, 'You're probably pregnant.' And I said, 'Oh no, you can't be pregnant unless you're married.'"[15]

This comment echoes those I heard as a child. Sometime in second grade, I mentioned casually to a couple of classmates that my parents were not married. They were dismayed and nonplussed, their fundamental conceptual categories challenged. "Then you can't have a father," one insisted, near to tears, meaning something like "then you can't exist." I thought them very stupid. Still, I learned that it was best not to upset people by mentioning my mother's marital status.

That it took me so long to learn that this fact was of any note is one of my mother's gifts to me. As with inherited wealth, the great dividend of my inheritance was obliviousness, total confidence in my own legitimacy. My mother never mentioned what it might have cost her to hold on to me. She treated me not as the source of her many difficulties but as her proudest accomplishment. She was far from a perfect mother. Our life was tumultuous, and she had many men over the years, but I always knew I was the most valued person in her life.

"If you murdered someone, I'd hide you from the police," she once said, those green eyes of hers fierce. She meant, *My love is unconditional.*

As I grew up, I began to see how rare this was. I saw mothers choose men over their daughters again and again, and their daughters absorbed this lesson, growing up to need the attention of men above all, betraying friends for the sake of unkind men, never quite trusting their own worth. This is brutally expressed in Dorothy Allison's *Bastard Out of Carolina*, in which a mother chooses the man she loves over the daughter he rapes and nearly kills. For me growing up, feminism was not just a political ideology but a deeply personal gift from my mother. It meant that I was precious.

So I am puzzled that families would dispose of their offspring. Class was part of the reason, in the context of the growing middle class after World War II. With wages rising, large numbers of families entered the middle class for the first time. Families were anxious about maintaining their newly gained status, which was threatened by an unwed birth. Also, the new nuclear family was already fragile, shrunken and atomized as it was. Concern about maintaining their new class status goes some way toward explaining the shocking willingness of families to send their daughters away and to give away their descendants. Frequently, the pregnant girl's grandparents were never told they had a great-grandchild. That was the case for Meredith Hall and for me: My grandmother refused to tell her mother of my existence, claiming (according to my mother) that it would be too shocking to my great-grandmother. My great-grandmother lived until I was thirteen, yet I never met her.

As a child, I did not know this—wasn't exactly aware that my great-grandmother was still alive. It was only later, when I looked through some family history documents and saw the dates of her life, that I realized what my grandmother had done.

My grandmother doted on me. She was full of pride in me. Yet she broke the chain of generations between me and my great-grandmother. I do not know how to square these facts.

I first read Meredith Hall's account of giving up her child shortly after I gave birth to my first child. When I reached the scene in which, parted from the baby who was meant to suckle from her, she expresses milk from her impacted breasts into the bathroom sink, I began shaking, full of the visceral horror at the severing of what I now experience as a living bond between mother and child. That severing is inextricably bound up with the breaking of the bond between Hall and her mother. Hall's mother, who had largely abandoned her daughter to her own devices the summer Hall was seduced, reacted with anger to the news that Hall was pregnant, sent her away during the pregnancy, and offered her no choice but to surrender her child. This devastating destruction of the mother-daughter bond is crystallized in that bathroom scene. Her mother finds her crying as she expresses now-useless breast milk into the sink.

> "Oh, sweetheart," she had said. "My poor sweetheart."
>
> I whipped around and hissed at her, "Get out." They were the first and only tears I had shed throughout the pregnancy and birth and the terrible, terrible drive from the hospital. We had moved beyond mother and daughter forever. Whatever she felt, watching me cry, could not help me now.[16]

I find reading this part of Hall's account nearly unbearable. The injustice of her mother's behavior is the most intolerable element in the devastating story. The willingness of mothers to inflict this devaluation on their daughters demonstrates the profound depths of self-hatred that women internalized, and it seems to me that, at least in this respect, misogyny reached its worst depths in the postwar era.

It was a system full of hidden violence. Many of the sexual encounters that led these women and girls to become pregnant were hardly consensual. Where the Seattle Crittenton Home annual reports reveal the ages of those served, they tell a disturbing story: In 1946, the year it reopened after the war, seven of the seventy girls it served were thirteen to fifteen years old. In 1966, the home served six thirteen-year-olds and thirteen fourteen-year-olds. In 1968, the home served a twelve-year-old, two thirteen-year-olds, thirteen fourteen-year-olds, and thirty-seven fifteen-year-olds. In the 1956 report, intimate violence looms under nauseating euphemism: "When Lucy was thirteen, her father first made advances to her." Lucy, we are told, felt betrayed by her mother. Lucy then got pregnant by her boyfriend, although we are supposed to understand that she got herself pregnant as a result of her unresolved psychological conflict, which will be resolved by surrendering her baby.[17]

Nor was the decision to surrender a child freely made. Women who said they wanted to keep their babies were told they were selfish. Parents refused to help their daughters keep their babies and instead insisted that their daughters give them up. They were aided by institutional power. A maternity home administrator put it this way: "Consciously or unconsciously pressure is put upon her by the caseworker and she accepts the established point of view, namely that adoption is best for the baby and therefore for her, or she is asked to remove her child from the care of the agency."[18] If mere pressure wasn't enough, brute compulsion was used. A woman interviewed by Fessler found that, when she decided she wanted to keep her baby and got her mother to agree to help her care for it, the social worker told her she could take her baby only when she paid all the hospital, doctor, foster home, maternity home, and counseling bills, adding up to thousands of dollars. The woman had no money to pay this ransom, and so she surrendered her child.[19]

That families would be willing to throw away their grandchildren still seems to me inexplicable—until you add the final, fatal piece of the puzzle. It's what it always is in America: race. "In 1968 you were considered trash if you were pregnant. The symbol of being a good, white, middle-class family was a lily-white daughter," one woman explained to Fessler.[20] White families were so extreme in excising single pregnant daughters because unwed pregnancy equaled blackness. In this era, most unwed white girls gave their babies up for adoption, but nine out of ten Black girls kept theirs.[21] Most maternity homes did not accept Black girls (although Seattle's Crittenton Home did).

Black families did not, in general, spurn their pregnant unwed daughters or make them give away their babies. "It would be immoral to place the baby [for adoption]. That would be throwing away your own flesh and blood," one Black woman put it in 1962.[22] Having escaped an institution that ripped families apart less than a century before, the descendants of slaves would have no part of throwing away family members. The Black community in this era organized itself to accommodate single mothers and their children, while the white community organized itself to expel them. Yet in one of the many cruel ironies of racism, in this same era, white scholars accused African Americans of having a broken family culture. According to the 1965 Moynihan report (see below), Black family structure was the fundamental cause of worsening inequality between Black and white people. Just as an unwed mother was "not a mother," families that held on to their own were "not families." With autonomy of both individual and family ascendant, bonds could freely be broken, erased, and re-formed.

If Black families resisted giving up their babies, it was also true that there was less demand from the market for them to do so. Under slavery, Black women's fertility and the babies they bore were valuable commodities. Not so, once slavery was ended.

Racism associated Black people with sexual license and constructed Black women as unconstrained wanton breeders. Resistance to the desegregation of schools was linked to anxiety about white girls being "infected" with Black girls' "sexual license." For example, in 1956 congressional hearings on the desegregation of Washington, DC, schools, Southern congressmen focused on an assumed rise in teen pregnancies in the year since desegregation, then wrote a triumphant report recommending that segregation be restored because of the prevalence of unwed mothers among Black school girls.[23] A 1957 editorial in the *Richmond News Leader* wrote that "one of the more significant reasons for the South's resistance to integration of the schools" was the "sobering unpleasant fact" of Black "illegitimacy" rates, which were unaffected by advances in Black peoples' income, education, and housing.[24]

Of course, white girls were already widely infected with license, as the data on premarital sexual experiences show. The cultural response to this unacceptable fact was to cleanse and excise through adoption: By surrendering their illegitimate babies, white girls could regain their whiteness. Once race is added to the mix, the inexplicable becomes explicable: Families were willing to destroy their daughters and throw away their own descendants to avoid blackening the family. It was necessary to destroy the family to save its whiteness.

It was a solution that did not last. In 1965, Senator Daniel Patrick Moynihan warned that Black and white families were diverging, with disastrous implications for African Americans. It turned out that it was the white family that had taken an unsustainable detour. In 1964, white women were twenty-seven times more likely to surrender babies for adoption than Black women were. Today, rates of surrender among white people have dropped to about the same rate as those among Black people.[25]

One of the most haunting aspects of this history is how quickly the practice of forcing white girls to surrender their babies ended. It exploded and then suddenly ended: Seattle's Crittenton Home expanded in 1956 and again in 1965, but it closed in 1973 for lack of demand. The pattern was the same throughout the country. What later would be referred to as the Baby Scoop era was over. As of 1973, with the legalization of abortion, a single woman could freely end her pregnancy. Or she could keep the baby. If she had the right not to be a mother, the logical corollary was that she also had the right to be a mother. In 1971, in *Ordway v. Hargraves*, the Supreme Court ruled it illegal to expel pregnant girls from school, and in 1975 Title IX barred schools that didn't follow *Ordway* from receiving federal funds. An unwed girl in 1970 had no choice but to give up her child. By 1975 she could simply keep her child. Lorraine Dusky, for example, recounts that she gave up her daughter in 1966, in total secrecy, not even informing her family. But by 1974, still single, she was publicly searching for her daughter. Between 1945 and 1973, one-and-a-half to two million babies were relinquished to stranger adoption.[26] Thinking of these numbers is like walking along Maya Lin's Vietnam War wall. I imagine reading the final names and think, *So much pain in the service of a failed war to preserve—what, exactly?* Control of women's reproductive capacities, racial hierarchy, and a rigid, man-centered definition of the autonomous family.

By all accounts, the pain of surrendering a child is profound. "The grief was so intense that I remember thinking that I would die," one woman recounted to Solinger. Another said, "I never even read the relinquishment form. I was too crushed and just signed it . . . I was already a zombie just going through the motions of being alive . . . I felt dead inside."[27] Most women who give up children find a measure of healing only in being reunited with them. A quick internet search yields list after list of adoptees seeking birth parents, birth parents seeking surrendered children, children seeking siblings adopted away.

There are many from the time of my birth, several of whom were adoptees given up at the Seattle Crittenton Home.

In the morning, stiff and cold from a night under the willow tree, my mother did not walk to the Crittenton Home. Instead, she got on a bus to California—toward, not away from, her disapproving mother, refusing to be hidden, insisting that she was a mother and that we were family. After I was born, she went on welfare, lived on rice and beans, located the local women's movement, and helped found a feminist newspaper. My grandmother soon forgot her disapproval of my existence and became a doting grandmother, showing me all the love my mother felt she had never gotten. Lucky, because I would be the only grandchild.

My mother's refusal to give me up was at once a rejection of the myth of autonomy—she and I were not autonomous from each other, and our bonds of dependence were of infinite value—and an assertion of her autonomous right to be a mother without dependence on a man.

The Baby Scoop arose as a method of social control. It served, for a time, to contain the effects of loosening social mores, bolster the autonomous male-headed nuclear family, and maintain gender and racial hierarchy. But its brutality would help generate resistance as more and more women rebelled against a myth of the autonomous family that left no room for women's autonomy.

CHAPTER 7:

A Right Unknown

The practice of forcing single mothers to give up their babies for adoption subsided rather suddenly with the 1973 issuance of *Roe v. Wade*, so it may seem as if Justice Blackmun, with the stroke of a pen, ended the Baby Scoop and closed the book on the bad old days. Or at least it seemed so until 2022, when suddenly the undead past arose hideous from its coffin. Justice Alito, in the *Dobbs* decision, announced that women have no right against forced reproduction and claimed that "such a right was entirely unknown in American law."[1] Always and forever "in this Nation's history and tradition" (a phrase that appears hundreds of times in his decision), abortion was criminalized, he asserts.

In fact, our nation's history is a series of contests over what its traditions will be, of swings between increased freedom for women and reaction against it. This is cause for both fear and hope. Precisely because women achieved unprecedented freedom in recent generations, the backlash we face now is greater than ever before. In past eras, although abortionists were sometimes criminalized, aborting women were almost never criminally punished. In the new era, women may be sent to jail for exercising reproductive autonomy.

But such dark periods have begun and ended before, and not at the whim of Supreme Court justices. In 1973, the Court was pushed to issue *Roe* by a mass feminist movement that demanded the end of women's sacrifice before the altar of the autonomous family, and the decision was one element in a great social shift.

Justice Blackmun's opinion was not an unambiguous feminist victory. Rather, it was a compromise resolution to contesting social forces, which included not only feminists and conservative defenders of patriarchy, but also doctors trying to maintain their power while caught between the sexual revolution and the old regime of shaming and punishing women's sexuality. In his decision, Blackmun managed to accommodate these interests within the framework of the autonomy myth.

It was a strange decision. For one thing, *Roe* medicalized a profound moral question. Yet at the same time, the decision also divorced abortion from the main strands of medical law on informed consent and bodily autonomy. Blackmun based the decision on privacy—not the woman's privacy but the privacy of the doctor-patient relationship. This value was counterbalanced by a state's interest in fetal life that becomes significant at the point of the fetus's viability. This was the first time the Court recognized such an interest in fetal life.

By the time I got pregnant with my first child, shortly after the 2004 presidential election, the contradictions within *Roe* were in full flower. Prominent abortion-rights supporters began speaking of the need to accept right-to-lifers into the Democratic Party and "moral" questions into the discussion of abortion. Indeed, the Democratic Party repeatedly put money and muscle into ensuring that antiabortion candidates defeated more progressive abortion-rights supporters. In 2005, Catholics for a Free Choice president Frances Kissling published an essay entitled "Is There Life After *Roe*? How to Think About the Fetus," in which she argued that the pro-choice movement must acknowledge the moral value of a fetus. In 2022, the one piece of *Roe* that *Dobbs* left in place was the assumed value of the fetus.

I am sick of the fetus. The right wing worships the fetus and demands that the rest of us bow down before it too. Meanwhile, concern for children and grown women is at an all-time low. In the US, it has never been harder or more expensive to get full-time, quality daycare, reproductive healthcare, or a decent-paying part-time job that is compatible with being a parent, not to mention income support sufficient to make caring for your child your full-time job. There's an inverse relationship between respect for fetuses and respect for women. This is not an accident. A fetus is a creature that can exist only in dependence upon a woman, so to worship it as an independent being is necessarily to denigrate women.

I wish the fetus had never been invented. Make no mistake, it was invented. The invention happened in the mid-twentieth century, and it's possible to date it quite precisely: April 30, 1965, when *Life* ran a series of photographs of the "drama of life before birth . . . A living eighteen-week-old fetus shown inside its amniotic sac." The photos show a figure in a transparent balloon floating in what looks like a starry sky. Yet there's a falsehood here, as Barbara Duden points out in her remarkable book *Disembodying Women*. The technology for photographing fetuses in situ did not yet exist, so the pictures were actually of corpses, taken from dead women or tubal pregnancies. These pictures of "the beginning of life" in fact show the beginning of death. No wonder the images stripped away the necessary environment of a living woman's body.

By 1990, when *Life* ran another series of pictures of fetuses —"the first pictures of how life begins . . . The first days of Creation"—the technology for photographing in vivo had been honed. Yet what the photographs "show" looks as much like interstellar blobs as anything else and requires heavy captioning to help one see the images as pictures of conception and development. The captions repeatedly use metaphors from space travel: "Like an eerie planet floating through space, the woman's ovum has been ejected . . .", "like a lunar module, the embryo facilitates its landing on the uterus . . ." The invention of the fetus coincided with the invention of space travel—in 1965, two weeks before *Life* ran the photos of "life before birth," *Gemini*'s liftoff graced the magazine's cover. Just as space travel quickened the impulse to escape from the earth, images of the fetus heightened the drive to conceive fetuses as detached from women's bodies.

Prior to the second half of the twentieth century, conception and development were known only through pregnant women's visceral experiences. Through most of human history, it was a woman's announcement that she felt quickening—movements of the fetus within her—that established her status as pregnant. Indeed, this pretty much was the definition of when life began; in most countries, you could be accused of the crime of abortion only after quickening. But you had to take a woman's word for it. (Unsurprisingly, in the *Dobbs* decision, Justice Alito dismisses the notion of quickening, dispatching it in a footnote.)[2]

Abortion was not criminalized in the US until the late nineteenth century. The first statutes on abortion in the US, passed in the early nineteenth century, were designed to protect women from being poisoned by abortifacient drugs, which were often deadly. These laws punished purveyors of the drugs, not women who used them. For example, the 1827 Illinois law prohibiting abortifacients was listed under "poisoning."[3] Similarly, in William Blackstone's definitive eighteenth-century compendium of English law, he discusses a criminal abortion case only to explain how an abortionist who accidentally kills the woman while trying to cause an abortion can be found guilty of murder. Weirdly, Justice Alito quotes this commentary at length in *Dobbs,* apparently to demonstrate that because Blackstone didn't bother to use the term "quickening," it had no relevance to abortion—rather than, as seems more likely, that Blackstone took the concept for granted.[4] Washington state passed its first abortion law in 1854, making it a crime to administer "to any woman pregnant with a quick child any medicine, drug, or substance whatever; or use or employ any instrument or other means with intent to destroy such child," and it wasn't until 1909 that it removed the reference to quickening.[5] As late as 1970, when Washington legalized abortion, the new law reinstated the concept of quickening by legalizing abortion for women "not quick with child," language that stayed in place until 1991.[6]

In the mid-nineteenth century, the newly organized American Medical Association launched a crusade to criminalize abortion at every stage of pregnancy. This was part of the battle between "regular" physicians (organized into the AMA) on the one hand, and those they saw as competitors on the other hand: midwives (echoing the witch hunts), homeopaths, and patients themselves in the form of the Popular Medicine movement. The fight against abortion was a battle for market share and power, and it was both misogynistic and racist. Dr. Horatio Storer, the leader of the medical campaign against abortion, warned that if white Protestant women continued to practice abortion, the Western frontier regions would be filled with Mexicans, Chinese, Blacks, Indians, and Catholics. "Shall they be filled by our own children or by those of aliens? This is a question our women must answer; upon their loins depends the future destiny of the nation," he wrote, conjuring an early version of the great replacement theory. The editor of the Seattle *Mail and Herald* expressed a similar opinion: "The embryonic children of our 'most refined' families are being strangled by their parents by the tens of thousands."[7] The nineteenth-century antiabortion crusade coincided with, and was a reaction to, the first American feminist movement, which had been demanding not only votes for women but also freedom from compulsory childbirth, an end to the sexual double standard, and the admission of women to the professions—including medicine. Storer attacked women who sought "undue power in public life . . . in domestic affairs . . . or privileges not her own," and he took part in the fight to exclude women from medical schools. The first antiabortion movement was, like later such movements, a backlash against feminism.[8]

The antiabortion campaign set out to denigrate women's experience as a source of authority. That meant destroying the idea of quickening, which Storer sneered at as nothing but a sensation. By the 1870s, the campaign had succeeded: Numerous states passed laws eliminating the common-law concept of quickening and criminalizing abortion at all stages of pregnancy. In 1873, at the behest of Anthony Comstock, founder of the New York Society for the Suppression of Vice, Congress enacted "An Act for the Suppression of Trade In, and Circulation of, Obscene Literature and Articles of Immoral Use," which contained no definition of obscenity but criminalized publishing, distributing, or even possessing information about birth control and abortion.[9] Moral panics are evergreen: Like Ron DeSantis in 2022 pushing for his "Anti-Grooming Bill," Comstock warned Congress to suppress information to prevent the corruption of children. Comstock then got himself commissioned as a special agent of the Postal Service, vested with the power to arrest and granted free train transportation so that he could speed around the country enforcing the law. He later bragged that he had sent enough people to prison to fill a sixty-one-coach passenger train.[10][11]

On the other hand, the new laws contained a crucial exception: They generally allowed doctors, or at least "well known and respectable practicing physicians" (in the words of the Illinois statute) to perform abortions for bona fide medical reasons, such as to save a woman's life.[12] The regular doctors of the AMA had won themselves a monopoly on abortion, successfully wresting pregnancy from woman's private, felt experience and turning it into a public item that could be understood only with the help of medical experts—technicians, doctors, and nurses.

Ironically, by the middle of the twentieth century, many doctors came to regret the victory. By mid-twentieth century, the medical profession had been enlisted to enforce the criminal abortion laws. Hospitals created policies for reporting likely abortions and requiring a woman who wanted a legal abortion to come before the hospital board and go through the humiliating ritual of proving she would kill herself if she didn't get an abortion. In other words, you had to be suicidal to get an abortion. In addition, in the post–World War II era, for the first time, doctors began to be prosecuted for providing abortions even when no woman died. While the women who got abortions were not prosecuted, they were punished in another, prurient way: Prosecutors hauled women who had gotten abortions into court as witnesses, forcing them to discuss their most intimate secrets in open court.

This was the era of McCarthyism, of sending women home from their factory jobs to have babies and keep house, of cracking down on both political and sexual deviance. (Playwright Arthur Miller was right to see the Salem witch hunts as an apt metaphor for McCarthyism. But because he gave little attention to gender, he did not notice why it was so apt, or that the links were not merely metaphorical.) Until then, abortionists were quietly tolerated, and indeed in the 1930s they were not-so-quietly tolerated, as the Depression increased the demand for abortions and everyone understood the financial desperation driving that demand. But increasingly, in the 1940s, '50s, and '60s, police conducted raids on abortion clinics, arresting abortionists and grabbing their clients.

For example, in Chicago in 1947, as a thirty-eight-year-old factory worker named Clara walked away from an abortionist's apartment, two detectives seized her by the arms and dragged her to a doctor's office, where she "submitted" to a gynecological exam in the presence of a policewoman. After the doctor confirmed that Clara had had an abortion, the detectives took her to a police station and interrogated her, along with eight other women who had been apprehended as they left the abortionist's office. Clara later was forced to testify at the abortionist's trial, where the prosecutor pressed her to describe—publicly—exactly where a catheter had been inserted:

> Q: . . . Will you tell us where she inserted that rubber tube, into what part of your body?
> A: Well, I don't know. I would not know what to say.
> Q: Was it between your fingers?
> A: No.
> Q: Tell us what part of your body the tube was inserted into.
> A: In between my legs.
> Q: At the knees?
> *A:* No.
> Q: Well, where? This jury I think will understand.
> A: It was inserted in my privates.

As Leslie Reagan recounts, Clara had to testify in open court about her genitalia twice, the second time when the abortionist's conviction was overturned and the prosecutor retried the case. Juries did not necessarily like sending abortionists to jail.[13]

More and more women were caught in police raids on abortionists' offices. The police sometimes interrupted abortions midway through, leaving women bleeding, with catheters inserted. More women like Clara were forced to testify in court, a form of ritual humiliation. And as this repression pushed abortion deeper into the shadows, it became more dangerous—more women died. This was so because competent practitioners were pushed out of the business by prosecution, or the fear of it, and because women in their desperation tried to self-induce abortions.

Women, especially women of color, faced an additional danger: being sterilized by doctors as the price of granting an abortion. For example, in 1969, Theresa Williams went to a hospital in Seattle that had a progressive reputation, to seek a "therapeutic" abortion (that is, not an "elective" one, which was illegal). The board agreed that she was a candidate for such an abortion, because, although she was white, she was poor, on welfare, and a single mother of a multiracial child. Therefore, the hospital board believed she could not manage her own life. It agreed to offer her an abortion but only if she was simultaneously sterilized. In desperation, she agreed. However, afterward, she told her story to a women's liberation group, which then demanded a meeting with the hospital's director. He defended the hospital's actions as being consistent with its policies, citing other similar cases—all involving African American women. Aghast, the women listening realized that there were many other victims.[14]

Women's rage grew.

Doctors found themselves in an untenable position, caught between women's demand for abortion and an increasingly repressive criminal regime. As Dr. Harold Rosen wrote in 1965, arguing for the decriminalization of abortion, any discussion of "the abortion problem" must "stress the legal and medical hypocrisy involved . . ."[15] Some abortionists tried to resist. This included Dr. Edgar Keemer, whose Chicago office was raided by police in 1950. He put on a vigorous defense at his trial, insisting that his work performing abortions was legal, but he was convicted. He had no money for an appeal and refused to allow fundraising to collect money for one—he saw his case as an individual one, not a collective political issue.[16]

It was when women started treating abortion as their collective political problem that the abortion issue came to a head.

In the early 1960s, women created organizations to collectively subvert abortion bans and offer each other safe, affordable abortions—the two main such organizations being the Society for Humane Abortion in California and Jane in Chicago. Without at first using the terms "feminism" or "women's liberation," these organizations nevertheless were revolutionary in directly challenging the state's power to ban abortions and, by creating healthcare run for and by women, the medical establishment's authority over women's healthcare.

Founded by Patricia Maginnis, the Society for Humane Abortion (SHA) proclaimed for the first time that abortion was a right—part of women's right to control their reproduction. While SHA advocated for the repeal of abortion bans, Maginnis also created an underground arm of the organization that ran abortion classes, distributed leaflets with the names of abortionists, and sent thousands of women outside the US to get safe abortions. In order to use these services, women were required to write letters to their legislators demanding that abortion bans be repealed.[17]

University of Chicago student Heather Booth, along with a group of Chicago women active in Left politics, started what became known as Jane or the Service, which was initially a referral service to connect women with safe abortions. They then began to negotiate as a collective with abortion providers for lower prices and eventually learned how to perform abortions themselves, thereby eliminating the profit in illegal abortion and cutting out the male-dominated medical profession.

These two organizations were groundbreakers for a central premise of what became the women's liberation movement: that women themselves were experts on their experience, their bodies, and abortion. The movement adopted the abortion speak-out as a tactic. It was highly effective political jujitsu. In place of the forced outing of individual aborting women through terrifying and humiliating raids, gynecological exams, and court testimony, women erased shame and secrecy by shouting their own abortions. By doing so collectively, they transformed abortion from a personal problem into a political issue.

Washington state, which was one of the first states to legalize abortion, in 1970, serves as a good example of how change got made. Initially, in 1967, a group of doctors who were frustrated by the medical harm caused by the criminal abortion statute got together to form the Citizens' Abortion Study Group. Quietly, behind closed doors, they then lobbied for legislation to reform the state's abortion laws to allow physicians more flexibility to terminate early pregnancies. This would have ameliorated the system without fundamentally restructuring it, leaving power over abortion in doctors' hands. It was progressive for the time, but feminists were demanding much more radical change. That same year, the National Organization for Women (hardly the most radical of feminist groups), passed a resolution endorsing "the principle that that it is a basic right of every woman to control her reproductive life, and therefore NOW . . . urges that all laws penalizing abortion be repealed."[18]

When the reformers' bill was introduced in the Washington state legislature, women's liberation groups got wind of the effort and blew the reformists' cover. They organized raucous, multiracial demonstrations at the state capitol and interrupted the "expert" testimony of doctors who were assuring legislators that doctors would not be "stampeded into performing abortions at the mere whim of a pregnant female." Feminist activist Jill Severn told the chair of the legislature's rules committee that women were tired of being lectured by men and should be able to control their own bodies. The chairman objected to this idea, because "women are of varying intelligence." A quick-thinking demonstrator yelled, "So are legislators." The doctors' bill got bottled up in committee until feminists staged numerous, bigger demonstrations, at which point legislators agreed to send the question to the voters. What legislators approved was an imperfect reform: Abortion would be legal up to four months but only for those who had resided in the state for at least 90 days, married women would have to get their husbands' consent, and minors their parents' consent. An antiabortion legislator attempted to require that a woman would be able to get an abortion only upon the review and approval of three doctors—review boards assessing women's desert of abortion case by case, entrenching the existing system of control over women's reproductive lives. With continued public pressure, that amendment was killed.[19] As imperfect as the bill was, it represented a fundamental shift in the terms of abortion.

Despite the bill's limitations, once it was sent to the voters, feminists led a public campaign. They publicized Theresa Williams's case. They doorbelled and leafletted department stores, workplaces, and even University of Washington football games. They participated in an "Afro-American Abortion Assembly" at a Seattle public high school and published a pamphlet called *One in Four of Us Has Had or Will Have an Abortion*. They organized a counter-demonstration at a Voice for the Unborn rally on Halloween in 1970. Feminists came dressed as witches and faced down mostly young men from parochial schools, who carried signs that read "KILL KILL," above "THE BILL" in smaller letters. These men chased the women and hit them with signs. When Voice for the Unborn ran ads on billboards and buses showing a tiny fetus cupped in a large hand, abortion rights supporters corrected its copy: "LET ~~HIM~~ HER LIVE!" In November 1970, the people of Washington state voted in favor of the referendum, legalizing abortion throughout the state.[20] Most of the limitations in the law were overturned by *Roe* just a few years later, and in 1991 the state's electorate voted to enshrine abortion rights in the state's constitution.

Finally in 1971, Congress repealed the Comstock laws' prohibition of birth control—but left in place the ban on mailing even information about abortion, and the dire criminal penalties for it.[21]

As late as 1972, Chicago police raided Jane, taking nearly fifty people into police custody for questioning and arresting seven Jane members. This shocking move actually served to advertise the organization, and, unlike those caught in earlier abortion raids, Jane had the support of a mass political movement. This was the last gasp of the reign of terror.

When the Supreme Court issued the *Roe v. Wade* decision in 1973, announcing a constitutional right to abortion, it was a mixed bag. Justice Blackmun's majority opinion did not overturn doctors' control over abortion but rather engineered an accommodation between feminist demands and doctors' power by granting—to doctors, as much as women—a right to abortion limited by the medical concept of viability (not quickening). Blackmun did not ground the right to abortion in equality. Instead, he cited the line of cases finding fundamental rights of personal privacy in intimate areas such as marriage, procreation, family relationships, childrearing and education, and contraception—the legal framework supporting the autonomous family as a privatized container for dependency.[22] But this was an odd fit, because feminists had been critiquing these very relationships and women's lack of power within them and demanding women's individual freedom to control their own reproductive powers. So Blackmun did the neat trick of replacing husbands and fathers, whose control over women's reproduction was now being contested, with doctors as the governors of reproduction. Now women's reproductive needs and capacities would be contained within the privatized doctor-patient relationship, and they would be autonomous as consumers of healthcare. Women were now free to "choose" without the government's stopping them—but also without any social support to provide the conditions for meaningfully free choice and with ominous limits to their freedom built in.

The Court in *Roe* grounded the right to abortion in the right of privacy, the right to keep the government out of the doctor-patient relationship.[23] The Court decisively rejected the idea that a fetus is a person accorded rights under the Fourteenth Amendment, but Blackmun stated that "this right [to abortion] is not unqualified and must be considered against important state interests in regulation."[24][25] Just what those interests were is not clear. Blackmun characterized these interests as "safeguarding health, in maintaining medical standards, and in protecting potential life."[26] Blackmun never explained the nature of the state's interest in "potential life," nor why the state has it. One could interpret the first two interests innocuously, as referring to state standards for ensuring that abortions, like any other medical procedure, are performed safely. These regulations would further rather than conflict with patients' rights to elect abortion. But the next sentence asserts that the state's interests may "become sufficiently compelling to sustain regulation of the factors that govern the abortion decision." This phrase is opaque yet ominous, suggesting that Blackmun had in mind regulations to forbid, deter, or inhibit "factors" that allow women to exercise their right to abortion.

Blackmun supported his non sequitur that, in contrast to the situations in marital privacy, procreation, and education, "the pregnant woman cannot be isolated in her privacy" with a reference to a medical dictionary.[27] He did not explain how any of these other situations involve a single person in isolation. Perhaps what he meant is that these other situations involve individuals that he could imagine being. Blackmun could imagine himself as a husband, a father, a student, a teacher, and even, one suspects, a fetus—but never a pregnant woman. She simply can't really be an individual, which is why he accorded the state this unexplained interest in the "potential life" inside her body.

Blackmun refused to decide when life begins, as a metaphysical matter, and he ignored the notion of quickening, with its emphasis on women's felt experience. Instead, he selected the medical concept of "viability" as defining the moment when the state's interest in the potential life of the fetus becomes compelling and distinguished the level and type of permissible state interference with the abortion right by trimester.[28] Even before viability, the freedom from government intrusion belongs not to individual women, nor even to women in consultation with their doctors, but to the "physician, in consultation with his patient."[29] Even this limited role for the pregnant woman drops away by the time the holding is summarized a few pages on. During the first trimester, "the abortion decision and its effectuation must be left to the medical judgment of the pregnant woman's attending physician."[30]

These two interests that Blackmun's decision balanced against each other—consumerist doctor-patient privacy versus "potential life"—never really seemed equivalent. Like an equation that balances only with the arbitrary introduction of a constant, Blackmun's test came out for women's rights thanks only to that line drawn at viability. And by focusing on viability rather than birth, Blackmun's decision refused to acknowledge the unique geography of pregnancy.[31] Until birth, any contact between state and fetus must go through the woman. Therefore birth would seem far more salient than viability. Blackmun treated the fact that at viability a fetus *could* survive outside a woman's body as equivalent to its *actually being* outside a woman's body, a strange leap, as it were, around the birth canal.

Roe was not a firm foundation for women's rights. It did not reliably protect women's ability to access abortion. Immediately after the decision, states began passing restrictions: barring or limiting abortions later in pregnancy, establishing onerous requirements for abortion clinics, mandating parental involvement for minors, and allowing institutional and individual providers to refuse to participate without requiring them to refer women for the services they needed. The very first limitation was the most catastrophic and total: In 1976, Congress passed the Hyde Amendment barring federal funding for abortions, eliminating the public funding that would allow poor women to actually exercise their right to abortion. And, in 1977, the Supreme Court ruled that it was just fine for a state Medicaid plan to refuse to cover abortion, even if it covered childbirth.[32] The Hyde Amendment remained in place throughout the entire *Roe* era and beyond.

Nevertheless, activists immediately tried to use *Roe* to achieve broader reproductive justice, including the right to bear children. In one of its darkest hours, the Supreme Court had blessed forced sterilization with its 1927 decision in *Buck v. Bell.*[33] In 1942, as the Nazis' eugenics practices came to light, the court reversed course and ruled, in *Skinner v. Oklahoma,* that procreation is a fundamental right.[34] Yet *Skinner* involved not a woman but a man, who faced sterilization as punishment for committing multiple crimes of "moral turpitude." The decision muddled procreation and marriage together even though marriage wasn't at issue in the case. Nor did it explicitly strike down *Buck v. Bell.* In the 1960s, as the US government began providing states with funds for family planning services, states began using the funds to advance racist eugenics policies, coercively sterilizing thousands of mostly Black and brown women (but also some poor white women, as in Theresa Williams's case). This occurred nationwide, but with regional flavors of racism. In the South, Black women were targeted, to the point that about 20 percent of married Black women had been sterilized as of 1970. In Puerto Rico, 35 percent of women of childbearing age were sterilized. In California, Mexican American women were targeted, beginning as far back as 1909, when California enacted one of the first eugenics laws.[35]

In the early 1970s, a medical student alerted Mexican American activists that doctors at the Los Angeles County USC Medical Center were sterilizing Mexican American women against their will and in many cases without their knowledge. The head obstetrician told staff that his department had received a federal grant "to show how low we can cut the birth rate of the Negro and Mexican populations in Los Angeles County." Doctors approached the women while they were in the throes of labor and heavily medicated, in some cases while they were still under anesthesia from C-sections, to demand, again and again, that they sign the papers for sterilization. Witnesses later recounted that a doctor would "hold a syringe in front of the mother who was in labor pain and ask her if she wanted a pain killer; while the woman was in the throes of a contraction the doctor would say, 'Do you want the pain killer? Then sign the papers. Do you want the pain to stop? Do you want to have to go through this again? Sign the papers.'" Many patients had limited English skills and were handed consent forms they could not read.

When Georgina Hernández arrived at the hospital bleeding and in pain, medical staff demanded she consent to sterilization at the time of her admission, which she refused to give, but later, when the doctors decided to perform a C-section, the doctor again asked her to agree to sterilization. Hernández again refused, but the doctor simply asserted that she had agreed. Finally, "this lady came, I don't remember seeing her face, I just remember her voice telling me, '*Mijita*, you better sign those papers, or your baby could probably die here.'" Hernández learned she had been sterilized only when she returned to the hospital three weeks later for follow-up care.

While Jovita Rivera was groggy from anesthesia, a doctor told her she should have her "tubes tied" because "her children were a burden on the government." Some of the women consented to the procedure thinking it was reversible (that "tubes" that had been "tied" could be untied). The doctors did not explain that the procedure was permanent, and in some instances actively lied, telling women that the procedure could be reversed in a few years. Other women never signed consent forms at all.[36]

In 1975, a Chicana organization filed suit against the medical center, alleging that, by sterilizing women against their will, hospitals, doctors, the state of California, and the federal government that funded the procedures had violated their rights under *Roe*. They argued that the right to reproductive freedom included the right to choose to birth as well as not to give birth. The activists behind the case used the litigation as part of a broader public campaign, publicizing sterilization abuse that was rampant in California as well as throughout the country. A judge granted their demand to enjoin the state from further sterilizations, and the state agreed to reform its sterilization practices.

Unfortunately, that judge died and was replaced by Judge Jesse Curtis, a wealthy Nixon appointee who lived aboard a yacht. Curtis did not dispute the volumes of testimony and other evidence of acts of coercion and abuse. Indeed, Curtis recited examples of the coercive circumstances—including a doctor who demanded Dolores Madrigal's consent again and again, telling her husband in front of her that she might die if she had another pregnancy, then telling her that her husband had consented to the procedure, and demanding again that she sign the forms. Curtis concluded that the physician who performed the surgery relied on the signed form to support his "bona fide belief that Mrs. Madrigal had given her informed and voluntary consent, and that his belief was reasonable." He found in each woman's case that the doctor's asserted belief that she had consented was reasonable. Curtis defined consent so narrowly that all surrounding coercion was irrelevant, and he placed the burden of communicating consent (or its lack) on the patient, effectively blaming the women for their own suffering:

> There is no doubt that these women have suffered severe emotional and physical stress because of these operations. One can sympathize with them for their inability to communicate clearly, but one can hardly blame the doctors for relying on these indicia of consent, which appeared to be unequivocal on their face and which are in constant use in the Medical Center.

Curtis dismissed all the women's claims.[37] As a result, none of them received any compensation for the harm they suffered.

On the other side of the country at around the same time, the National Welfare Rights Organization and the Southern Poverty Law Center filed suits on behalf of involuntarily sterilized welfare recipients. The cases were consolidated as *Relf v. Weinberger.* Again, activists used the cases to publicize sterilization abuses, successfully pressuring the federal government, before the case was decided, to rewrite regulations on the use of federal funds to actually require "indicia of consent" to sterilization.

When the cases were decided by Judge Gerhard Gesell, he was far more thoughtful than Judge Curtis about consent. Gesell found that poor people had been coerced into accepting sterilizations under the threat that welfare benefits would be withheld or had agreed after doctors made consent the condition of giving medical care. He wrote that involuntary sterilization threatens the right under *Roe* against government intrusion into decisions whether to bear children and that "federally assisted family planning sterilizations are permissible only with the voluntary, knowing, and uncoerced consent of individuals competent to give such consent." Gesell found even the revised regulations inadequate to ensure genuinely voluntary consent. The federal family planning law had always included a requirement that services be "voluntarily requested," and Gesell noted that even the dictionary definition of the word "voluntary"

> assumes an exercise of free will and clearly precludes the existence of coercion or force . . . and its use in the statutory and decisional law, at least when important human rights are at stake, entails a requirement that the individual have at his disposal the information necessary to make his decision and the mental competence to appreciate the significance of that information.

Because the federal regulations failed to require that recipients of services be provided with both oral and written assurances that benefits could not be withheld because of a refusal to consent to sterilization, Gesell found that sterilizations funded under the regulations were unlawful.[38]

This was a great victory. However, Gesell stressed that he was deciding the issue under the family planning statute and therefore did not have to reach the question of whether the Constitution would permit the federal government to fund involuntary sterilizations. In any case, the government appealed his decision and, while the appeal was pending, withdrew the challenged regulations, telling the appeals court it would issue new ones. The appeals court then found the issue moot and ordered the case dismissed. As a result, no binding legal precedent against sterilization was created. Although coercive sterilization receded, it never really ended. For example, California continued coercively sterilizing women prisoners until as late as 2011.[39] Again, activists publicized the abuses, locating prisoners to speak out about their experiences, and pressured the government to stop the practice; eventually, the state agreed to end it and issued a public apology.

These coerced sterilizations were profound violations of women's liberties. They also denied women equality. What they didn't have much to do with was privacy. Justice Blackmun's basing reproductive rights in privacy missed the point. Sure, privacy is a good thing and we need it, as far as it goes. Like any healthcare procedure, my abortion is nobody's business but my own. But privacy is relevant to abortion mostly because violating the privacy of abortion-seeking women and enacting a theater of shame and exposure is a time-tested technique for keeping women in line. In the lead-up to *Roe*, feminists resisted this technique not by insisting on abortion privacy but by foregoing it—shouting their abortions, thereby refusing to be controlled by shame. *Roe*, even as it based the abortion right in privacy, made privacy less crucial by reducing the stigma of abortion, and thereby of unwed motherhood. With the collapse of the regime of shame, in the years following *Roe*, rates of abortion dropped and rates of adoption plummeted. But opponents of women's autonomy did not forget the efficacy of shame.

CHAPTER 8:

No Fault of Her Own

One of the reasons it was just possible, in 1971, for my mother to become a single mother was welfare. She had some family support, but she also depended on the lifeline of modest welfare checks for the first year of my life. Once upon a time, as a never-married woman, she would not have qualified. Into the 1960s, 40 percent of states enforced "suitable home" rules, barring aid to "illegitimate" children.[1] But thanks to activism, largely led by Black women, that began to change. In 1968, the Supreme Court ruled, in *Levy v. Louisiana*, that states could not discriminate between "legitimate" and "illegitimate" children in the amount of welfare benefits they granted.

Interrupting diatribes, or mere sneers, about welfare mothers—by mentioning that my mother and I survived on welfare when I was a baby—tends to stop the ranters in their tracks. They assume that because I am white and well-educated, my mother could not possibly have taken welfare. But then they say, "Oh, but only for a little while, right?" When I admit this is true, their faces clear. They have successfully made my exception prove their rule.

But in depending on welfare for only a little while, my mother was like most welfare mothers. Before the 1996 end of welfare as we knew it, about half of welfare mothers received benefits for one year or less, while 70 percent were off welfare within two years. My mother was also typical of the majority of welfare recipients in that she was white.[2]

What we now call welfare began as "mother's pensions," which were first enacted by states at the beginning of the twentieth century. The idea was to assist families that were missing the breadwinner role, whether through the husband's death or abandonment. As a presidential commission would later put it, what would become welfare was "aimed primarily at families with absent or incapacitated fathers."[3] The economic dependency of mothers and children was assumed and approved, the problem being that they had no man to depend on, "through no fault of their own." This paralleled the unemployment system, which helped male breadwinners when they lost jobs through no fault of their own.[4] When a family was missing the breadwinner role, the government would step in as the breadwinner, while allowing mothers to continue in their role as care providers.

To apply for a mother's pension, you had in some sense to admit your family was broken. Still, mothers were seen as deserving the help, and it was assumed that a mother was fulfilling her social role and contributing to society by caring for her children. It was no accident that, until the 1960s, African American families were generally ineligible for welfare assistance, or that in many places only widows, not the unmarried or abandoned, were eligible. Mothers' pensions recognized the value of mothers' care only when they met certain cultural, racial, and moral standards. They never provided enough money to fully replace a man's wage. Still, mothers' pensions represented a small recognition that care work had value. They were modeled on veterans' pensions; the idea was that, just as men who served their country in war deserved support from the state, a woman should receive government support in exchange for her service to the state through child rearing.

The first mothers' pensions were local, through private charities and cities. Illinois was the first state to pass a mothers' pension law, in 1911, although all it did was allow for counties to use public funds to create pensions. Even so, the private charity industry vociferously opposed public mothers' pensions, railing against the subversive idea of social support as a right, which would cause "pathological parasitism" that would "inevitably create a new class of dependents."[5] Nevertheless, the idea spread rapidly to other states, and, by 1934, forty-six states had some form of mothers' pensions, with state governments providing about 20 percent of the money and localities the rest. In 1935, FDR's Committee on Economic Security took up the idea, proposing mothers' pensions as part of a broad program of social insurance. The committee noted that the name was misleading, because they were "not primarily designed to help mothers, but to protect children." Mothers' pensions were designed not only to "keep [children] from falling into social misfortune, but more affirmatively to rear them into citizens capable of contributing to society."[6]

Fatefully, the committee proposed that the new federal money be in the form of federal grants to states to support these programs—not a direct, uniform national program. Civil rights advocates pressed for the Social Security Act to require equal treatment on the basis of race, for mothers' pensions as well as other forms of social insurance, and child welfare advocates in Roosevelt's Children's Bureau initially wrote the bill to include federal oversight that would have barred differential treatment based on either race or marital status. But pressure from Southern states ensured that these provisions didn't make it into the law, nor did a requirement that welfare benefits pay a "reasonable subsistence compatible with decency and health."[7] [8] As part of the deal FDR made with Southern Democrats, states would be free to run programs themselves, mostly without federal oversight, and to exclude African Americans. This meant that existing local racist structures, which as of 1931 kept African Americans to only 3 percent of welfare recipients, could stay in place—or expand with the help of federal money.

In 1935, the Social Security Act included mothers' pensions in the form of Aid to Dependent Children. The law made state participation in ADC voluntary, with the result that as late as 1939, eight states had no ADC programs. Even where a state had a program, the white power structure in a given locale with a large fraction of African Americans might decide not to establish an ADC program there.

In 1939, the same year that Social Security was amended, the US Board of Tax Appeals held that childcare expenses are not deductible as work-related expenses, and that no income results from childcare.[9] As described in Chapter 1, the board refused to consider childcare anything other than a personal concern.

Meanwhile, Aid to Dependent Children, later Aid to Families with Dependent Children (AFDC), remained a meager and stigmatized assistance, only sneeringly referred to as an "entitlement." Unlike Social Security survivor benefits, with AFDC, you had to prove your poverty to qualify. Americans have always been concerned with welfare fraud and with limiting welfare benefits to those who "deserve" it. There has always been an assumption that the poor are to blame for their own poverty and only those who can be shown to be blameless deserve a handout. This assumption goes hand in hand with the myth of autonomy, that families should be autonomous. Indeed, they naturally are autonomous, and only in exceptional cases where something in the family has broken should they need outside assistance.

Hard as it is to believe now, the concern with fraud was initially focused on able-bodied men receiving benefits. In the 1930s, common terms used for welfare cheats were "family men" or "reliefers." After World War II, the worry shifted to Southern migrants moving north and claiming benefits, migrants who could be either men or women.[10] A 1951 *Saturday Evening Post* article entitled "The Relief Chiselers Are Stealing Us Blind" discussed "grafters," "leeches," "racketeers," and "professional paupers" and was particularly concerned with unemployed or underemployed men who refused to support their children.[11] As Rickie Solinger describes, a poor single mother might be considered a slattern or a slut, and certainly she was low-status, but her motherhood at least made her a figure of pity; she wasn't considered an aggressor or enemy of the people.[12] That role was more plausible in a man.

Furthermore, until the mid-sixties, when newspapers and magazines pictured "the poor," they were usually depicted as white, which was accurate given that the majority of the poor, and those on welfare, in the US have always been white. For example, a 1952 *Saturday Evening Post* article about "federal relief" showed pictures of nicely dressed white children heading to church.[13] However, depictions of the poor began darkening in 1965. Twenty-seven percent of published photographs of poor people in 1964 were of African Americans, but in 1966, 53 percent were, and by 1967, 72 percent of the photos of poor people were of African Americans. Furthermore, when publications described poor people sympathetically, they used photos of white people, whereas when articles demonized the poor, they used photos of African Americans.[14]

The turning point happened in 1964. That was the year when California Governor Ronald Reagan began to create the figure of the "welfare queen" and use it to rile up crowds. He newly placed the focus on female welfare cheats. In a 1964 speech, he described a young woman who had come before a judge to get a divorce, because her husband earned $250 a month, and on welfare she could get an $80 raise, to $330 a month. She got the idea, he said, from two other women in her neighborhood who had already done the same thing.[15] Part of what was new was to depict the welfare mother as alienated first from men and then, worse, from her own children. She was equated with a prostitute, in that she had sex for money. That is, she had sex to get pregnant, have more children, and thereby get more welfare money.

Part of the irony is that it was the very stinginess of American welfare that allowed for the demonization of welfare mothers: How could any mothers support their families on the tiny sums public assistance doled out? The answer must be that they were doing something underhanded and improper.

Although American skepticism of families in need of outside assistance was not new, the late 1960s shift to demonizing welfare mothers and racializing that demonization was. Rickie Solinger explains that in the 1960s and '70s welfare rolls significantly expanded, in part because states began to allow African American women to claim benefits. Until this point, you couldn't demonize welfare recipients as Black, because in general African Americans were ineligible for public assistance. Agricultural and domestic workers, who were disproportionately African American, were excluded from New Deal relief programs, and they weren't allowed to claim Aid to Dependent Children in the South, where most African Americans lived.

But civil rights litigation and activism, combined with LBJ's War on Poverty, changed this. In 1960, 3.1 million people received AFDC. That rose to 4.3 million in 1965, 6.1 million in 1969, and 10.8 million in 1974. The amounts expended rose from $800 million a year in 1958 to $11 billion in 1977.[16] Much of this expansion was the result of the new inclusion of African Americans.

This inclusion didn't just happen. Black mothers fought to receive welfare and to raise benefits to levels that would support dignified life—the original "reasonable subsistence compatible with decency and health" that the Children's Bureau had once promised. They also fought against degrading treatment by welfare administrators. Johnnie Tillmon, who became a leader of the welfare rights movement, had supported her six children by working in laundries, then reluctantly accepted welfare when she was hospitalized with severe tonsillitis. Having already earned her political stripes—she was a union steward, worked on voter-registration campaigns, and joined her housing project's community association—she found the disrespect of the welfare officials intolerable. After a night when welfare officials showed up unannounced at her house to rifle through her belongings and check for signs of a "man in the house" or unreported income, she decided she'd had enough. In 1962, she began organizing her Watts neighbors to demand better treatment from the welfare offices and within the next year had created one of the first welfare rights organizations in the country, thereby seeding a movement that spread nationwide. In June 1966 (the same month the National Organization for Women was formed), the National Welfare Rights Organization (NWRO) launched with the 155-mile Walk for Decent Welfare across Ohio to the state capitol, ending with a rally attended by local politicians, union leaders, and the activist and comedian Dick Gregory. Hundreds of NWRO chapters formed around the country. Tillmon's organization became a chapter, and she became the founding chair of the NWRO. By the late 1960s, the NWRO had more than twenty-five thousand dues-paying members, and they were marching, staging sit-ins at local welfare offices, and suing for increased benefits, for the right to move from state to state while still maintaining their benefits (a right to travel, by the way, arguably enshrined in the First Amendment), but most of all for self-determination and respect. As Tillmon wrote, "The ladies of NWRO are the front-line troops of women's freedom. Both because we have so few illusions and because our issues are so important to all women—the right to a living wage for women's work, the right to life itself."[17]

Reporters in 1966 gave almost as much coverage to the welfare march as to the civil rights march from Selma to Montgomery. The welfare rights movement inspired feminists worldwide. In the 1970s, under the banner of "wages for housework," an international feminist movement took the claim of US welfare mothers—that their mothering had value—and universalized it. All mothers, whether on welfare or otherwise, deserved recompense for the value they created. Started in Italy and Britain, the movement spread back to the United States. A New York Wages for Housework Committee poster in 1975 stated, NO TO WELFARE CUTS. YES TO WAGES FOR HOUSEWORK FROM THE GOVERNMENT FOR ALL WOMEN.[18] Margaret Prescod and Wilmette Brown founded Black Women for Wages for Housework in 1976.[19]

In 1977, as part of International Women's Year, Congress provided millions of dollars to support a National Women's Conference in Houston. It was led by Congresswoman Bella Abzug, and its attendees included three current and former first ladies as well as Coretta Scott King, Betty Friedan, and Maya Angelou.[20] But also present, and united for the first time, were leaders of the welfare rights movement and the wages for housework movement. The Carter Administration was proposing to require (waged) work from welfare recipients to "ensure that work will always be more profitable than welfare"—a fateful definition of mothers' work as not-work. As historian Emily Callaci recounts, Prescod and Brown came to the conference with the objective of changing the conference plan of action to include demands to defend and increase welfare and recognize it as a wage. They joined forces with Johnnie Tillmon and NWRO cofounder Beulah Sanders to lobby attendees, many of whom were invested in Democratic Party politics and opposed to any criticism of the Carter Administration. Remarkably, they won. The plan of action issued at the end of the conference stated, "We support increased federal funding for income transfer programs. And just as with other workers, homemakers receiving payments should be afforded the dignity of having that payment called a wage, not welfare."[21]

But by this time the NWRO had folded and a vicious backlash had arisen. Phyllis Schlafly held a counterconference across town at the same time as the National Women's Conference.[22] The women's movement would be identified with the (white) women of NOW, and the women of NWRO forgotten. The very existence of a vibrant, powerful Black mothers organization would be erased, its existence evident only in the lingering rage it stirred up. But, for a moment, Black mothers dared to speak up for the right of all mothers to receive support for care work, and, for just a moment, America listened.

Meanwhile, civil rights activists were pushing for integration in employment and better work opportunities for African Americans, and President Lyndon B. Johnson was trying to reduce poverty. An obvious solution to both problems was jobs. The federal government could have created a major program to provide direct employment, like the jobs programs created by Roosevelt during the Great Depression, except this time, offering equal opportunity in hiring to African Americans and women. But this was too big a lift. Instead, Johnson's administration promoted job training. Like so many efforts to solve fundamental problems on the cheap, this seemed easier at the time but set the effort on a path to long-term failure.

First, a focus on training as the solution allowed the white establishment to ignore the fact of discriminatory hiring and the structural interests served by poverty wages. It implied that poverty was caused by African Americans' and the poor's own failings—their lack of skills—rather than by racism, sexism, and capitalism. This narrow focus on training has been favored by Democrats ever since, one fruit of which has been the explosion of student debt in the early twenty-first century. What happened to LBJ's job training program showed, early on, that it was a disastrous choice for the Democratic Party and for the prospect of reducing poverty and racial and gender disparities in employment.

Job training programs were dominated by trade unions, which systematically excluded African Americans. Control over apprenticeship programs and the path they gave to stable work at a family wage—that is, a wage that would allow a man to support a non-wage-earning wife and children, making his family autonomous—was a fiercely protected trade union power. It was a working-class property right, passed on from (white) father to (white) son. In fact, it was an attribute of masculine identity for the white working class. As one construction worker put it, "Some men leave their sons money, some large investments, some business connections, and some a profession. I have none of these to bequeath to my sons. I have only one worthwhile thing to give: my trade . . . For this simple father's wish, it is said that I discriminate."[23] To take away this right to pass on his trade to his sons was to unman him. In the absence of serious programs to expand employment, Johnson's efforts at integrating apprenticeship programs and entry to the trades felt to working-class white men like a zero-sum attack on their hard-won rights, on their very manhood. Predictably, white-controlled trade unions strongly resisted and resented integration. Richard Nixon would soon exploit this resentment, tapping into both misogyny and racism. Welfare would offer the perfect target.

Urban uprisings in the late 1960s led to much wringing of white hands about urban poverty, especially unemployment among Black men. In 1967, Johnson created the National Advisory Commission on Civil Disorders, known as the Kerner Commission, which in 1968 found that participants in the "riots" were mainly young African American men, who were in a state of crisis because of chronic unemployment and low wages. It concluded that the riots were a response to African

American poverty caused by racism.[24] Viewed from today, it is startlingly sympathetic to the plight of poor African Americans, recipients of welfare, and the poor in general. It advocated dramatic increases in government spending on housing and public schools, boosting welfare payments to a livable level, and creating a million new government jobs for which African Americans would be given priority. Yet the commission, all but one of whose members were men, focused on the denial to African American men of the opportunity to be successful breadwinners. Page after page in the employment section of the commission's report focuses on African American men's poor employment prospects, while African American women are mentioned only in a few paragraphs that bemoan their *high* rate of employment. Whole sections discuss the problem of fatherlessness. "Men who are chronically unemployed or employed in the lowest status jobs are often unable or unwilling to remain with their families. The handicap imposed on children growing up without fathers in an atmosphere of deprivation is increased as mothers are forced to work [*sic*] to provide support."[25] It proposed to support the nuclear family by expanding welfare eligibility to "intact" families (that is, families with both a mother and father present) and to reverse recently enacted requirements for welfare mothers to work (for pay).[26] There is a not a single reference to childcare in the entire 431-page report. The commission did not question the model of the autonomous family. In any case, none of the Kerner Commission's recommendations was put into place.

It was around this time that the concern with undeserving welfare recipients began to shift to women, specifically to African American women. Wages had begun to stagnate. From 1948 to 1972, wages grew at almost the same rate that worker productivity did. But beginning in 1973, while productivity—American workers' output of goods and services per hour worked—kept growing, wages did not.[27] This was partly due to deindustrialization, the resulting loss of well-paid factory jobs, and the decline in labor unions, which tightly correlated with increasing inequality. All these trends hit African American men hard and increased the numbers of poor women heading families and needing welfare. In this situation, welfare rolls kept expanding, and this provided a focus for racial, gender, and economic anxiety.

In the US, we are willing to provide social support for dependent caretaking when we see it as providing reciprocal benefits. We will provide support for childrearing if we see those being raised as *our* children. But white America does not consider Black children as theirs. Backlash against welfare rose during the 1960s and '70s when there was a perception that those who were being helped by it were Black.[28] While Black people never represented a majority of those on welfare, the numbers of Black people receiving it did rise in the 1960s and '70s. Right-wing politicians seized on white resentment of these shifts and stoked it.

In tandem with the Kerner Commission, Johnson also created the Commission on Income Maintenance Programs, known as the Heineman Commission, to conduct a study of all existing welfare programs and how to reform them. Made up of corporate executives, economists, and union leaders, as Jill Quadagno recounts, it considered and rejected a jobs-creation program because it would be too expensive and wouldn't address the poverty of the millions of working poor, including the ten million workers who earned less than minimum wage.[29] This, of course, begged the question why there should be such a thing as a job that doesn't pay minimum wage or that fails to pay enough to raise a worker out of poverty. Nor did it address whose interests were served by low wages.

An even stranger blind spot in the commission's report is women. It barely acknowledges that they exist, referring repeatedly to welfare programs as benefiting "the blind, the aged, the disabled, and dependent children," then finally obliquely adding, in a later recitation of this list, "spouses" and "people who have dependent children." It's as if women were a sort of negative space, not worth mentioning directly and defined only in relation to others. The report noted that welfare programs were "residual" to the New Deal social insurance programs, designed to offer some slight assistance to those who were "unemployable for noninsured reasons."[30] It did not address the question of why the needs of those providing care to dependents should be noninsured. Rather than propose fundamental changes to the American economic, racial, or gender structure, the Heineman Commission settled instead on a universal income supplement for the working poor, while eliminating the existing welfare program. As Quadagno notes, this was compatible with business interests and was an idea popularized by the conservative economist Milton Friedman. But because it would provide only enough to supplement wages, and was designed to incentivize (low-)wage work, it would only minimally help those who were too busy caring for children or elders to take on waged work. At best, if benefits for poor mothers were kept the same as welfare benefits, they would be no worse off. But with welfare replaced by a system no longer focused on the needs of poor mothers, it was unlikely their benefits would be maintained. In Nixon's hands, the idea became a stalking horse for dismantling the hated welfare system.

In August 1969, in a speech unveiling his version of the universal income supplement—what he called the Family Assistance Program—Nixon introduced the word *workfare* into popular lingo.[31] It was his first major speech on domestic policy, and in it he proposed to reform welfare to incentivize work and shift even more authority to state and local governments. Welfare—that is, aid to women and children—as well as food stamps and other in-kind support would be replaced with a universal basic income that phased out with increased wage earnings.

From the perspective of an America now shifted dramatically to the Right and with a social safety net shredded to the point of irrelevance, the proposal seems at first glance astonishingly humane. It would have dramatically helped the newly enfranchised white working poor in the South, where wages were so low they kept masses of working people, both Black and white, in poverty and where poll taxes had been common until their challenge by the civil rights movement.[32] By providing sufficient income to lift every American out of dire poverty, it would have freed us all from the brutal fear of disaster, one missed paycheck away. Today, it seems downright socialist. The terms of debate were different then, the liberal Left dramatically more powerful. To pass anything, Nixon would require the support of congressional liberals, and no doubt he designed his FAP to get it.

But the proposal was also meant to tap into white working- and middle-class resentment of the "nonworking" poor in both the North and South, to build a lasting Republican coalition. The FAP would have redistributed welfare benefits from non-wage-earning women and African Americans to working-class whites, especially men.[33] Whereas welfare went nearly exclusively to single-mother-headed families, FAP would have provided benefits to families that included a wage-earning husband, with the aim of encouraging marriage and traditional gender roles. The Nixon administration was explicit that the FAP's employment elements were designed first and foremost for men, because it wasn't worth it to try to help women get employed:

> In general, we would support giving higher priority to the training and employment of men than women. Given the greater employment opportunities for men generally available, they are more likely to achieve self-sufficiency. Moreover, training and employment will often be

much more expensive for women, if child care must be provided.[34]

Nevertheless, the proposal required both male and female recipients to seek either waged work or training. Initially mothers of children under six were exempted, but in the 1972 version of the bill that was cut to age three.[35] [36] Those who didn't meet the work or training requirements would have their family's benefits cut. For mothers to take waged work, of course, daycare would have to be provided. But America was still extremely ambivalent about mothers in the paid workforce, and therefore ambivalent about—or downright hostile to—daycare.

The federal government had provided some childcare funding during the Depression, to create jobs for unemployed teachers, custodians, and nurses. In 1941, with America's entry into the war and the need for women to work in the defense factories, Congress enacted the Lanham Act, which gave grants for building and operating daycare centers. But within months of the war's end, the funding was ended, and 2,800 daycare centers closed. The official rhetoric was that women should now go home and take care of babies. The rhetoric didn't match reality; women's labor force participation kept going up in the 1950s. But women were on their own to find childcare. It wasn't until 1962 that any federal funds went to support daycare.[37] Even after that, there was no national system for providing high-quality daycare to all who needed it.

In 1969, Nixon made a half-hearted proposal for a daycare system alongside the FAP, allocating far less funding than would have been necessary. To top it off, daycare beneficiaries would also experience a corresponding cut in their FAP payments.[38] In 1971, Shirley Chisholm and Bella Abzug introduced a bill for a fully funded, comprehensive system, and Congress voted for a stripped-down version, but by then Nixon had lost any interest in childcare and vetoed the bill.[39] To this day, America has no national daycare system.

Soon, the entire FAP came under fire, particularly from the Southern establishment. Southern wages, especially for African Americans, were so low that the modest sums the supplement would pay would have dramatically altered the Southern economy and power balance. Most African Americans in the South worked in jobs that actually paid less than minimum wage, because Southern legislators had seen to it that the types of jobs they were relegated to—maids, cooks, gas station attendants, bus boys—were exempt from the minimum wage law. The income supplement would pay more than these jobs, allowing African Americans to turn these jobs down—or at least not to worry about losing such jobs, depending on how the work requirements were written into the bill. In the South, welfare officials had often granted field hands welfare during the winter months but kicked them off in spring and summer; the income supplement, on the other hand, would come all year long. Georgia Representative Phillip Landrum said when he voted against the bill, "There's not going to be anybody left to roll those wheelbarrows and press those shirts."[40] Louisiana Representative Russell Long put it even more personally, wailing that if the FAP passed he wouldn't be able to get anyone to iron *his* shirts.[41]

By providing African Americans (and poor whites) with money that wasn't locally controlled, the income supplement would also have upended the Southern political structure. African Americans who tried to register to vote or engaged in civil rights activities were often cut off from welfare by local officials, and counties in the South with high Black voter turnouts were those where Black people depended least on whites for their livelihoods.[42] Such weapons of control would have been far less effective if African Americans could count on a federal income supplement. As Quadagno puts it, a federal income supplement "threatened to emancipate the Southern labor force."

Southern members of Congress lined up against the bill, as did the Chamber of Commerce. The women of the NWRO also opposed it, because they thought its payments too stingy and because of the work requirements for mothers. They staged a sit-in at the office of Secretary of Housing, Education, and Welfare and a "wait-in" to speak before the Senate Finance Committee. Many liberals also opposed the bill, because of its penalties for refusing low-wage work, elimination of other forms of aid, and requirements that mothers of young children seek paid work. Although many Americans were anxious about expanding welfare rolls, America wasn't quite ready to end welfare. There was still a lingering belief that mothers, even poor ones, should be at home caring for their children.

In response to this multifaceted opposition, Nixon quickly dropped the FAP and it sank nearly without a trace—except for its antiwelfare rhetoric. Nixon avidly hung on to that, using it successfully to stir up the "Silent Majority," and inventing language that would work for Republicans for decades. There is some evidence that Nixon was never in earnest about the FAP and proposed it only for cynical political purposes. H.R. Haldeman wrote in his diary that Nixon "wants to be sure it's killed by Democrats and that we make big play for it, but don't let it pass, can't afford it."[43] In any case, Nixon would have the last laugh, when the antiwelfare elements of the FAP, stripped of its humane income supplement, would become the basis for a Democratic president to end welfare twenty-five years later. Nixon's administration would also play another crucial role in welfare: In 1975, a former Air Force researcher and member of the Nixon administration named David Mastran would found a company called Maximus to root out fraud in Great Society programs. In 1987, when Los Angeles County signed the first contract with a private, for-profit entity to administer welfare, it was with Maximus. Mastran was prescient to spot a growth industry in the obsession with supposed fraud by the poor.[44]

The irony of the FAP was that although Nixon touted it as encouraging work, it would have helped prop up a structure in which work didn't pay enough to lift people out of poverty and, by ending what had once been known as mother's pensions, would have eliminated that small, grudging recognition of care work as work. Although the FAP died, the idea that reproductive labor wasn't work did not. Instead, it took root.

One factor in that shift was that women's participation in the paid market kept growing and the fraction of women who did reproductive labor exclusively, without working for wages, shrank. Despite Ozzie-and-Harriet rhetoric, this had been true even through the 1950s—in fact ever since World War II. Women's workforce participation grew steadily until 1999.[45] The effect of this was to mask the flattening of wage growth; family income kept growing, but only because families now often had two earners instead of one.[46] Family income growth ceased in about 1999, right about the time women's workforce participation leveled off. Thanks to women's wages, families did not see as much of a decline in living standards as they might have. This muted what might have become a demand for employers to raise wages. Instead, capitalism got a pass, thanks to women. In fact, it was largely thanks to mothers. From 1975 on, the workforce participation of mothers increased much more steeply than that of women overall, with the sharpest increase among mothers of children under age three.[47] Yet because wage growth stagnated and there was still no system for subsidized, good-quality childcare, many families were struggling under the combined weight of too little money and too little time.

In the American context, in which the only way families maintained their incomes was to increase the hours worked by every adult in the family, time spent providing care without earning wages began, in the late twentieth century, to seem like a luxury. Welfare mothers, who were doing care work instead of wage earning, began to seem newly anomalous, and it was natural to resent them for getting to do what most families could not afford. Instead of asking why minimum wage jobs paid so little that a mother could receive more money from welfare, many asked why welfare should pay so well and whether welfare mothers deserved to choose welfare over wage work. People even began to ask: Do welfare mothers have babies in order to get welfare checks? Like Reagan, many on the Right said yes, treating welfare mothers (read: Black mothers) as grotesquely rational economic choosers, trading sex and pregnancy for federal dollars.

Economic choice is a favored language in America. Yet Rickie Solinger argues that there was a particular reason that this language began to be applied to welfare mothers in the 1970s and '80s: Beginning with *Roe*, abortion was framed in terms of choice, in a consumerist framework, rather than one of rights or equality.[48] While feminists were not the first to frame abortion this way, white feminists in the decades after *Roe* embraced the language of choice. This set the ground for what would otherwise seem a bizarre misapplication of the language of consumer choice to pregnancy and childbirth. This misapplication was, for abortion opponents, the point: "It's a child, not a choice." But the real vitriol would be applied to so-called welfare queens who chose to have babies for welfare checks. Poor African American mothers were portrayed as bad choosers, rational yet immoral and disgusting. In confluence with increasing welfare rolls and a lack of structural analysis of an economy in which wages were falling, for the first time welfare mothers were seen as enemies of the state, bleeding taxpayers dry.

By the time Ronald Reagan ran for president, in 1976 and 1980, he had honed the racial coding of his welfare queen stories. He incessantly used the term, describing in speech after speech a woman with multiple aliases, four husbands, driving a Cadillac, and she was of course from Chicago's South Side. In the 1980s, Democrats also trafficked in these stereotypes, often at the very same time that they distanced themselves from them; in 1988, Senator Joe Biden wrote in an op-ed, "We are all too familiar with the stories of welfare mothers driving luxury cars and leading lifestyles that mirror the rich and famous." He went on, "Whether they are exaggerated or not, these stories underlie a broad social concern that the welfare system has broken down—that it only parcels out welfare checks and does nothing to help the poor find productive jobs."[49] This is a deft maneuver. First he suggests that other people tell such stories, even as he tells one himself, then he admits that the stereotypes might not be true, but he ends by saying that it doesn't matter.

In 1992, when Bill Clinton was running for president, the groundwork had been laid and the conditions were finally ripe for eliminating welfare. As Arkansas's governor, Clinton championed welfare "work" requirements (reproductive labor being not-work) and time limits on benefits. When he ran for president, he made welfare reform a central plank of his platform. Like the Heineman commission report earlier, his speeches on welfare hardly mentioned mothers and children. For example, in Clinton's 1991 New Covenant speech, although welfare was a central topic, the word *mother* does not appear: "The New Covenant will say to people on welfare: We're going to provide the training and education and health care you need, but if you can work, you've got to go to work, because you can no longer stay on welfare forever." This sounds like welfare is some general poverty program for "people" who mysteriously, listlessly fail to look for work. Listening to this speech without context, you would have no idea what or who welfare was *for.* His listeners, having been primed by Reagan and Biden's welfare-queen tropes, didn't need it spelled out. Clinton could count on their knowing exactly who it was for. He could be gentler, vaguer, though also firmer: "In a Clinton administration, we're going to put an end to welfare as we know it," he said. "Welfare should be a second chance, not a way of life"—as if welfare recipients had somehow committed a royal screw-up and could be given one more chance by the long-suffering taxpayers but not a lifetime pass.[50] But consider that what he was talking about was mothers' pensions. The screw-up in question was children, or the delusion that caring for them is valuable work.

Around this time, the Republicans called Clinton's bluff. They issued their Contract with America, proposing strict lifetime limits on welfare benefits, denial of added benefits to families if another child was born, denial of benefits to mothers under eighteen, and wage-work requirements. Then they began to pass bills containing these provisions. Clinton vetoed the first two of these as too draconian, but by the third round he caved. The Personal Responsibility and Work Opportunity Reconciliation Act (PRWORA) provided a five-year lifetime limit on benefits, required waged work after two years of benefits, and turned the program from an entitlement into a block grant to states, to use as they saw fit. The act did not require states to spend their entire block grant on assistance for poor mothers and children or require states to offer all or even most aid in the form of direct cash assistance. States would not be required to show that block grant money was reducing poverty or even increasing marriage rates (one of the act's stated goals). The only measure of success they would be held to was the "work participation rate"—the percentage of aid recipients participating in "work" activities, not including childcare or eldercare.

The law also included an astonishing throwback to older times, in a requirement that mothers tell the government the names of their children's fathers, echoing the pressure women dying from botched abortions once faced to "name their seducers." If they refused, they faced a 25 percent cut in benefits. The intent was for the state to go after the fathers for child support, regardless of whether the mother wanted this. Although the rationale was that child support is a "key factor in increasing self-sufficiency among low-income families," the law eliminated an earlier requirement that states pass on some of the child support funds collected to the welfare mother and her children.[51] As of 2002, fewer than half the states passed any child support money on to the welfare recipients on whose behalf it was ostensibly collected.[52] This aspect of the law is not only cruel but perverse, in that it insists on treating the nuclear family as a unit in the very moment that, by definition, it has ceased to be a unit. It also insists on the autonomy of the family, without regard to the autonomy of those who comprise it.

Clinton signed the act into law in 1996. With that, mothers' pensions came to an end. What had begun as the demonization of poor African American mothers had spread outward to become hostility to all mothers in need. These are the continuing fruits of what W.E.B. Du Bois called the American preference for the "public and psychological wages" of racial superiority over a decent safety net for all.

PRWORA made it official: Care work was not work, and dependency was bad. As Clinton said, the act "gives us a chance we haven't had before to break the cycle of dependency that has existed for millions and millions of our fellow citizens, exiling them from the world of work. It gives structure, meaning, and dignity to most of our lives."[53] Johnnie Tillmon had died the year before, but she had given an answer to this kind of rhetoric decades earlier: "The truth is a job doesn't necessarily mean an adequate income. There are some ten million jobs that now pay less than the minimum wage, and if you're a woman, you've got the best chance of getting one." Or, with the federal minimum wage now nearly worthless, the best chance of getting a minimum wage job.

The same year that Congress passed PRWORA, eviscerating support for mothers' care work (and recognition of it as work), Congress also enacted the Telecommunications Act of 1996, further deregulating the phone industry. Yet Congress refused to deregulate women's reproductive capacities, rejecting Representative Pat Schroeder's proposal to include in this bill a repeal of the Comstock Act, the nineteenth-century law banning communication about abortion. Congress never did repeal the Comstock Act, not even as it became clear that the Supreme Court was poised to overturn *Roe*.

In 1996, I turned twenty-five. I was full-grown, out of my mother's house, graduated from college, and I had no children. My mother, healthy at forty-nine, didn't need care, and my grandparents, though aging, had enough money to cover what care they needed, thanks in large part to the GI bill, Social Security, state pension systems, and Medicare. My autonomy was at its peak and our family's cycle of dependency was at an ebb. But it was not ended. Within a few years, my grandmother would need 'round-the-clock care, I would have children, and my mother would face several health crises requiring intensive, ongoing care.

We were lucky. Lucky because of our race and class privilege, of course, but also in timing. Had my mother given birth to me earlier, as an unwed mother she could not have claimed welfare. Had she given birth later, there would have been no welfare for her to claim. Without welfare, she would have been utterly dependent on social norms and on her family, or on my father and his family. She could not have made her decision to raise me by herself. This is what is missing from standard discussions of welfare's evils. Welfare dramatically enhanced women's autonomy. It recognized, at least implicitly, that reproductive labor is work.

Clinton was right that work gives structure and meaning to our lives. Sometimes it gives dignity, especially if it is recognized as work, and better yet if it is paid well. I and other American mothers, poor and otherwise, know what it is to feel exiled from the world of (wage) work by motherhood. Despite Clinton's promises, the end of welfare did not "break the cycle of dependency." The cycle of dependency is the cycle of human life, which will be broken only when the human race perishes.

CHAPTER 9:

Faulty Vessels

As the welfare safety net, which had enabled women to choose to mother, was being eroded and then eviscerated, physical coercion of reproduction persisted and took new forms. Women whose reproductive capacities were regarded as undesirable were still sometimes subject to coercive sterilization, and women whose reproduction *was* desired were subject to other forms of medical coercion. Thanks to medical advances, particularly in the 1980s and '90s, doctors' ability to intervene in pregnancy increased, something that Justice Alito would eventually cite as a reason for striking down *Roe*'s line drawn at viability. Conflicts between doctors or hospitals and pregnant women, between our mythology of autonomy and the bodily autonomy of actual pregnant persons, increased. Many of these conflicts became court battles over whether pregnant women could be subject to forced medical care in the interest of promoting birth. Long before *Roe* fell, women often lost these battles.

These cases are wildly inconsistent, but I've found that women have been likely to succeed in protecting their freedom from forced medical care if they can convince a court to apply ordinary medical-law doctrines of informed consent—as in the *Relf* case, discussed in Chapter 7. However, to the extent that the facts of the case push the unique features of pregnancy to the fore, judges tend not to find in favor of the pregnant woman. Judges often have a hard time seeing a pregnant person as a person. Informed consent is a well-developed framework for protecting bodily autonomy, and using this framework highlights the crux of the issue: If you don't believe that pregnant women are entitled to the bodily autonomy accorded to others, then you don't believe in women's equality. Grappling seriously with informed consent means talking about the context of consent as a foundational political question.

Cases involving compelled medical care of pregnant women to promote birth fall into three types: First, there are cases involving compelled C-sections.[1] Second, courts have issued orders to compel pregnant women to submit to treatment to save their own lives (and therefore those of their fetuses).[2] Third, courts have issued orders to compel treatment to maintain pregnancies.[3]

In one Tallahassee case from 1999, a federal court upheld a state court's order that a woman not only be compelled to receive a C-section, but be forcibly transported to the hospital.[4] Laura Pemberton had had a previous C-section, and because that surgery had been performed using a method that created a heightened risk of uterine rupture in subsequent vaginal births, she had been unable to find a doctor who would attend her in a vaginal birth. She was able to find a midwife who would attend her in a home delivery, but, during a slow labor, she became dehydrated and went to the hospital to receive intravenous fluids.[5] She was told that she required a C-section, but refused and left. Indeed, she snuck out, an astonishing act of wherewithal in the midst of this strenuous and disorienting athletic event.

When Laura Pemberton made it home, she would have thought for a moment she was safe. But the hospital had set court proceedings in motion. Within hours, a judge had granted the hospital's request to force Pemberton to have a C-section. The police took her from her home and brought her to the hospital, where doctors strapped her to an operating table and cut into her body against her will.

Pemberton later filed suit against the hospital in federal court, alleging violations of her constitutional right to bodily integrity, privacy, and due process; professional negligence; and false imprisonment. The district court noted the right to abortion, but engaged in a balancing test of the state's interest in preserving the life of the fetus against Pemberton's rights. The court found the intrusion of having a compelled C-section to be much lower than the intrusion of bearing an unwanted child, and therefore overridden by the "baby's" interest in living.[6] It's as if a court were to decide that it was OK to send you to jail by arguing that going to jail is less intrusive than being executed, when of course the real question is whether you deserve to be punished at all. The court dismissed all of Pemberton's claims.

Sadly, Pemberton's case is not unique. For example, a DC court in 1986 granted a hospital's petition for an emergency order for a C-section on a Muslim woman having her first child.[7] Her membranes had broken forty-eight hours earlier, creating a risk of infection, but there appears to have been no sign of actual infection or of any actual problem with the labor except its slow progress.[8] [9] The court cited precedents finding no right of a parent to refuse lifesaving treatment of a child and treated this as such a case.[10]

The second type of case is where doctors believe a woman will die unless she receives medical care, such as a blood transfusion. These cases frequently involve Jehovah's Witnesses refusing for religious reasons, and sometimes involve post-partum women as well as pregnant women.[11] Two New York decisions, with opposite conclusions, are illustrative. In *In re Jamaica Hospital*, a court in 1985 ordered a woman who was eighteen weeks pregnant to have a transfusion over her religious objections.[12] The court there said it did not reach the issue of this single mother's duties to her ten living children (!), on the grounds that the fetus's interests were decisive.[13] A few years later, in *Fosmire v. Nicoleau*, a court overturned a lower court's granting of an order to transfuse a woman who had just given birth by C-section.[14] The court declined to find that a child has a right to two parents and distinguished a mother's refusal of medical care from intentional abandonment of a child. It noted that a patient's right to refuse medical care is not conditioned on having no dependents.[15]

The pattern in this sort of case is that appellate courts generally find that a fetus's interests override a woman's wishes but that live children's interests do not.[16] In other words, fetuses carry more weight than live children. At first glance, this is puzzling. Even if you think a fetus is a person, that should gain it only as much value as any other person in the world. But it is precisely because a fetus is contained within a woman that its personhood tends to swallow the pregnant woman's. To ignore where fetuses *are* requires ignoring women, or demonizing them. Judges identify with the fetus. In the words of one judge in 1999, the fetus is "literally captive within the mother's body" (yet another instance where the word *literally* doesn't mean what it used to mean).[17] Some judges see pregnant women only as vessels or hostile captors.[18] Meanwhile, courts have nearly uniformly recognized fathers' rights to refuse medical care of themselves.[19]

The third type of case is where intervention is ordered to maintain the pregnancy. *Burton v. Florida*, a 2010 case, involved a woman in her fourth month of pregnancy who already had two small children and was ordered to stay in the hospital on bed rest for the remainder of her pregnancy. Neither trial court nor appeals court seem to have noted the fact that, in protecting the supposed interests of the fetus, they harmed the interests of Burton's living children. Days after the court order was issued, she delivered a stillborn baby.[20] The state appeals court overturned the order, finding that the right of a person to determine what happens to her body can be overridden only by a compelling state interest using the least intrusive means possible. Citing *Roe*, it noted that the state's interest in the life of a fetus becomes compelling only at viability and found that the lower court had failed to make a showing of viability.[21] The appeals court in *Burton* suggested that compelled medical care is categorically impermissible prior to viability. *Burton* is rare in rejecting a balancing of a woman's rights against a fetus's. But it does so only up to viability, a line no longer drawn after *Dobbs*.

Taft v. Taft involved a husband who, in the early 1980s, sought a court order compelling his wife to have a purse-string operation—to sew her cervix shut so that she would maintain her pregnancy (her cervix had been "incompetent"—yes, that really is the medical term—in previous pregnancies, and several of her children had been born after she'd had purse-string operations). The hearings judge appointed a guardian ad litem for the fetus, and he granted the husband "the authority to force [Mrs. Taft] to undergo the surgical procedure."[22] The judge ordered Mrs. Taft to "submit forthwith," but she appealed rather than submit. She got the order stayed, making this one of the few cases where a woman not only won on appeal but never had her bodily autonomy violated in the first place.[23] The appeals court, noting both the right to have an abortion without a husband's consent and the lack of any cases ordering a woman to submit to medical treatment to carry a not-yet-viable child to term, found that no state interest in requiring a competent adult woman to submit to the operation had been established.[24] [25] The decision is affirmative of women's rights to autonomy. However, the court left open the possibility that there might be a case in which forcing a woman to submit to medical treatment to carry a baby to term would be justified.[26]

It likely mattered that the plaintiff requesting the order was a husband, and not a doctor or hospital. Because of courts' deference to doctors, the outcome might have been different if it had been a doctor demanding submission.

A variant on this type of case is that of a pregnant woman who is terminally ill or in a vegetative or brain-dead condition.[27] As of this writing, nine states automatically invalidate women's advance directives when they are pregnant, and another twenty-one exclude pregnant women in some fashion from their advance-directive laws.[28] This means that hospitals in these states will not respect pregnant women's wishes about medical treatment at the end of life and can use women's bodies as incubators for fetuses. In 2014, Marlise Muñoz was fourteen weeks pregnant when she was rushed to a Texas hospital after likely suffering a pulmonary embolism. Two days later she was pronounced brain dead, and, in accordance with Muñoz's previously expressed wishes, her husband and parents requested that she be taken off life support. The hospital refused, citing Texas's advance directive law, which provided that "a person may not withdraw or withhold life-sustaining treatment under this [advance directive] subchapter from a pregnant patient." Muñoz's husband sued and, nine weeks later, won the right to cease life support and take her body home. But the court's ruling did not overturn the advance directive pregnancy exclusion. Instead, the court held that the exclusion did not apply to a person who had been pronounced brain dead, because a dead person was not a patient, thus the treatment was not life-sustaining.[29] This was a limited victory, applying only in the tragic situation of brain death. But the decision did hoist Texas legislators on their own petard, exposing the statute's hypocrisy. The court's decision took the statute at its word by focusing on the pregnant woman as patient, even though the legislators who drafted the statute had clearly been focused on the fetus as patient, seeking treatment of pregnant women to sustain fetuses' lives rather than their own.

This was what courts and lawmakers allowed to be done to pregnant women even before *Roe*'s demise. Courts typically cited *Roe* to justify interventions late in pregnancy, as if the defeasibility of the abortion right postviability justified actively intruding into women's bodies, which does not follow. It's one thing to bar a woman from intruding into her body to end a pregnancy, another to allow someone else to intrude into her body against her will.[30] [31] Courts upholding forced interventions early in pregnancy simply ignored or dismissed *Roe*.

Justice Blackmun in *Roe* sought to avoid difficult moral and political questions by treating abortion as a purely medical question. Yet, oddly, his decision never discussed the jurisprudence of informed consent for medical procedures. The single allusion to this issue was when Blackmun rejected "the claim asserted by some amici that one has an unlimited right to do with one's body as one pleases" and cited cases upholding the right of the state to compel vaccination and sterilization, without mentioning the terrible history of forced sterilizations of Black, brown, and poor women.[32] Nowhere did the opinion acknowledge either that doctors are fallible or that their expertise is properly a means of furthering the health interests of patients, including pregnant ones.[33]

In 2022, the new right-wing majority on the Supreme Court finally pounced on the weaknesses in the *Roe* regime. In *Dobbs v. Jackson Women's Health Organization*, the Court struck down *Roe* and with it the constitutional right to abortion, by exploiting *Roe*'s own flawed logic.[34] Writing for the Court, Justice Alito took as given *Roe*'s valuation of "potential life," found viability to be an entirely arbitrary line, and dismissed the existence of any privacy right to abortion. According to Alito, because abortion is nowhere mentioned in the Constitution, for such a right to exist it must be found to be "deeply rooted in the Nation's history and traditions."[35] Because the *Roe* abortion right is based on the Fourteenth Amendment, which was enacted in 1868, Alito looked to the late nineteenth century's laws in search of a deeply rooted abortion right. Not surprisingly, he did not find it. In that era of antifeminist backlash, he found numerous statutes criminalizing abortion, which he listed for twenty-nine misogynistic pages—without acknowledging the historical battle this "tradition" reflects. Alito even went all the way back to the witch-hunting centuries, repeatedly citing Matthew Hale, the late seventeenth-century judge whose orders for some of England's last executions of witches inspired the Salem witch hunters. For Alito, rights are one-way ratchets, accorded only to those who have always had them, and history is the victor's story. Tradition, as Alito uses the term, is the inverse of democracy: Democracy is the ongoing giving of consent, whereas tradition, for Alito, means never having to get consent.

Alito was also selective in his respect for tradition. He ignored the deep tradition of medical law, dismissively framing the purported abortion right as unique and narrow—a right to abortion, not to reproductive or bodily autonomy (much as the Supreme Court once dismissed gay rights as "the right to engage in sodomy")—as part of his aim of cabining abortion from all other rights and claiming that his decision would not have broad effects.[36] But abortion cannot be disconnected from the rest of medical law, which has roots deeper than *Roe*. Taking the medical law tradition seriously—more seriously than either Blackmun or Alito did—leads to fruitful insights about autonomy.

The common law has long recognized medical interventions to which one does not consent as forms of battery.[37] Federal courts have recognized the right to make healthcare decisions as of constitutional magnitude and interpreted the right to consent as implying the right not to consent.[38] Informed consent developed as an extension of the fundamental and "sacred" right to bodily integrity and freedom from interference.[39] If the government has no other purpose, it must at least protect one from physical injury by others. "Our society, contrary to many others, has as its first principle, the respect for the individual, and that society and government exist to protect the individual from being invaded and hurt by another," a court wrote in upholding the right of a person to refuse to donate bone marrow.[40] As in so many other areas, the doctrine assumes—as the default—separate, independent adult persons who are fully capable of knowing and acting on their own interest as long as no one interferes.

Informed consent becomes problematic when this default fails to obtain, such as when persons are incompetent to make decisions because of disability or age. But courts have developed tools for dealing with this problem without assuming that the disabled or the elderly have no right to autonomy. Among these tools is the idea (one might say the fiction) of substituted judgment.[41] Incompetent persons retain their rights to bodily integrity, but someone else takes on the duty to act as the decision maker on their behalf. Crucially, this decision maker must determine not what would be in the best interests of the incompetent persons but what decisions such persons would make for themselves if they could.[42] In practice, the distinction frequently vanishes, as when there is no information about what the incompetent person would have wanted and there is little controversy as to what a reasonable person would want. But some cases have hinged on the distinction. These cases fall into two categories: where the person will die without medical intervention, and where someone else will die unless the incompetent person donates an organ or other body matter. Outside the pregnancy context, courts respect a person's bodily autonomy in both these situations.[43] Apparent exceptions (other than in pregnancy) actually involve courts finding that the incompetent person would want to make the organ donation.[44] Courts in more recent cases have refused to allow such organ donations for the benefit of relatives.[45] The trend has been toward increasing respect for the bodily autonomy of both competent and incompetent persons.

While one in general has a right to refuse medical care for oneself, parents may not refuse to authorize necessary medical care for their children.[46] This is despite the recognition of a right of familial privacy and freedom in childrearing. Courts have distinguished the freedom of an individual to determine what is done with his own body from the freedom to determine the fate of another's body. The lack of a right to deny medical treatment to another, even for the highest religious reasons, affirms the autonomy of the individual rather than violating it.

Courts frequently misapply this doctrine in cases of compelled medical care of pregnant women.[47] The lower court in *Burton* reasoned that "as between parent and child, the ultimate welfare of the child is the controlling factor," but it misapplied parental refusal of care for children to the case of the pregnant woman refusing care for herself.[48] One of the few court decisions to recognize pregnant women's existence distinct from their fetuses involved the state of Idaho's advance directive law and the state's interpretation of it as categorically requiring medical treatment of a pregnant woman regardless of her directive. The judge explained that those seeking to enforce a pregnant woman's advance directive were not "seeking an abortion of the fetus, but rather are seeking the proper administration of that woman's choice of her own end-of-life care." The judge acknowledged that, under *Roe* and its successor case *Planned Parenthood v. Casey*, the government could limit women's decisions to end pregnancies.[49] But the Idaho law did not just limit women's choices; by invalidating women's advance directives and forcing medical treatment on them, "Idaho's pregnancy exclusion completely denies the choices of women." He found the state's interpretation of the law unconstitutional, violating women's rights to their own medical decision-making. The decision issued in 2021, just a year before *Dobbs*.[50]

Organ transplant cases raise the issue of the duty to rescue. In US law, there is no duty to rescue another whom one sees in peril, unless one caused the peril.[51] One of the few exceptions to the rule is where there is a "special relationship" between the persons.[52] Although "special relationship" suggests a familial relationship, in the court cases these relationships are usually less intimate (I imagine that is because family members generally do rescue each other and don't sue each other). For example, a social companion who witnesses his friend being severely beaten has a duty to obtain medical care for his friend or at least notify someone.[53] Common carriers have a duty of reasonable care to their passengers, employers to their employees, innkeepers to their guests, and jailers to their prisoners.[54] Masters of ships must attempt to rescue crewmen and guests who fall overboard.[55] A common theme is that where you control the situation in which the person comes to peril, you incur a duty of care, and especially where you control the instrumentality of rescue (as in a boat), you must use it.

This duty to rescue would seem at first glance to apply to pregnant women and their fetuses. A relationship doesn't get more special than that. A number of commentators have treated the complete dependency of the fetus on the woman as self-evidently creating a duty on the part of the woman to undergo medical intrusions for its benefit.[56] This misunderstands the nature of the duty to rescue, which is, as noted above, a duty of reasonable care. It is not a duty of self-sacrifice. Masters of ships are not required to put themselves (or the rest of their crew) in danger to rescue a crew member or passenger who has fallen overboard, nor is a person who sees his friend being beaten under a duty to offer himself for beating instead.[57] The duty of rescue is limited even when no one else is in a position to help the person in distress. Nor is any invasion of one's body at issue in these cases.

Transplant cases provide the best analogy to pregnancy. As far as I am aware, courts have uniformly found there is no duty of a person to provide body parts for the use of another, even when that other will die without the aid, where the potential donor is the only one capable of giving the aid, and where the two persons are family members.[58] Indeed, courts have found the notion of compelling one person to submit to a medical procedure for the benefit of another person deeply repugnant. "For a society which respects the rights of *one* individual, to sink its teeth into the veins or neck of one of its members and suck from it sustenance for *another* member, is revolting to our hard-wrought concepts of jurisprudence," a Pennsylvania court wrote in 1978, in *McFall v. Shimp* (emphasis in the original).[59]

As I note above, both *Roe* and *Dobbs* assumed the existence of a generalized state interest in "preserving life" and even in "potential life." These decisions do not explain or justify this interest. When courts do attempt to pin down this interest, it vanishes. For example, in the Nancy Cruzan case, involving a woman who had entered a permanent vegetative state as a result of a car crash, the Supreme Court in 1990 wrote that "there can be no gainsaying" the state's interest in preserving life, but the discussion following is about protections to ensure that persons' wishes are truly being respected in allowing them to die (tellingly, Alito's decision in *Dobbs* does not cite the Cruzan case).[60] Similarly, in the discussion of preservation of life in *St. Mary's Hospital v. Ramsey*, a Florida court stated that a competent person's right to decline lifesaving treatment can be overcome only by some distinct reason to preserve his life, which amounts to saying there is no freestanding interest in preserving life itself.[61] The state has at most a minimal interest in protecting individuals from themselves.[62] The actual state interest is in protecting persons from injury by others.[63] As described above, this does not translate into any right to press others' bodies into service to sustain one's life. Thus, whether or not you consider a fetus a (unique type of) third person, a woman has no duty to sacrifice her body to it or save her own life for its sake, and there is no state interest in life itself that counterbalances her interests.

There are occasions other than pregnancy when state interests can override an individual's autonomy, when the state will sink at least a needle into the veins of an individual over his objections. Courts have upheld the state's power to compel vaccination, to administer breathalyzer tests, and to require use of seat belts, in the interest of public health and safety.[64] Both the insane and accused criminals can be locked up and even drugged or operated on against their will for public safety (which raises the question why the law treats pregnant women like criminals and crazy people). But even this area of state control is subject to significant limits and protections for individuals' bodily autonomy.[65] Even where the state has an interest sufficient to override an individual's autonomy, it may vindicate that interest only by the means least intrusive to individual rights.[66]

Courts are far more blithe in overriding pregnant women's rights and frequently fail to require the least intrusive means to the state's ends. But there is another, fundamental difference. In every other context besides pregnancy, it is only community interests—the interests of the generalized many—that can ever override an individual's interests. This, at least in principle, still treats every individual as equally valuable and can be justified in terms of reciprocity: Such impositions benefit us all, including the individuals imposed upon. What the court in *McFall* found so repugnant was the notion that the government could subordinate one individual to *another individual.* Refusal to subordinate one individual to another is deeply rooted in our legal tradition and enshrined in the Thirteenth Amendment's ban on slavery.[67]

It is also evident in contract law. As I've mentioned before, courts refuse, except in special circumstances, to order specific performance of contracts. This is based on "the principle that one cannot coerce the labor or personal service of another, even if the labor or personal service was initially voluntarily engaged in."[68] Yet a number of proponents of compelled medical care of pregnant women make a contract argument: that a pregnant woman, by virtue of not having an abortion, has contracted a duty to undergo forced medical care in the interests of the fetus.[69]

There is a problem of locating the agreement to this imputed contract. Perhaps women like me who chose to get pregnant and birth a baby could be said to have, by virtue of that choice, agreed to the contract. But that's a rare and privileged situation. Throughout human history, most women didn't have access to reliable birth control or abortion, and still don't. They frequently don't know when they're pregnant, and sometimes they do not control whether and how they have sex. In any case, I do not recall being given any contract to sign when I got pregnant, in which I agreed to give up decisions about my body, in the fine print or otherwise.

But even setting aside the origin problem, there is no place in our contract jurisprudence for a duty to submit to medical care in the interests of another. It would be a contract for the most intimate slavery. No matter how innocent or endangered another is or how unique one's ability to offer aid, there is no relationship so special that it creates an obligation to allow one's body to be used by another. No relationship, that is, except pregnancy. This is to say that arguments for compelled medical care of pregnant women—or against the right to abortion—devolve into the bare and circular assertion that, because women can become pregnant, they have a duty to sacrifice their bodies to fetuses. The contract was signed when you were born a girl.

We are, therefore, back to the issue of equality, the road not taken by *Roe* and dismissed by *Dobbs*. Judges seeking to treat likes alike can point to the uniqueness of pregnancy to justify treating pregnant persons differently. Our notions of bodily integrity assume the separateness of bodies, which can lead judges to assume that, because another body is forming inside hers, a pregnant woman has no bodily integrity worth respecting.[70] That follows only if we treat the way each of us came into existence as an exception to the normal human condition, and the power to bring forth life as precluding human dignity. But if we define women out of our principles, there must be something wrong with our definitions, not with women. To subject pregnant persons to violations of their autonomy—whether compelled medical care, coerced sterilization, or forced pregnancy—is to subordinate women.

Advocates of abortion rights have tied themselves in knots arguing whether abortion is best seen as a matter of liberty or equality. Ultimately abortion rights are a matter of both liberty and equality: Liberty, because to be subject to compelled childbirth is to have one's freedom violated in the deepest way; gestation is work (profoundly intimate work at that), and to be compelled to perform work is enslavement. Equality, because without the freedom to decide whether and when to have children, women cannot participate in society as equal citizens. To attain this equality requires not just the negative right to keep the government out of my bodily decisions—the right to *choose* an abortion—but the positive right to *get* an abortion, or to have a child, with social support and funding. This is the kind of autonomy we need and will have to fight for in the coming years.

CHAPTER 10:

The Prisoner's Dilemma

After welfare, what happened? Certainly middle-class tax-payers did not get a boost in money or free time, even though welfare queens were no longer sponging off their tax dollars. Nor did former welfare recipients suddenly find liberation from dependency in remunerative work. Mostly, what happened was that mothers and children got poorer. Especially, more Americans became desperately poor; the number of families living on less than two dollars per person a day more than doubled between 1996 and 2011.[1] As Kathryn Edin and H. Luke Schaeffer describe, without welfare, poor parents get by selling plasma (in 2014, which was not even a recession year, plasma "donations" hit an all-time high at 32.5 million, having tripled over ten years), collecting tin cans or trading away their food stamps, at the going rate of fifty or sixty cents on the dollar. They trade sex for cash or the payment of their cell phone bill, a room to stay in, a meal.

In the first few years after welfare was ended, many poor single mothers got jobs. But the jobs were mostly at or just above the minimum wage, with unpredictable schedules and no benefits.[2] All mothers in the US were going to (waged) work for longer and longer hours. Yet none of the structure was in place to make work fit mothers' needs: no system of affordable childcare, no nationally guaranteed sick time, no limits on sudden changes of schedule. In fact, the trend was the opposite: toward fewer bounds on bosses' freedom to fire, to grant no leave (paid or otherwise), to schedule at the last minute, or to call employees *independent contractors*. More and more employers favor Orwellian-named "no-fault" attendance policies, which really mean it's always your fault, even if you miss the end of your shift because you have a heart attack on the job or you have to rush home to care for a suddenly ill child. Perhaps the most telling statistic is that a 2000 study found that former welfare recipients who were working were *more* likely to have trouble getting enough food than those who were still receiving welfare or even those simply without work.[3] Work—getting there, dressing for it, paying for childcare—is expensive.

Welfare functioned as a kind of governmental stand-in for the family-wage-earning breadwinner and, by providing an alternative to poorly paid work—even if meager and stigmatized—created some pressure against the worst exploitation the market would bear. Congress, by ending welfare, announced that everyone must take and keep any job on offer, regardless how dangerous, low-paid, or incompatible with family needs. This tilted power toward employers, affecting every worker, not just the twelve million people receiving welfare benefits in 1996. It helped discount care work especially. In some instances the connection was direct, as former welfare mothers got low-paid jobs providing care, in childcare centers, nursing homes, and hospitals (remember Emma Mae).

For some, the end of welfare as we knew it was highly profitable. Maximus, the company founded in 1975 to root out fraud in social programs (mentioned in Chapter 8), won its first welfare contract in 1987 and had already reached $19 million in annual revenue by 1990. But the big bonanza came with the end of welfare in 1996, with its added work and child support requirements. In 1997, Maximus went public and posted $128 million in revenue. The company's annual report describes its targets: 6.5 million people receiving federal disability assistance, requiring $2 billion in administrative spending per year; 28 million people on food stamps at $3.7 billion in overhead; plus Medicaid, welfare, and child support collection. All told, Maximus spotted a $21 billion human misery market in the US alone. The Affordable Care Act, with its subsidy of the private insurance industry and complex eligibility rules, became another bonanza for Maximus. By 2018, Maximus had won 180 contracts from forty-four states and the federal government, mostly for means-tested social service programs, such as Medicaid and the Children's Health Insurance Program.[4] Its crucial insight was that profit could be made in the discord between society's inability to completely ignore dire human need and the imperative to privatize everything.

Maximus is now just one among numerous companies that reap billions from all varieties of human need for care, from health insurance companies profiting from illness, to nursing homes profiting from aging, to hospice agencies profiting literally from death. Three-quarters of hospice agencies are now for-profit, many of them owned by private-equity firms that siphon 25 percent returns from the $17.7 billion that Medicare paid for hospice care in 2017.[5] Some of the profits of the misery industry come from preventing people from accessing the care they need, but to the extent people actually receive care, the profits come off the backs of exploited, underpaid care workers. For example, when my mother, at the end of her life, lived in facilities run by the for-profit senior living chain Aegis, we were billed according to my mother's care needs and told that the billing corresponded to staffing. But Aegis has been sued repeatedly for allegedly setting staffing at inadequate levels in order to ensure profit margins. In 2021, it settled one such lawsuit for $16.25 million.[6]

The elimination of welfare was only one instance of decreasing social support for care work and increasing penalties for engaging in it. For example, between 1948 and 1960 the value of the federal tax exemption for dependents was so high that most families with children paid no federal income taxes, but after this period the inflation-adjusted value of the deduction shrank. The tax rate for families with two children increased about 43 percent from 1960 to 1985, while the average tax rate for those without children stayed the same. Even efforts to counteract this were stingy and disproportionately benefitted the wealthy. In 1998 Congress added a small per-child tax credit whose value increased with income and was only partially refundable (that is, paid as a grant, not just as a credit against taxes owed), so those who earn too little to pay taxes get little to no benefit from it.[7] In 2017, Congress doubled down on the regressivity, extending the credit to six-figure earners without helping the poor by making it fully refundable. In 2021, during the COVID pandemic, Congress finally made it refundable—but only temporarily, for that single year.[8]

Even as the government has withdrawn support for parents, the costs of parenting grow. These include both the direct costs of raising a child (food, clothing, diapers, a bigger house, education, etc.), but also the indirect costs and risks. As I note above, having children cuts into a woman's earnings, and the more children she has, the less she earns, even if she is somehow able to work the same number of hours (yet having children traditionally raised a man's earnings). Precisely because women now earn more than before the women's movement and antidiscrimination laws, they have more to lose when they take time out of the paid labor market to engage in child or elder care. This increases the care penalty. This is one reason, as Nancy Folbre notes, that the overall costs of care have gone up; we can no longer get it on the cheap from women.

Elizabeth Warren and her daughter Amelia Warren Tyagi, in their work on bankruptcy, have found that having children was the single best predictor of whether a woman would go bankrupt, and the likelihood was, unsurprisingly, greatest for single mothers. We have grown so used to female poverty that these figures don't really shock. But it is startling that the association between parenting and poverty is stronger than it used to be, and it seems to have begun to spread beyond mothers to fathers. From 1981 to 2001, bankruptcies skyrocketed, and those in the worst financial distress were parents of young children. Only sixty-nine thousand women filed for bankruptcy in 1981, but in 1999 nearly five hundred thousand women went bankrupt. Part of the reason is that so many women are now parenting solo, without the aid of a man's wages. It has always been hard to be a single mother, and there are a lot more single mothers than there used to be. But that isn't the whole story; from the early 1980s to 2001, things got harder even within the group of single mothers. Bankruptcy rates for single mothers skyrocketed. And even two-parent households are increasingly going broke. A family—two-parent or otherwise—with children is now 75 percent more likely to be late on credit card payments than one without children, and families with children are more likely than anyone else to lose their homes to foreclosure. "Having children has become the dividing line between the solvent and insolvent," Warren and Tyagi write.[9]

Warren and Tyagi explain that, even as mothers moved into the workplace over the last forty years, modern two-earner families now have less discretionary income and less savings than one-earner families did. On the one hand, men's incomes haven't risen at pace with inflation and, on the other, fixed costs of living, especially for housing, *have* risen. Warren and Tyagi explain that the extra earnings of the second earner enabled a bidding war on housing, while the bidding was made desperate by families' drive to find housing in safe neighborhoods with decent schools. Two-earner families are now, paradoxically, more vulnerable to financial ruin than one-earner families. Partly this is because the margin between cost of living and earnings has shrunk—even in two-earner households.

But Warren and Tyagi argue that it is also because both two-earner and single-parent families lack a crucial safety net that two-parent single-earner families once had: the stay-at-home mom. Mom was the safety net in multiple ways. She was available to provide care, to a sick or injured spouse, to a child, or to elders, at no additional cost, and if the wage-earner lost his job (yes, mostly his), she could go into the workplace to make up for at least some of the lost income. Warren famously recounts the story of her own mother, who went back into the workforce after her father was disabled by a heart attack, thereby saving the family from losing their home. When all adults in a family are already in the workforce, there is no such protection against job loss. To top it off, a two-earner family has double the risk for one of them to lose a job (in fact, more than double the risk that single-earner families of yesteryear faced, because companies are now faster to cut workers).[10] Warren and Tyagi argue that this shift of families into greater risk happened in part because nobody, on the Left or the Right, noticed the economic value of the stay-at-home mother.

Unfortunately, at this point in their argument, Warren and Tyagi's feminism goes shallow, both historically and conceptually. Plenty of feminists did, in fact, notice the economic value of the housewife. Warren and Tyagi feebly protest that they aren't advocating for sending mothers back out of the workplace because they personally like their careers, and anyway it's unlikely to happen. They don't seem to consider whether women ever wanted to be the "all-purpose safety net" or why the role was (and still largely is) assigned by gender. Nor do they consider the power imbalances that this assignment of roles depended on and created, let alone the deeper analysis of the essential role this reserve workforce of the unwaged plays in holding wages down under capitalism and diverting demands for a social safety net.

As I mention in Chapter 8, in the 1970s an international feminist movement did draw all these connections and began demanding "wages for housework." Activists such as Mariarosa Dalla Costa, Selma James, Silvia Federici, Margaret Prescod, and Wilmette Brown called attention to housework's economic value as work, like that done in the office and factory, rather than as love or women's identity. To do so required identifying what that work produced: "The product that our housework produces is people . . . We produce and reproduce in other people and ourselves the ability to work and go on working, we produce labour power," wrote British wages for housework activists in 1975. Wage work depended on unwaged housework in several senses: Unwaged housework created and maintained the supply of workers, and it did so at a discount that enabled workers to be paid less while employers profited from the discount. When that discounting reduced wages below subsistence or bosses decided outright layoffs would increase profits still further—or, as in Warren's situation, the breadwinner became unable to work—the housewife was there to step into the wage market and make up the difference, no government safety net required. In addition, with wife and children dependent on a husband's wages, the male worker was more tied to the necessity of keeping his job and less willing to quit or strike.

Wages for housework activists rejected the idea that liberation would be found in women's taking wage work, noting that wage work for housewives was a *second* job, on top of their existing unpaid care work. These activists also intended the demand to be paid for care work as a step toward liberating women from being compelled to do it: The demand "makes clear this is a job like any other, and that we can refuse like any other."[11] Federici titled one of her articles "Wages Against Housework."

The wages for housework movement focused more on provocation than policy programs. Their pamphlets were sprinkled with all caps and sometimes read like ransom notes: "WE WANT IT IN CASH, RETROACTIVE AND IMMEDIATELY, AND WE WANT ALL OF IT!"; "WE WANT OUR WAGES AND WE'RE NOT WAITING."[12] Although it was not usually made explicit who would pay the wage for housework, often proponents suggested that they wanted a universal basic income paid by the state—universal, that is, to women.

Whether you label it housework or care work, demanding an accounting of this work is the first step toward upending the unjust privatization of care. Warren and Tyagi have missed these insights. As a result, despite their accurate description of the economic havoc being wreaked on parents, when they get to proposed solutions, their analysis goes bankrupt. They reject socially supported universal childcare, because it would discriminate against single-earner families—by which they mean two-parent, one wage-earner families (forget single mothers). Despite being economic scholars, they fail to notice that two-parent, one wage-earner families get their own subsidy, in the form of getting the value of the non-wage-earning parent's care tax free, not to mention an extra 50 percent return in Social Security benefits. Warren and Tyagi instead propose further privatization—school vouchers, especially—and modest regulation of the worst excesses of the financial services industry. They do not propose any social solutions. Even as they acknowledge that the desperation of the housing bidding wars revolves around the quest for decent schools, and they acknowledge the decline of public schools, they don't seriously consider the obvious solution of reinvesting in good schools for all. Nor do they address race, that elephant in any conversation about real estate in America. The bidding wars for housing occurred not only as mothers streamed into the workplace but also as legally enforced segregation ended. Support for public schools eroded when white Americans no longer saw them as places for "our" children. As good public schools, along with all other public goods, grew scarcer, Americans have been pitted against each other for scraps, further fraying social bonds. Scapegoating was a natural response, and right-wing politicians exploited it.

Increasing atomization and privatization deepen this vicious circle. Only social solutions will get us out. It is, at bottom, a kind of Prisoner's Dilemma. Folbre suggests we imagine the situation of a fictional Robin and Terry, two people working for the same company and in competition for a promotion, who each want both a good job and time for family. Their employer naturally would like to extract as much value from them as possible for the lowest wage possible. One of the easiest ways to do that is to get them to work more hours. This is so whether they are salaried or hourly, because even paying overtime is cheaper than hiring more people to whom benefits have to be given. Furthermore, demonstrating a willingness to work more hours also signals dedication to the firm and a likelihood of continuing to give value in the future. Therefore, all other things being equal, the employer is likely to give the promotion to the person who demonstrates a willingness to work more hours. If Robin and Terry could coordinate and agree that neither would work overtime, they could protect their nonwork time while still being in the running for promotion. But if they aren't sure of each other, they will both work more and more, in an arms race that will be lost by the one most constrained by the need to care for dependents—and also by society, because all this time at wage work means less time for the care work that society, and the economy overall, depend on. In a one-off Prisoner's Dilemma, a ruthless or lucky prisoner may win a round. But in a series of continuing rounds, in which the prison can keep offering worse terms as the prisoners' situation gets more desperate, the only way to beat the house is through solidarity.

We have tried privatized solutions—it's called "the autonomous family." That solution worked only to the extent that it rested on social systems of coercion and oppression—racial segregation, abortion bans, forcing women to provide unpaid or discounted care. The Christian Right continues to pursue this strategy, seeing in "pro-family" policy the way to fix America's decline. Sometimes this is dressed up in pretty, modern trappings, as when J. D. Vance promotes childcare subsidies or the Heritage Society advocates tax-free "family flexible spending accounts." But at the same time, Vance didn't bother to show up for a vote to expand the child tax credit, and Project 2025 sought to gut Head Start, the tiny but successful national program that offers quality childcare to poor parents. Within the first one hundred days of the second Trump administration, it quickly began doing just that. The Right seeks to bolster the "traditional" family, which is to say the autonomous nuclear family that safely contains breadwinner, care provider, and children—preferably lots of them. And the modest carrots offered are always quietly paired with more powerful coercive sticks. For example, Project 2025 seeks a nationwide ban on abortion pills and restricted access to birth control.

Folbre's thought experiment demonstrates the link between care work and the essential role of communities in stabilizing capitalist economies. They have always been linked, but now the role is urgent in a new way: If we are to both respect women's autonomy and ensure that care work is done, we must make social provision for care. Another way to put this, as I write in Chapter 1, is that capitalism is prone to a contradiction between its pursuit of unlimited accumulation and the reproductive processes on which capitalism depends. Capitalism seeks to get the most value out of labor for the lowest wage, leaving less and less money and time for labor to reproduce itself—for parents to go home and take care of their children, their elders, or their communities. But without this care, there can be no more labor from which to extract surplus value. One way this tension was managed for a time was domesticity, as I describe in Chapter 4, and the related concept of the "family wage," the insistence that a male breadwinner be paid enough to support a non-wage-earning spouse and their children (and therefore have the right to wield authority over them). Both of these solutions have fallen apart, for related reasons. Few families now have a non-wage-earning angel in the house, and with wages stagnating, one person's wages alone can't support a family. The angel has left the house.

Economists have assumed that care is an inexhaustible and inelastic resource, meaning that it is simply a given, unaffected by changes in incentives or penalties. They have made this assumption because they did not notice the severe social constraints enforcing women's role as givers of care. Women had few options for wage work (teaching or nursing, mostly) and these were low-paid. Furthermore, a woman who didn't wish to do care work was considered unnatural, defective. My grandmother, who was brilliant with money and would have made a great investment banker, instead became a nurse and preschool teacher, despite having little aptitude for those professions other than gregariousness. A few centuries ago, women had no options but becoming wives and mothers. The dark subtext running beneath the romance of such books as *Pride and Prejudice* is that an upper- or middle-class woman had to get married—to a man with money—or she would be both destitute and without a social role. Meanwhile, working-class women would provide both wage labor at discounted rates and free labor in the home to support their husbands' wage earning. This served to put a discount on care work and ensured that care was always there. So capitalism could depend on it, and did. As Folbre puts it, "Patriarchy was not simply a means of privileging men. It was also a means of ensuring an adequate supply of care." Our economy has depended on women's lack of autonomy.

Even as women have gained greater freedom to enter the workplace on men's terms, courts have been reluctant to extend autonomy into the family. The moment I gave up on contract law was when my contracts class got to a 1993 case involving Michael Borelli, who needed twenty-four-hour-a-day care after a stroke. He desperately wanted to stay out of a nursing home, so he told his wife, Hildegard Borelli, that if she provided care for him at home he would will her more of his property when he died. She cared for him, and he died at home—but he broke his promise and left his property to his daughter instead. After his death, Hildegard went to court to enforce their agreement, but the court refused, citing "the long-standing rule that a spouse is not entitled to compensation for support." It also waxed poignant that "even if few things are left that cannot command price, marital support remains one of them."[13] In an echo of the 1939 Tax Board point that husbands ordinarily get childcare from their wives for free, the court found that because husbands already own wives' care work, the contract was unenforceable for lack of consideration (a contract-law principle that an agreement in which one side receives no benefit is unenforceable). This being 1993 rather than 1893, the court insisted that ownership of care was mutual and gender-neutral; each spouse, of whatever gender, owed the other care. The dissent mocked this idea by having us imagine President Clinton being legally obligated to drop his presidential duties in favor of caring for Hillary. The court vaguely described this as "marital care," rather than doing laundry, emptying bedpans, and so on. It took the dissent to remind readers what precisely was owned: labor, and dirty, exhausting, traditionally female labor at that. This case exposed for me not only the incoherence of contract law (some promises are more promises than others) but also the rot at the foundation of marriage law. The results of care work often are embodied in people who are in no position to bargain for their care and therefore can't be expected to repay the care—babies most especially. But this case involved a grown man who *did* bargain for his care. If even he could not be held to his bargain, something is deeply wrong. Ultimately, at the heart of the autonomous family, is force: Someone, usually a woman, must be forced (tricked, denied any other option) into providing care.

As I note in Chapter 3, women have long been subject to strange types of contracts. Marriage was first a contract *for* a wife and, even when brides became parties to the deal, marriage was the only contract a woman could make, and it was a take-it-or-leave-it agreement to give up all of her rights. In recent years, courts have extended these historic forms of coercing women's reproductive capacities into new arenas.

Right around the same time as the California appeals court decided the Borelli case, courts began having to deal with surrogacy. In the 1980s, with the invention of IVF and therefore the possibility of separating pregnancy from sexual intimacy and genetic relationship, contracting with women to bear babies for hire soon became common. Some of these contracts turned into legal disputes. Faced with these disputes, courts proved unable to admit that these *were* contracts, even as they began enforcing them. The California supreme court, in a 1991 decision that influenced other states' treatment of surrogacy, couldn't even use the word *contract*, because then it would have had to face head-on the truth that surrogacy means the purchasing of babies and renting of wombs. Instead, it referred to Mark and Crispina Calvert's "intent" that surrogate Anna Johnson should carry a baby for them, and therefore held them, not Johnson, to be the baby's legal parents. In a bizarre nod to the Aristotelian belief that men are the creators of babies and women only passive vessels, the court argued that the Calverts' intent made them "the first cause, or the prime movers, of the procreative relationship."[14] Of course, by "intent" the court meant the terms of the contract. The Calverts' instigation of the contract that brought the baby into being made them the baby's parents. The court ordered Anna Johnson to hand over to the Calverts the baby that she had gestated and birthed.

In doing so, it thus enforced the contract, effectively determining without analysis that surrogacy contracts are legitimate contracts. It begged the first question at issue: Is a surrogacy contract really a contract at all, rather than a human trafficking crime, as a New Jersey court had earlier suggested, or is it simply unenforceable?[15] But it also begged the second question at issue: As I explain in Chapters 3 and 9, even when courts enforce contracts, they ordinarily allow parties to forfeit money as the penalty for backing out of a contract, rather than requiring "specific performance" of the contract. Yet here, the court ordered Johnson to engage in the specific performance of handing over the baby that she had created within her body, without any analysis of why an exception to the bar on specific performance should apply. Finally, as law professor Jennifer Hendricks points out, in analyzing disputes in which both parties to a contract accuse the other of breaches, courts normally address how each side's alleged breaches affect the contract's enforcement. Yet here, both sides accused the other of breaches—the Calverts accused Johnson of failing to turn over the baby, and Johnson accused the Calverts of failing to buy a life insurance policy and treating her badly. But the court ignored Johnson's accusations and did not engage in contract analysis at all. It thus established the full freedom of wealthy people to purchase women's reproductive services, while denying gestating women a crucial element of autonomy that contract law normally protects: the freedom to change one's mind. As Hendricks astutely notes, the court did not even acknowledge that Johnson had changed her mind. Instead, it referred to her only as having had a "change of heart," treating it as an emotional rather than a legal problem.[16] Numerous states initially banned surrogacy contracts, but after the *Calvert v. Johnson* case, they steadily dropped those bans. As of 2025, only Louisiana still prohibits commercial surrogacy.[17]

A crucial step in creating a viable surrogacy market has been the disappearance of gestating mothers' care work. In an echo of the earlier treatment of unwed mothers, courts have consistently treated gestating mothers as not-mothers. In cases of what are called *full surrogacy*, in which a woman is impregnated with someone else's egg, and therefore is genetically unrelated to the resulting baby, courts typically do not recognize her as the baby's mother and in fact treat her as completely unrelated to the baby. Anna Johnson was genetically unrelated to the baby she carried, and this was one reason the court rejected her status as the baby's mother. The trial court found the Calverts to be the "genetic, biological and natural father and mother" of the baby. Similarly, in a New York case, when a lab mix-up led Donna Fasano to become pregnant through in vitro fertilization with Deborah Perry-Rogers's embryo, the court ruled that Fasano's work of gestation and birth created no relationship with the baby and she had no rights to it.[18]

This ignores the nine months of intimate work a woman does in gestating and then birthing a baby (work that marks her entire body forever). This work not only creates a profound relationship, but in fact, in scientific terms, shapes the physical identity of the baby. A branch of biology known as *evo devo*, that is, evolutionary developmental biology, has found that organisms are the products not only of their genes but of the precise and unique choreography in which those genes get expressed to develop the organism.[19] In humans, that choreography occurs first and most importantly in women's wombs.

Therefore, the genetic essentialism courts have embraced is scientifically inaccurate: Gestating mothers, even if they do not contribute genes, are nevertheless biological mothers to their babies.

This combined erasure of gestational labor and coercion through specific performance has served to create a viable surrogacy market and to cheapen surrogacy. If contracting parties faced the risk that a surrogate might change her mind and keep the baby, they would have an incentive to pay her well to help ensure that she wouldn't change her mind. If she can't change her mind, they have less reason to pay her well. In 2022, the *New York Times* featured a couple who paid $200,000 for a surrogate baby, but most of that went to IVF and the surrogacy agency; only $35,000 went to the surrogate mother.[20] In 2023, the going rate for surrogates in the US was about $30,000 to $100,000.[21] If you turn that into hours, twenty-four-seven work for nine months, that amounts to only $4.50 to $15 per hour ($30k or $100k divided by 6,570 hours)—even at the top end, less than the minimum wage in my hometown of Seattle. Given that you can do this work only a few times in a lifetime, with gaps for recovery between pregnancies—and that it involves risk to life and health, along with lifetime effects on one's body—those are exploitatively low wages. Surrogacy contracts are the old coercion of care in a new bottle.

There is another subsidy that supports the surrogacy market, one that all US taxpayers pay: An outsized portion of surrogate mothers are military wives, who are considered in the industry to be ideal surrogates. Because surrogacy is unregulated in this country, it is difficult to find accurate statistics on it. But researchers and surrogacy agencies themselves estimate that 15 to 20 percent of surrogate babies are carried by military wives, even though active-duty military members make up less than 1 percent of the population.[22] Part of the reason for this is that military families are forced to move frequently, making it difficult for military wives to find steady work—an extreme version of the old norm that the wife followed the husband's career. Yet military pay is low, so these families need other income to supplement it. Also, military wives are inculcated in values of sacrifice and service. But there is another, bottom-line reason surrogacy customers seek out military wives: They have some of the best health insurance in the United States, through the military's TRICARE program. Even though, like most insurers, TRICARE eventually banned coverage for surrogacy pregnancies, it is an open secret that TRICARE does not enforce that ban. TRICARE coverage saves a surrogacy customer tens of thousands of dollars, even as much as $100,000, per pregnancy; surrogacy agencies sometimes offer military spouses a fraction of the savings as an incentive.[23] Media coverage of the issue is afflicted with telling blind spots. This sentence appeared in a *New York Times* article on surrogacy: "Applicants who are deemed overly dependent on the compensation provided, including those who receive government assistance, are screened out as surrogates."[24] By "government assistance," the writer apparently meant welfare, Medicaid, food stamps—but not TRICARE. Karen Synesiou, director of the Los Angeles–based Center for Surrogate Parenting, touts military wives as good surrogates because they are "independent" and "self-sufficient."[25]

Some subsidies are visible, while others are made invisible. When Transportation Secretary Pete Buttigieg and his husband, Chasten, welcomed twin babies into their family, the photograph they provided to the media showed them sitting in a hospital bed holding the babies and wearing hospital bracelets on their wrists—as if they had just given birth. Most articles did not so much as mention that a woman gave birth to the twins and relinquished them for adoption.[26]

When the supply of a natural resource plays out—when the Texas oil fields have been sucked dry or the giant trees of the

Pacific Northwest felled—the market seeks new sources. Sometimes, new sources are created, such as by making something previously unsaleable into a marketable good—as the government in England did long ago by enclosing formerly common lands, or as US courts have done in the last twenty years by enforcing surrogacy contracts with specific performance and holding gestational mothers to be not mothers at all.

Often markets seek sources abroad, preferably where environmental and labor protections are lax. This has certainly been true of the market for care. As women's reproductive labor in high-income nations has become increasingly expensive or unavailable, immigrant women are now supplying a large fraction of the reproductive labor in the United States.

Welfare reform played a role in this process. As described in Chapter 8, Black women were, in the twentieth century, the most visible targets of the quest to end welfare. But immigrants were also targeted, even then. Like Black welfare mothers, they could be attacked for their choices. Immigrants have chosen to come to this country, and undocumented immigrants have chosen to come illegally. Therefore, they can be blamed. (Never mind the desperation pushing these choices, and the role US policy plays in it.) The worst blame would be reserved for those who chose to come to this country and then dared make a claim for social benefits.

In the 1996 welfare reform law, the statement of purpose heading the section on immigrants reads, "Self-sufficiency has been a basic principle of United States immigration law since this country's earliest immigration statutes." Then it recites a pinched inversion of Lady Liberty's creed: "It continues to be the immigration policy of the United States that aliens within the Nation's borders not depend on public resources to meet their needs, but rather rely on their own capabilities and the resources of their families, their sponsors, and private organizations"—as if community and government don't exist to boost those capabilities, or at any rate immigrants can take no part in them. It then waxes outraged that "Despite the principle of self-sufficiency, aliens have been applying for and receiving public benefits from Federal, State, and local governments at increasing rates," thereby "burdening" the public benefits system. This section of PRWORA then goes on to make undocumented immigrants ineligible for nearly all government benefits, including the threadbare remnants of welfare, and even immigrants with papers are ineligible for benefits for five years after arrival. To paper over the cruelty of these provisions while ensuring that most immigrants won't actually get benefits, the law provides various complicated exceptions.[27]

As described earlier, PRWORA writes into law that care for one's own family members is not work. Although it grudgingly allows brief, minimal support for care work—no more than five years at best—it pronounces immigrant families valueless by excluding them from this last tatter of the social safety net. PRWORA establishes the principle that immigrants can be cut off from social solidarity, which would echo six years later with the Supreme Court's ruling in *Hoffman Plastic Compounds, Inc. v. NLRB* that immigrants can be fired with impunity for exercising their right to form unions or otherwise act together at work to improve working conditions.[28] These measures ensure that immigrants have no alternative but to accept any work, no matter the terms, and are available to provide cheap care for others' families—which, unlike work caring for your own family, is still work after welfare reform. Just like the rest of the welfare reforms, these provisions serve to discipline labor and shift power to employers.

There is another structural reason that immigrant labor can be had on the cheap: The labor to raise immigrants into productive care workers has been provided by other countries and the communities within them. Other countries' mothers birthed them; other countries' parents, grandparents, aunts, and uncles reared them; and other countries' teachers educated them. When these workers leave their countries, the chain of social reproduction is broken, because they can't in turn provide care for elders or children in their countries of origin. That care goes to the United States and other First World countries, creating what Arlie Hochschild and others call a *care drain*.

The connections can be traced quite directly: A mother in a high-income country works for wages, so she needs childcare and probably housecleaning too. Perhaps her own mother isn't available to provide care because she, too, is working in the wage market. The US offers mothers no social solutions—no paid leave, no public daycare system, no break from the expectation to work long hours to get ahead or simply to keep their jobs. So a wage-earning mother will need to hire care, and at a lower rate than her own pay. Enter an immigrant woman. There's a good chance she will have left children of her own back in her country of origin. According to Hochschild, 30 percent of children in the Philippines live in households where one or more parents have gone overseas, and many Latin American, Sri Lankan, and African children similarly lose parents to overseas work.[29] These children will be left in the care of some other family member, perhaps a grandmother, or maybe their immigrant mother will hire someone to care for them, at a lower rate than her own pay in the US, thus continuing the downward slope of privatization, commodification, and surplus care extraction. Except, of course, there is nothing surplus about any of it. The children left behind simply lose their mothers' care.

For example, Rowena Bautista took a job in 2000 as a nanny for a child named Noa, in Washington, DC. She had to leave her own two children, Clinton and Princela, behind in the Philippines. There, they lived with their grandmother, but, since the grandmother worked long hours as a teacher, Bautista hired Anna De La Cruz to cook, clean, and care for the children. De

La Cruz in turn left her teenage son in the care of her eighty-year-old mother-in-law. At the time Bautista was profiled in the *Wall Street Journal*, she had not seen her children for two years. She sent money home to her children, but she could not send them her care. "I give Noa what I can't give my children," she said.

She also gives Noa what many Americans cannot afford to give their children and elders. Only a privileged minority of Americans can afford to hire nannies. Like Rowena Bautista's children, the children of those Americans who aren't so privileged go without care when their parents work long hours or make long commutes. A political analysis demonstrating the parallels and linked fates of Bautista's children and the children of working-class Americans might have prompted solidarity and demands for new social supports. Instead, what happened has unfolded with the predictability of a horror film or Greek tragedy: Just as racialized resentment of "welfare queens" was stoked for political ends in the 1980s and early '90s, so resentment of immigrants who take "our" jobs is now being stoked in the current century. PRWORA's punitive exclusions are just the beginning.

CHAPTER 11:

Orphan Trains and Immigrant Cages

In 2018, during the height of the first Trump administration's brutal separation of immigrant children from their parents, protesters gathered outside the Michigan headquarters of Bethany Christian Services, one of the main foster care agencies placing children taken from their parents at the border. The protesters demanded that Bethany end its contract with the US Office of Refugees until ICE stopped separating families. Organizer Katy Steele Barone said, "The system is not meant for kids who are purposely taken away from their parents."[1] But Barone was wrong. Bethany is a prominent part of a system that was designed precisely to take children away from their mothers.

Many Americans reacted with shock at the appalling images and sounds of children being ripped away from their mothers at the border. But only a generation ago, America practiced a policy of systematically separating a different group of mothers from their children: unwed white women, like my mother. Then, we mostly turned away from these mothers until we turned them into not-mothers, applying the rhetoric of autonomy to mothers and babies for the first time and twisting it into a tool for denying women the autonomy to raise their own children.

This required an infrastructure to do the practical work of transferring babies from unwed mothers to married couples and ensuring that women and girls fell into line. This included maternity homes in which families could hide their pregnant daughters until their babies were born, social workers and psychiatrists to tell these women they were selfish or unbalanced if they kept their babies, and adoption agencies to facilitate the adoption of their babies. Sometimes one organization performed all these functions—as did Bethany Christian Services, established in 1944, right at the beginning of the Baby Scoop era.

Lorraine Dusky, in her memoir about surrendering her baby for adoption in the 1960s, writes that when she began to speak out about the experience, someone at a seminar asked her if there were commonalities among mothers who surrendered babies. She answered no, but wishes she had said instead, "Yes, we all had sex." This is not the answer the questioner was looking for, because it turns attention back to the straightforward causes, and therefore to men: Who did all these women and girls have sex with? Just as the president and the border guards were uninterested in why mothers and children were showing up at the border, during the Baby Scoop era, those who separated unwed mothers and children were uninterested in addressing the causes of these births. Erasing causes was precisely the aim.

Today, Bethany still runs a home for unwed mothers. It is the largest adoption agency in the country, and it has won millions of dollars in federal contracts for foster care and refugee resettlement services, including placement of children taken from their immigrant mothers at the border. It thus conferred a veneer of humanitarianism on the Trump administration's family separation policy. A banner on its website during the first Trump administration's attacks on immigrant families invited the reader to "learn how Bethany helps reunify children separated at the border—and donate to help." Bethany's slogan is, "Bringing and Keeping Families Together." Disconnected from the organization's history, these slogans' Orwellian meanings show only in the odd phrasing of "children separated at the border." Separated from whom?

Bethany has a seventy-five-year track record of successfully erasing mothers. Susan Hays, the former legal director of Jane's Due Process, which has been involved in efforts to ensure detained immigrants have access to abortion and other reproductive services, expressed concern that the Trump administration's family-separation policy was intended to get babies away from their mothers for adoption. She questioned whether she was being paranoid.[2] Extraction of adoptable children may not have been the primary purpose of anyone crafting the policy. On the other hand, Bethany had close ties to the Trump administration through Education Secretary Betsy DeVos, whose family members have served as board members and a vice president of Bethany and donated millions to the organization.[3] In any case, making immigrant children available for adoption is a predictable result of a policy designed, among other things, to demonstrate the worthlessness of immigrants' family ties in ways that have deep historical precedents.

As I describe in Chapter 6, the practice of taking babies away from unwed white women in great numbers ended rather suddenly, with the rise of effective birth control, abortion rights, and feminism. The tide that surged in 1944, the year Bethany was founded, peaked in 1970 at 170,000 and then began to drop, falling to half that number by 1975. When the Baby Scoop era ended, the number of American children available for adoption plummeted. Today, the rates of surrender by white women have dropped to about the same rate as those of Black women, and nearly half of all American babies are raised by unwed mothers. Meanwhile, white anxiety about maintaining status persists in new forms. And the market for babies did not vanish. Because our society never confronted the practices of the Baby Scoop era, the infrastructure built to enable it was never dismantled. It was ready and waiting to be turned to other purposes.

This infrastructure included laws requiring that adoptees' birth certificates be sealed, mandating short windows for birth parents to withdraw consent to adoption, and creating tax incentives for adoption and the network of adoption agencies. The agencies that had thrived on this industry—including Bethany Christian Services—remained, in need of a new supply of babies once the progeny of unwed white American women were no longer available in large numbers.

This infrastructure in need of a purpose coincided with a rising conservative Christian evangelical movement at the turn of the twenty-first century. That movement was strongly identified with opposition to abortion and frequently accused of caring about babies only before they were born. For the Christian Right, the answer to the criticism was adoption.

There is a history in America of seeking to solve complex social problems without profound social change through adoption. Or rather, as historian Laura Briggs has explained, adoption has been used to prevent social change. Modern American adoption was effectively invented in the mid-nineteenth century by Charles Loring Brace, a minister who was appalled by the huge numbers of homeless and vagrant children roaming the streets of New York City. Industrial capitalism and waves of immigrants had created new inequality in the Eastern US, with the result that many parents could not support their children. The problem was especially acute in New York City, which grew exponentially in the nineteenth century, from 33,000 inhabitants in 1790 to 1.5 million in 1890. Thousands of children had nowhere to sleep but on the streets. Many worked as newsboys, shoe shiners, in factories where their small hands were prized, or as thieves and prostitutes. There were no child labor laws, child protective services, or juvenile justice systems, so many children ended up in adult jails and prisons. Brace believed this only bred further crime. He hit on what he believed to be "the cheapest and most efficacious system" for solving the problem of the "dangerous classes": He would collect children from the streets of East Coast cities and send them to farm families in the Midwest that needed laborers. They would be "help," but also adopted as family members to "draw them under the influence of the moral and fortunate classes."[4] Brace established the Children's Aid Society (CAS), which sent more than 250,000 children west on what came to be known as "Orphan Trains" between 1854 and 1929.[5] Thousands more children were sent on Orphan Trains by other organizations inspired by the CAS.

At the time, there was no official structure for adoption in the US. When children's parents died or were unable to care for them, the children would typically be taken in by extended family or the community, without any legal formalities, and given back to a parent or other relative if the family regained footing. Brace aimed at a very different solution: to take these children completely out of their (immigrant and mostly Catholic) communities, severing ties entirely. This was Brace's great innovation, what distinguished his solution from adoption as practiced by most cultures throughout the world and across history. In place of caring for children within communities, preserving their dependence on the community and enabling that community to continue, this version of adoption severs ties between parents, children, and communities. Indeed, this severance is precisely its intended function. Brace saw the taking of immigrant children out of their communities as a way of controlling unruly immigrant populations. In this way, as Briggs argues, the Orphan Trains must be seen as one episode in the American tradition she calls "taking children," that is, removing children from their mothers and severing family ties as a method of controlling communities that are considered insurgent against existing power systems and social structures. The origins of this technique lie in slavery, which crucially involved taking children from their mothers and breaking family ties as a method to prevent resistance.

Because no formal legal requirements had yet developed to regulate Brace's new practice, he could collect children by the thousands—without any system to assess whether they were really orphans—and send them off to be selected by farmers. The adoptive parents were supposed to be vetted by churches and communities, but in most cases, they simply showed up to claim children, who were paraded in what amounted to auctions. According to Brace's own estimates, 40 percent or more of the children sent on the Orphan Trains by the CAS had one or both parents living.[6] There was little to no follow-up by CAS to ensure that children were being well-cared for.

Catholic immigrant groups considered Brace a baby snatcher who aimed to get children under Protestant influence. The Orphan Train movement also provoked hostility from those who believed the orphans were taking jobs from adults and that the orphans were destined by their bad blood to become criminals. As a result, eventually several states passed laws barring interstate placement of children. The last Orphan Train arrived in Texas in 1929, and the movement was over by 1930. But a hundred years later, Brace's book, *The Dangerous Classes*, is still recommended by Christian adoption advocates.[7] Brace's particular innovation, the invention of the US institution of stranger adoption, took root.

Brace's model also inspired the taking of Native American children as a method for controlling that dangerous class. Beginning in 1879, taking Native children out of their communities and sending them to boarding schools became a method to permanently subdue Native tribes, both by blocking the transmittal of Native culture to the next generation and as a general technique for causing terror. As the War Department put it, children should be taken as "hostages for tribal good behavior."[8] In the 1950s to '70s, taking a page from Brace's book, the Child Welfare League of America's Indian Adoption Project—in concert with the US government's Bureau of Indian Affairs—relocated between 25 and 50 percent of Native children from reservations to white adopters, orphanages, and foster homes. Although these efforts were designed to erase Native communities, they did not succeed, and in fact they inspired a movement to publicize the horrifying methods and devastating effects of taking Native children—and to resist. This movement culminated with the passage in 1978 of the Indian Child Welfare Act, which strictly limits adoption of Native children outside of their tribes. In 2001, the Child Welfare League formally apologized for its part in this history.[9]

One after another, sources of adoptable children in America closed up, as communities rebelled against the taking of children. But stranger adoption never lost its allure. With the rise of conservative politics in the late twentieth century, adoption would get a boost.

Beginning in 1980, the US government began giving financial incentives for adoption. The Adoption Assistance and Child Welfare Act created a tax deduction for adoption and a program of financial assistance to families adopting children from foster care. Tellingly, it specifically provided subsidies for adoption of children from welfare-eligible families. Initially, the amounts were modest, less than $400,000 total in 1981. But federal support for adoption expanded more than two thousand times over the next two decades, to $1.3 billion in 2002 and still growing.[10] A major turning point was the 1997 Adoption and Safe Families Act, signed into law by Bill Clinton. Like welfare reform, this legislation enacted a plank of the Republican Contract with America. The law turned the tax deduction for adoption into a full credit and increased it to $5,000. It also, for the first time, created a legislatively mandated preference for adoption over biological parents' rights. It created expedited timeframes for terminating biological parents' rights and financial rewards to states that significantly increased the number of adoptions over previous years.[11] In addition, while the 1996 welfare reform act capped money for welfare, it kept adoption subsidies unlimited. As money for poor women to raise their own children became a block grant, money for richer people to adopt the children of poor mothers remained a genuine entitlement.[12]

Adoption has been pushed heavily by conservatives and liberals alike, as an option they can unite around. Jimmy Carter championed the original adoption assistance act. More recently, Democratic Senator Mary Landrieu, herself an adoptive parent, has been a leading proponent of adoption incentives, along with Democratic Senator Amy Klobuchar. As a result, the subsidies have kept growing. The Tax Relief Act of 2001 gave a $10,000 tax credit to families who adopt a child with special needs. The tax credit is not reimbursement of adoption expenses; it is an outright gift. In 2020, the federal tax credit for adoption expenses was a maximum of $14,300 per child. Because it is nonrefundable, only wealthier families can claim this much.[13] In addition, many states have gotten into the act, offering their own tax credits, in some states as high as $20,000.[14] These incentives are now so high that they can make adoption nearly free.

Around 2000, adoption blossomed into a central cause among American evangelicals. It was a ticket for Christians to claim moral authority in reproductive politics, and it was a natural fit with evangelical Christian theology. Numerous New Testament verses speak of Christians as being adopted as sons by God, and evangelical Christians speak of being "born again" and thereby adopted by God. "This means that it is not the children of the flesh who are the children of God, but the children of the promise are counted as offspring." (Romans 9:8.) In evangelical understanding, one is a "spiritual orphan" if one hasn't found Jesus. This has the effect of making birth from an actual mother less important than spiritual birth through God the father. Furthermore, father-centric "family values" are central to conservative Christian politics.

In 2002, Rick Warren, the pastor of Saddleback Church and author of the megaselling book *The Purpose-Driven Life*, with his wife, Kay, announced their concern for AIDS orphans. "What God does to us spiritually, He expects us to do to orphans physically: be born and adopted," Warren said.[15] In 2004, Jedd Medefind established the Christian Alliance for Orphans, and in 2007, the Alliance held a summit on adoption at Focus on the Family. As journalist Kathryn Joyce recounts, dozens of books for evangelicals on adoption were published between 2008 and 2011, and thousands of churches began to participate in Orphan Sunday every November. In 2009, the Southern Baptist Convention passed a resolution, "On Adoption and Orphan Care." In 2010, Bethany announced that its adoptions had spiked 26 percent in the first half of the year. Christian families that were already large became huge through the adoption of six, seven, eight orphans. Adoptive parents refer to these children as coming to their "forever families."[16] A few of these children came from the United States. Bethany, for one, had never gotten out of the business of separating unwed American women from their babies. To this day, it provides "pregnancy counseling services protecting unborn children." These services reprise the tactics of the Baby Scoop era. This includes hiding pregnant women away in its Bethany's House maternity home or housing them with "shepherding families," who isolate the women and first convince them not to murder their babies, then insist that they give their babies up. Kathryn Joyce recounts numerous stories of women allegedly subjected to coercive adoption practices by Bethany. For example, in 1999, when Carol Jordan (a pseudonym) had second thoughts about giving up her baby, she was told by a Bethany counselor that if she kept the baby she'd end up homeless and lose the baby anyway, then was hustled through the relinquishment paperwork before she was discharged from the hospital.

Even as the old institutions for facilitating adoption of vulnerable women's babies persisted, the Christian right pioneered new ones—with the cooperation of liberals. In 1999, Texas Governor George W. Bush signed what was called the Baby Moses law, allowing women to abandon newborns anonymously at police and fire stations, hospitals, and the like, without fear of prosecution. Under the sanitized name "safe haven laws," lookalike bills quickly swept the country; by 2008, every state had enacted one. The laws were typically enacted in the wake of a highly publicized discovery of a dead, discarded newborn and were offered as the solution to this horrifying problem. Once outrage was whipped up, legislators acted with speed, typically taking no more than a few months—and in some cases only a few weeks—to introduce and pass the laws, with no opposition. Not one vote was cast against safe haven laws in at least ten states.

It was all done under the banner of *the culture of life*, a term deployed insidiously by the Christian Right as shorthand for opposition to abortion. The phrase was coined by Pope John Paul II in 1991 and then used effectively by George W. Bush in the 2000 presidential campaign. No one, of course, is against a culture of life, any more than anyone is against protecting abandoned babies from death. That's probably why Democrats and the pro-choice movement jumped on this bandwagon. In my home state of Washington, the prime sponsor of the original safe haven law, passed in 2002, was a liberal Democrat, Jeanne Kohl-Welles.[17] In other states, Planned Parenthood and Right to Life united to back safe haven bills.[18]

But safe haven laws quietly frame unwanted pregnancy as a matter of a choice between killing babies and relinquishing them for adoption, thus blurring the distinction between abortion and infanticide. Democrats may not have noticed where the wagon was headed, but the antiabortion movement certainly did. An amicus brief submitted on behalf of twenty-six antiabortion members of the House of Representatives in defense of the Partial-Birth Abortion Ban Act of 2003 put it, "The frequency of abortions throughout pregnancy, the grotesque and barbaric methods of destruction of children in the womb, and the consequent cheapening of human life in the eyes of society, [are] reflected in the widespread phenomena of 'dumpster babies.'"[19] In 2022, the Supreme Court outed safe havens as crucial to the antiabortion right's long game. First, in Justice Amy Coney Barrett's comments at oral argument in *Dobbs v. Jackson*, and then in the Court's decision in that case that eviscerated the right to abortion, the Court took the position that safe haven laws make abortion unnecessary.

Stories of dead babies found in public bathrooms or in dumpsters are shocking but very rare. A 2003 study put the rate of babies killed or left to die at two per one hundred thousand births. Murder or abandonment of babies is not a major cause of infant death in the US. It doesn't even rank in the top ten. Lack of prenatal care and maternal smoking, to name just two factors, kill many more babies.

Safe haven laws take funding and attention away from reducing these more significant causes of infant mortality. They also discourage women from getting prenatal care while putting them in a double bind: For a woman to take advantage of the supposed inducements of safe haven laws—anonymity and immunity—she must conceal her pregnancy for its entirety, foregoing prenatal and obstetric care, while somehow managing to deliver her baby alive and healthy. These laws typically grant immunity from prosecution only if the baby shows no sign of neglect or abuse. This may explain why so few women make use of them.

In Washington state, the number of babies surrendered to safe havens since 2002 numbers in the dozens: Forty-three babies were turned over to safe havens in Washington between 2009 and 2016, about five per year.[20] Nationwide, about 3,500 babies were turned over to safe havens between 1999 and 2018, and about 115 in 2021, as compared to more than 600,000 abortions and about 100,000 adoptions per year.[21][22] Advocates say saving the life of even one baby is worth it. But even by that measure, it's not clear the laws work—no one knows what would have happened to these babies if not for the safe haven laws.

After passage of safe haven laws, babies are still occasionally found in dumpsters. For example, in Texas in 2019, ten years after passage of the first safe haven law, fifteen babies were illegally abandoned, five of whom died.[23] These incidents haven't undermined enthusiasm for these laws; instead, they serve as occasions for news articles on the mysterious depravity of pregnant women who refuse to use safe havens—reminding the public that women don't seem capable of using their choices properly and spurring calls for more funding for safe havens.

In Washington state, the safe haven law was broadened in 2014, after a dead infant was found wrapped in a blanket in the woods outside of North Bend. In 2016, the discovery of a live baby in a dumpster in Everett prompted news stories on Washington's safe haven law, with quotations from an adoptive mother who helped spearhead passage of the law and was "troubled" that the Everett baby's mother "failed to use the law."[24]

The latest move to broaden safe haven laws comes straight out of the middle ages—foundling wheels or drop boxes for babies. The ancient version was a revolving cylinder with a bell, in the wall of a church; the modern version is a climate-controlled box with an alarm, in the wall of a fire station or hospital. The boxes lock automatically as soon as the baby is placed inside and the drawer is closed; there is no changing your mind. There are only about one hundred of these baby boxes currently nationwide, but with the fall of *Roe*, safe haven activists are pushing for them in all fifty states.[25]

Safe haven laws may actually tend to increase the number of dumpster babies, by creating a feedback loop of shame. Through the association of unwed birth with secrecy and shame, safe haven laws suggest that unwed sex is shameful, and if unwed sex is shameful, then one certainly can't plan for it by using birth control. For that matter, if one cannot openly say yes to the sex one does want, it is more difficult to say no to the sex one doesn't want, all of which may lead to unwanted—and unspeakable—pregnancies. Perhaps this is why Texas, first in the nation to pass a safe haven law, has high numbers of both legal and illegal infant abandonments.

The "culture of life" teaches that premarital sex and unwed pregnancy are wrong, though they still occur even among those who have absorbed these teachings. Indeed, unwed pregnancy is more common among those who are taught that premarital sex is wrong.[26] The catch-22 between the shamefulness of both abortion and unwed pregnancy tends to induce paralysis in a pregnant, unmarried woman, as Merritt Tierce eloquently described in the *New York Times Magazine*.[27] A tiny number of these immobilized women abandon their babies in dumpsters.

In terms of the number of babies turned over to safe havens, these laws have been marginal, at least so far. Their real function is the cultural message they send to women. Safe haven laws are the camel's nose of the old regime of shame, which was essential to controlling women's reproduction. After *Roe*, the number of American babies given up for adoption plummeted. This decline cannot be attributed to increases in abortion—abortion rates initially rose modestly after *Roe*, but then fell to below their pre-*Roe* rates.[28] *Roe* helped destigmatize unwed pregnancy, freeing women to choose abortion or to keep their babies. It was as if America gave pregnant women a chance to vote and the result was a landslide: Women overwhelmingly expressed their new choices by declining to give up their babies for adoption. As Justice Alito would later put it in the *Dobbs* decision, thanks to abortion and destigmatization of single motherhood, the "domestic supply of infants" became inadequate. Given any other option, women do not choose to surrender their babies for adoption. So the key is to take away their options.

Safe haven laws were part of the misogynistic Right's cultural and legal strategy to do just that, by restigmatizing abortion, promoting adoption, and reinvigorating shame's hold on women. But safe haven laws haven't produced significant numbers of adoptable American babies in the short-term. In the meantime, there simply aren't enough vulnerable women in the United States to supply the adoption demand.

So adoption advocates turned to other countries. In the early 2000s, evangelicals began to speak of "143 million" orphans around the world in need of saving. This number alone became a shorthand for the cause of international adoption. For example, an organization named Project 143 offers "orphan hosting" and bumper stickers that read simply "143 million." Amazon offers "143 million" coffee mugs and T-shirts. The problem is that this number is a distortion. There are not 143 million children in the world who are without family and waiting for adoption. The number comes from a UNICEF report on "orphaned and vulnerable children," and UNICEF defines an orphan as a child who has lost one or both parents. UNICEF notes that the vast majority of orphans are living with a parent, grandparent, or other family member.[29] As UNICEF explains, it used the broad definition of *orphan* in the 1990s to highlight the vulnerability of children in the face of the AIDS crisis, not to indicate that there are 143 million children in need of adoption. UNICEF also notes that among the causes that make children "vulnerable" is problems with registering them, because without registration they do not legally exist. In some countries, single mothers are unable to register their children, because only a father can do so. This includes South Korea, which for decades has been one of the world's biggest suppliers of adopted children, precisely because of the country's high stigma and legal barriers to single motherhood. The more obvious and just solution to the vulnerability of these children than international adoption is reducing this stigma so that their mothers can keep them.

But the Biblical definition of an orphan is a "fatherless child." Thus, for conservative Christians, *all* children born to single mothers are orphans, by definition. So UNICEF's qualifiers did not stop the American Christian international adoption movement. Instead, it boomed. In 1998, about 14,000 children from other countries were adopted to the US. By 2002, that number rose to 21,459, and in 2004 it hit 22,220. The US has for decades been the country that adopts the largest number of children from abroad.[30]

International adoption is expensive, costing on average $20,000 to $35,000 per adoption in fees to adoption agencies alone. With all this money sloshing around, scandals abounded. Money and demand for babies created corrupt markets for them. It turned out that many of the babies sent to the United States for adoption were not orphans at all. For example, in 1990, only 257 children were adopted by Americans from Guatemala, but by 2007, one in every hundred Guatemalan children was adopted by Americans. Then it was discovered that Guatemalan women were being paid to give up their children, and in 2008, Guatemala closed down international adoptions. Almost immediately, Liberian adoptions to the US spiked. This brought history grotesquely full circle: Liberia was founded by freed American slaves sent to Africa because white liberals wanted to end slavery without integrating former slaves into American society. In 2006, Liberia became the eighth highest adoption-sending country in the world, although its total population was only three million people. Then Ethiopia became the hot adoption market, with adoption rates rising from 82 children adopted to the US in 1997 to 2,511 in 2010. Corrupt Ethiopian officials were bribed to overlook questions about whether adoptees were truly orphans. Ethiopian families were deceived into relinquishing their children, not understanding that adoption to the US would be permanent, and thinking instead that their children would go to the US to receive an education before returning home.[31] In 2011, the US State Department said 90 percent of Ethiopian adoptions that went through its embassy had to be investigated for misrepresentation or concealment of facts. In Haiti, children were just scooped off the streets in the chaos after the 2010 earthquake, then whisked out of the country without proper paperwork or proof that they were really orphans (Amy Coney Barrett was among those who adopted Haitian children during this chaos). Eventually even the narrative of China's foreign adoption program began to unravel. The story was that girl babies were abandoned on street corners and orphanage steps in large numbers, ready for foreigners to rescue them from Chinese misogyny. But eventually journalists and adoption advocates began uncovering numerous instances in which this story was false. Instead, many babies were stolen or coerced from their parents by the Chinese government.[32] Again and again as a scandal came to light, a country would close its borders to foreign adoption, or the US government would try to discourage adoption from whatever country was the scandal of the moment and then the market would shift from that country to the next hot market.

Many of these Black and brown children adopted from overseas became part of white Southern congregations, including many in the Southern Baptist Convention (SBC), a branch of Protestantism that came into existence in 1845 when pro-slavery members splintered from the Northern part of the denomination. In 1995, the SBC publicly apologized for its history of support for slavery and has been working ever since to rehabilitate its image.[33] Now many of its congregations are integrating—through their members' international adoptions. As Kathryn Joyce argues, that means the SBC is addressing its racism not by engaging with African American adults within their own country and community but by adopting Black and brown children from other countries. Bypassing deeply difficult conversations among equal adults about a shared history, the church and its members instead have been engaging with people of color from a position of power—as parents to children extracted from their communities of origin.

There are numerous gruesome stories of internationally adopted children being abused, including an Ethiopian girl who died at the hands of her fundamentalist Christian adoptive family near Seattle. Hana Williams was found malnourished and dead of hypothermia. Her adoptive parents sent her outside as punishment, then watched through their windows for hours as she stumbled toward her death in the forty-degree rain. They intervened only to beat her repeatedly. What sealed her death seems to have been her shameful female body: In her hypothermic delirium, she stripped her clothes off, and so her adoptive mother refused to allow her brothers to bring her inside.[34] Kathryn Joyce has reported dozens of other cases of international adoptees being abused. Twenty Russian adoptees are believed to have been killed by their adoptive parents. This was a factor in Russia's banning of US adoptions in 2012. There is no legal requirement for adoption agencies to check on the welfare of adoptees after adoptions.

Perhaps it is not fair to judge all international adopters by these extreme cases. Most adoptive parents do not abuse their adopted children to death. Yet in 2010, at least forty-one internationally adopted children were removed from their adoptive families and placed in state custody.[35] An astonishing 10 to 25 percent of domestic adoptions are either "disrupted" or "dissolved."[36] As far as I can find, no statistics are kept on rates of failed international adoption. But adoption of older children strongly correlates with higher rates of failure, and international adoptees are often older, so there is every reason to believe that international adoptions fail at a higher rate. In 2013, Reuters did an investigation into abandonments of adopted children in the US and found that 70 percent of children advertised on a Yahoo bulletin board as available for "rehoming" were foreign-born.[37] Every one of these failed adoptions represents a child who was either abused or, devastatingly, rejected.

In this context, although many evangelicals were likely appalled at the separation of children from their parents at the border in 2018, those separations have uncomfortable continuities with the extraction of children from other countries for the booming evangelical adoption market. Still, I do not believe that the Trump administration instituted its zero-tolerance immigration policy in order to procure babies for the adoption market. But that may turn out be a side effect. I also do not believe it was intended, or is likely, to "secure" our borders, any more than the social policies of the Baby Scoop era were intended or likely to reduce premarital sex and out-of-wedlock births.

Making unwed mothers surrender their babies was a kind of social theater designed to demonstrate the disposability of women, protect the fragile status of white middle-class families, and induce sufficient fear to ensure continued control over women's reproductive powers. I believe that Trump's border policy is also a social theater of fear. Trump's senior policy advisor Stephen Miller and others have said as much: These sights would terrorize prospective immigrants, deterring them from trying to come to the US. Yet I don't believe that prospective immigrants are the primary intended audience. Instead, the targeted audience is the US. The cruel border theatrics say to American voters that immigrants' bonds with their children have no value, providing a target for rage that many feel at being unable to securely support and spend time with their own children. As Miller clearly anticipated, even the outrage expressed by many against the 2018 border horrors was useful, confirming a sense among aggrieved Trump voters that liberals care more about immigrants than about working-class Americans. Trump stoked rage at a less deserving "other" who supposedly gets to do what working-class Americans cannot. Earlier, that other was the welfare queen, subsidized with tax dollars to stay out of the job market. Now it is the immigrant stealer of jobs.

A federal judge ordered the Trump administration to reunite all immigrant children under five with their parents immediately, and the rest within a few weeks. But the administration missed its deadlines, telling the judge that nearly half of the children under five had not been reunited with their parents, for various reasons. Some parents had already been deported, and some children had simply been lost. Five years later, many children were still not reunited with their parents; in 2022, seven hundred to one thousand children who had been taken from their parents at the border were still separated from their families.[38]

In recent years, amid repeated bad press over foreign adoptions and the closure of many countries to foreign adoptions, foreign adoptions in the US have dropped dramatically. Between 2004 and 2016, foreign adoptions to the US dropped by 77 percent, and by 2020 (accelerated by the pandemic) foreign adoptions in the US had dropped by 93 percent from 2004 levels.[39] The US's overall adoption rate also fell by 17 percent between 2007 and 2014.[40] In a kind of bookend on the international adoption boom, in 2024 China, which had been a huge supplier of babies to the American adoption market, ended its foreign adoption program.[41] But as one door closes, others are being opened.

The US Supreme Court's new right-wing majority has begun issuing decisions that serve to undermine women's reproductive autonomy and support the taking of children. First, in June 2022, the *Dobbs* decision erased the right to choose whether to gestate and birth a child. As described above, the conservative justices, both in oral argument and in the decision itself, explicitly drew the link between safe haven laws and abortion: The right to abortion and mechanisms to facilitate women's giving up their babies stand in opposition to each other. With abortion now banned at any point in pregnancy in twelve states and at some point before viability in another ten states, abortion is no longer an option for huge numbers of American women.[42] History suggests that the relinquishment of babies for adoption will surge when women no longer have a choice.

Also in 2022, the Court was poised to issue another devastating decision in which safe haven laws and the taking of children figured. On November 9, 2022, the Court heard arguments in *Haaland v. Brackeen*, in which three non-Native adoptive couples claimed their rights were violated by the Indian Child Welfare Act's (ICWA) preference for keeping Native children within their Native families and tribes. The ICWA, which was drafted to stop the practice of taking Native children out of their communities, requires child welfare agencies to prioritize placing children with family members and gives tribes the right to intervene in foster care and adoption proceedings.

The congressional findings for the ICWA are remarkable for recognizing the value of parental and community ties and the costs of sundering them through adoption: "There is no resource that is more vital to the continued existence and integrity of Indian tribes than their children."[43] As the Tribal Chief of the Mississippi Band of Choctaw Indians put it in a hearing on the proposed law, "Culturally, the chances of Indian survival are significantly reduced if our children, the only real means for the transmission of the tribal heritage, are to be raised in non-Indian homes and denied exposure to the ways of their people."[44]

Despite the ICWA, all but one of the adoptive parents were successful in adopting the babies. In one case, the state court ordered adoption outside of the tribe in spite of the law. In another, in the face of prolonged litigation and as childhoods passed by, the tribes gave up their claims. Yet the adoptive parents claimed that their rights were violated by the mere fact that the original family and tribe were considered at all. They argued that the ICWA violates their rights to equal protection because it grants preferences based on race—that is, they claimed that tribal preference was racial preference. As the tribes that filed briefs in the cases pointed out, tribes are cultural and political entities, not races. That is certainly true, yet of course it is not the whole truth—the ICWA is a remedy, among other things, for centuries of race discrimination. But given the current backlash against any efforts to remedy race discrimination, framing tribes as cultural entities was a strategic necessity.

One reason the white adoptive parents of one baby in the case (called Baby O) succeeded in adopting her was because Baby O was not initially identified as being Native American or as having family members who wanted to take her in—because she had been relinquished by her mother at a safe haven site. If the ICWA gives value to family and tribal ties, safe haven laws aim to erase them. The birth mother of Baby O was herself one of the plaintiffs, and she claimed that the ICWA violated her rights by preventing her from choosing her child's adoptive parents. Yet she surrendered her baby under a safe haven law that required her to relinquish all parental rights (she did not claim safe haven laws violate parents' rights). The plaintiffs omitted mention of safe havens from their filings in the case.[45]

Supporters of the ICWA were braced for the Court to eviscerate it, even though it has proven effective in raising rates of kinship placement, and children placed with kin are less likely to stay in or reenter foster care, to be shifted around, or to have mental health issues—such good outcomes that states have begun to model their child welfare policies on the ICWA. These are all effects of *not* taking children from their birthing families and communities, and so the ICWA stands in the way of the right-wing agenda of facilitating such taking.

Chief Justice John Roberts, himself an adoptive parent, chose fellow adoptive parent Justice Barrett to write the Court's decision.[46] The result seemed a foregone conclusion, yet when the decision issued in June 2023, the Court blinked, upholding the ICWA while evading most of the issues by deciding the case largely on standing grounds: The adoptive parents did not have standing to sue because they couldn't show any harm that could be redressed by the Court.[47] It's hard to know why the Court decided against striking down the ICWA or finding tribal preferences to be unlawful race preferences. Perhaps the law's success is too clear, or the case too shaky in its facts, to comfortably support a sweeping new precedent.

There were two dissenters: Justices Thomas and Alito. Alito, with his typical sneer, wrote that Congress "does not have the power to sacrifice the best interests of vulnerable children to promote the interests of the tribes in maintaining membership."[48] He seemed to consider relationships with parents and community irrelevant to the best interests of vulnerable children and tribes to be just a type of club worried about dues payments. Neither Alito nor Thomas are ones to give up, so the ICWA may not be safe for good.

While many Democratic politicians have recently rediscovered their support for abortion rights, there has been insufficient recognition that abortion is only one interconnected part of reproductive justice, or of the broader links between abortion, adoption, and shredded social safety supports for mothers. A woman who can be forced to bear a child because abortion is unavailable, either legally or economically, can also be forced to give that child up, by the law or by economic desperation.

To resist these assaults on reproductive rights, we will have to finally dispense with that optimistic American belief that social problems can be solved without deep structural change. There is no longer wide-open farm country to which we can send poor children. There is no frontier where we can escape our problems. We will solve them not by sundering, but by repairing, our connections to each other.

CONCLUSION:

Crisis and Opportunity

In early 2020, the COVID pandemic began its sweep through the world. In the US, by late March most governors had issued "stay-at-home" orders, banning large gatherings, closing all but "essential" businesses and all schools and childcare centers, and barring visitors from nursing homes. As if in a dystopian science fiction story, the virus and our responses to it targeted social connection, pushing Americans especially away from social goods and into isolation: We stopped going to shared workplaces, stopped using public transit, sidestepped each other on sidewalks. In my part of the country, even outdoor public spaces were closed—city, county, state, and national parks were locked off. In Seattle, city parks eventually reopened, but were emblazoned with threats: CROWDED PARKS LEAD TO CLOSED PARKS signs remained months after research had demonstrated that proximity outdoors carried minimal risk. Public bathrooms went the way of the dodo.

Systems of disconnection reached new heights of cruel absurdity. In the child welfare system, parents struggling to prove their fitness to reunite with their children were allowed visits—even with infants—only through Zoom, attempting to demonstrate through these bizarre sessions that they could connect normally with their children.[1]

The virus even got the last redoubt of public good in the US: The public schools remained closed in most parts of the country for more than a year (in Seattle, they remained closed for nearly a year and a half). Priorities were revealed. Whereas in Europe, schools were closed only briefly, as a last resort, in the US schools closed before bars, restaurants, and gyms and reopened well after them.[2] Childcare centers closed too. The chattering classes suddenly realized that schools *are* childcare. Predictably, these closures meant that many women had to quit their jobs.

Some private employers, particularly wealthy technology corporations, responded by granting parents leave to care for children while schools and daycare were closed. The backlash was swift: The *New York Times* reported that childless employees began complaining that it was unfair that parents were getting "special perks."[3] At Facebook, after the company granted ten weeks of leave for caring for children or elders because schools, childcare, or nursing homes were closed, and granted all employees the bonuses normally reserved for high performers, some childless employees complained that the policies were primarily benefitting parents and argued that those who worked harder should get higher bonuses. When Sheryl Sandberg, the company's chief operating officer, hosted a companywide videoconference in the summer of 2020, more than two thousand employees voted to ask her what more Facebook could do to support nonparents, because its other policies had benefited parents. Sandberg initially responded that she "disagreed with the premise of the question," but employees stated that more than a thousand employees agreed with it and insisted she answer. Around the same time, battles erupted on internal forums at both Twitter and Facebook in which certain parents were criticized for not pulling their weight. At Facebook, things got contentious enough that managers shut down the forums.

In one way, those resenting the benefits were right. A corporation is not a mutual aid society. It is a private, competitive endeavor, for the purpose of profit. The assumption when you take a job at a corporation is that you will be rewarded if you work harder or can claim contribution to higher profits (a distinction often glossed over). By offering what amounted to social benefits, corporations were stepping into a breach that should have been filled by government.

But the backlash revealed a confusion that has a lot to do with why American government doesn't offer these benefits. At Facebook, the leave was not limited to parents; it was for elder care as well. That a significant fraction of employees had no responsibilities for either elders or children says a lot about age and wealth segregation and shrunken nuclear families. That these employees had no shame in admitting their lack of responsibilities demonstrates how profoundly they have internalized a shrunken, competitive sense of self, to the point of economic irrationality: They complained about the equality of the bonuses even though all employees had received larger-than-normal bonuses. That is, what they resented was someone else's having gotten as much as they. This is the sense of fairness gone warped into the politics of resentment.

Even based on a sense that benefits should go only to those who "deserve" them, it fails. Parents deserve leave because they are doing valuable work that sustains even for-profit corporations; there won't be any next generation of Facebook or Twitter employees without parents. Not to mention that, as a parent at Facebook pointed out, taking leave for childcare is not exactly a vacay.

This misunderstanding isn't limited to the corporate world. At the government agency where I work, the issue of parental leave came up before COVID, during a round of snowstorms that shut down snow-hysterical Seattle, leaving employees unable to make it to the office. The agency directed employees to work from home if able, but if an employee was unable to work at home, such as because of power failure or lack of wi-fi or other equipment, and unable to get to the office due to the weather, the employee could take paid administrative time off. At the same time, the agency's existing policy barred employees from working from home when they lacked childcare or eldercare for a dependent they were responsible for. The agency even explicitly stated during the snowstorm that employees home caring for children because schools were closed could not receive paid administrative time off. That is, paid leave was granted for every reason that snow might make an employee unable to work *except for* the need to care for dependents. This policy parallels the eligibility rule in many unemployment insurance systems that a worker must be available for any and all hours of work. Of course, no one can actually work twenty-four-seven, but only limitations caused by childcare responsibilities will render a claimant ineligible. For example, a standard availability questionnaire used by unemployment judges in Washington state asks specifically about childcare responsibilities. These are vestiges of domesticity and the public-private distinction, in which ideal workers and care providers are opposed categories.

To add insult to injury, it was difficult to get people around me to understand this point. When I complained about the policy to a young acquaintance who called herself a feminist, she said to me that she would love to get to take a paid day off to play in the snow. She simply could not understand that childcare is work, that care for dependents is a necessity rather than a luxury, or that parents were being singled out to have their needs left unmet, despite the social value of their parenting. The care work may sometimes be fun and often is rewarding, but since when does being fun or rewarding render work not-work? In fact, in our society, some of the highest paid work is highly rewarding (consider star athletes, movie stars, or surgeons).

I wanted to suggest to my acquaintance that she come over and play in the snow with my children while I worked on the agency's business. The thought was not just snark. We all need to reconceive care work not only as work but as everyone's work. There is no need for everyone to have children (indeed, the planet needs us all not to), but we all share responsibility for our society's children and elders. A society that does not share this responsibility justly is on an ominous path toward dissolution.

Much was made of how COVID increased the visibility of essential care work and the burdens faced by parents. Under the pressure of the pandemic, Congress passed the Families First Coronavirus Response and CARES Acts, which for the first time created nationwide paid family leave. Yet tellingly, while most of the leave the laws provided was paid at 100 percent of workers' salaries, leave to care for children or others was singled out to be paid at only two-thirds of salary. The laws also exempted small businesses from the school and childcare leave requirements.[4]

Yet daycare centers closed by the thousands during the pandemic. Many never reopened. In addition, household workers, including house cleaners and nannies, suddenly without work, were left high and dry. This was especially so for the large number of undocumented workers among them, who could not claim pandemic unemployment benefits.

Congress took a significant step toward support for care work in 2021, with passage of the American Rescue Plan Act. The law gave billions in new money to childcare centers, to keep centers open, support worker pay, and reduce prices for parents. The law also took a step toward child allowances. From March through December 2021, the existing child tax credit was doubled in size and sent as monthly checks.[5] Millions of households didn't have to do anything to get these checks—the IRS sent the checks to any parent who had filed a tax return the previous year. Then America's dysfunctional politics took over. The child allowances expired when Congress refused to enact President Biden's Build Back Better Act, and the childcare funding expired in late 2023.[6] To top it off, many Americans were unaware of the payments, or had no idea whom to thank for them.

These payments were a tremendous aid to parents and children. The child allowances lifted 3.7 million children out of poverty as of December 2021. Parents used the money to pay their housing costs, feed themselves and their children better, to pay down debt, to pay for education, and to worry less. The money especially helped people of color and poor people, and yet it went to nearly all lower- and middle-income parents, which protected it from being tarred as "special benefits."[7] What it did not do was enable parents to work less. This, in America, is generally treated as a good thing, work being our supreme value.

But what if it isn't the only value? What if *not* working also has value? There were signs that Americans were beginning to have this thought during the pandemic, when many workers simply left their jobs. Some labelled this the Great Resignation, but it seemed in fact the end of workers' being resigned to working impossible jobs. More apt was the term "the Big Quit."

There is plenty of work that needs doing, of course, including care work. One step in ensuring the autonomy and dignity of those who perform reproductive labor is to recognize its value. But this step enables further steps: If reproductive labor is valuable, it should be paid for, and then those who do too much of it can do less, can reclaim some time for ourselves. Money is time, and time is possibility, as the feminist activist Selma James has explained. Under capitalism, an employer hires a worker's labor power, extracting value from it and paying only a fraction of that value to the worker. James put it in terms of purchasing labor power by the hour. She writes, "By buying the use of our labor power, the employer buys the right to tell us what to do for a fixed time, for the forty or fifty hours a week that it belongs to him, and to own all that we produce in that time."[8] But the point applies equally to piece work (a.k.a., gig work): The lower the rate of pay, the more hours a worker has to spend working in order to live. This leaves her with little opportunity "to learn, to invent, to create, and to develop and exercise talents," in James's words.[9] To develop autonomy, as Virginia Woolf almost put it, one needs time of one's own.

For this reason, another answer to my acquaintance's quip about wanting a day off to play in the snow is: Yes, so you should! Each of us should have time for play. But that means equitably sharing the work that needs to be done, which can happen only after a just accounting of work, including care work.

The wages for housework movement, of which Selma James was a leader, sought to begin that accounting—to demand that women be paid for housework as the first step toward sharing it equally. It was crucial that the wages for housework movement framed its principles as demands—not policy proposals, not requests or pleas.[10] Unlike those other modes, a demand is not neutral, nor is it polite, and it is directed not only at the powers that be but equally at those in the class on whose behalf the demand is made, in this case, women. A demand is a provocation, and the demand for wages for housework sought, among other things, to provoke women to feel entitled to a wage for their contributions to social good. By demanding wages for housework, the movement ultimately demanded not just money, but power and respect. That framework makes the perspective useful, even though its terminology now feels dated or even inaccessible.

The movement claimed that all women were housewives—that is, that whatever else women do, all women by virtue of their gender were required to do housework. It therefore assumed that there was no need to distinguish between paying women and paying for care work. That claim feels risky now.

For decades, feminists of color have critiqued the tendency of white feminists to make claims on behalf of all women that ignore differences of class and race among women. Many women now pay other women to do their housework.

Marriage once was our primary repository for dependency. It was a standardized deal based on status. It slotted parties into roles based on gender, with the husband providing the wage and the housewife providing the care. But that nuclear family system depended on the status coercion of women and the family wage system, both of which have collapsed. Marriage as a dependency container no longer works. The housewife is now a vanished figure, and the idea of one family member's income being enough to support a whole family seems terribly quaint. Nobody outside of trash TV wants to identify herself as a housewife. One part of the shift is simply a replacement of *housewife* with *stay-at-home mother* (or, even worse, the oxymoronic *nonworking mother*), which signals our shift of attention from house and husband to children. Feminism at least made it embarrassing for grown men to expect women to devote themselves to their care. But this still leaves care of children to women.

This vocabulary shift is just one more capitalist disappearing trick. With all adults in most households working full-time for wages and lip service given to women's equality, the official story is that housework is equally shared. Yet study after study has found that men do far less than half of household chores and care work. Somehow, behind the scenes, women are either doing the bulk of it or hiring others to do it (itself a task). At the same time, they have to keep up the charade of egalitarianism by pretending that extra work simply doesn't exist. The result is an even more profound erasure of women's labor than when it was "housework" and all women were "housewives."

A great deal of housework has in fact been pushed into the low wage market: Large fractions of Americans hire housecleaners, dog walkers, nannies, rideshare drivers, and food and package delivery. In a bitter irony, it's as if we *got* wages for housework, except that instead of the state paying us what we are worth or what we need, the market delivers those doing this work an unreliable pittance, leaving less time for family, self, what we will. This also serves to enable those purchasing this labor to work even longer hours themselves, thus diverting demands for shorter hours and better pay and pushing wages down for everybody. To be fair, increased low-wage work was precisely *not* what the wages for housework movement advocated.

There is another limitation in wages for housework that it shares with the movement for universal basic income: Wages for housework activists sometimes dismissed the demand for childcare and other social goods, seeing childcare either as just another way for the state to control childrearing, or as good but unimportant. James, for example, wrote that what was wanted was money so as to have time. Basic income schemes assume that we can buy everything we need on the market if we only have more money, and thus that the market can provide everything we need. This is simply not correct. The US childcare market was, until COVID, rickety, barely functioning, inadequate to meet the needs of everyone but the wealthiest. Then, with COVID, it collapsed. Similarly, nursing homes during COVID became, in many cases, death traps for both elders and workers, and their chronic understaffing grew to crisis levels, with no signs of relenting years after the pandemic began. Childcare and elder care cannot be provided adequately by the market. Nor can healthcare, or pretty much anything with *care* in the name.

"Free" markets in care simply don't exist. In America, government disciplines labor, first by providing no support for unwaged reproductive labor, thereby forcing mothers of even small children into the labor market at the lowest wages. The government also terrorizes immigrant workers, rendering them vulnerable to workplace exploitation. Meanwhile, government outsources care programs, such as Medicare Advantage, Medicaid, the Children's Health Insurance Program, welfare, and so on, to private companies. Companies like "government services" [*sic*] provider Maximus, insurer United Healthcare, hospice agency Kindred Healthcare, and nursing home chain Genesis Healthcare extract obscene profits from taxpayer subsidies, while delivering the least care they can get away with to the fewest people and getting the most care work out of workers for the lowest wages. Too, companies profit from the human impulse to repair, to provide care for each other, and take pride in work well done despite low wages. Think teachers buying their own school supplies, nursing home employees hurting their backs turning patients to prevent bedsores, mothers doing paid work late at night so that their children get attention before bedtime.

Elon Musk's attack on the federal workforce in 2025 was a logical step in the intensification of capitalism. It was an attack on social goods, through the public servants who provided those goods. Many liberal commentators mischaracterize these attacks as displays of incompetence or ignorance, but destruction and dysfunction are precisely the point. When decimated public institutions no longer successfully provide social goods, the breakdown will be used to justify further privatization and profit extraction from reproductive labor. Not coincidentally, Elon Musk is a supporter of universal basic income, because he believes that most human labor will soon become obsolete.[11] (He believes this even though he has fourteen children, all gestated and birthed by women. Presumably armies of nannies are helping to raise them. At least two of his children were procured in the distorted surrogacy market.)[12]

Wages for housework assumed that housewives would be paid for the reproductive labor they did but did not give attention to how such work would be measured, and anyway the housewife has nearly gone extinct. Basic income drops the assumption of the housewife and delivers an equal sum to all. This puts it in an additional difficulty, in that it fails to account for the unequal burdens of social reproduction. Providing social goods themselves rather than money with which to try to buy them avoids all these pitfalls.

We need socialized solutions for care work, that is, reproductive labor supported at a social rather than individual level, based on need rather than ability to pay. We need time, which is to say money, but, first and foremost, basic needs must be met directly through social institutions. As I describe throughout this book, we've been endlessly told since at least the Civil War, by everyone from Jim DeMint to Eleanor Holmes Norton and the commenters on my family leave article, that robust social welfare programs would foster dependency and interfere with liberty. In fact, such programs would promote liberty.

Our choice is not between autonomy and dependency. Rather, the choice is between a system of fairly shared social supports and a coercive system in which some achieve autonomy at others' expense. To make social provision for basic needs would enhance individual autonomy, as our most successful existing social welfare program, Social Security, demonstrates. At the same time, such social programs would protect the essential ties between people. Without the imperative to extract profits, we could start paying fair wages to those who perform reproductive labor. With respect, power, and decent working conditions, care workers could actually provide care. The wages for housework feminists weren't wrong to worry about state control of childrearing, but the answer is that these social institutions should be subject to democratic control. Childcare centers, like all public schools, should be answerable to the communities they serve.

Nowadays we should leave intimate relations between freely consenting adults to private agreement and contracts. On the other hand, dependency relations cannot be left to contract, because they don't involve equal adults at arm's length. Without social support for reproductive labor, care workers must sacrifice their autonomy by becoming dependent on individuals around them (including men, through marriage). Reproductive labor performed without equitable social support structures creates imbalances of power between care workers and those they depend on to provide financial support for their work. It is not liberty that is threatened by social support for reproductive labor but coercive power.

Society depends on reproductive labor. Therefore, justice requires that society as a whole provide support for that work. To meet human need, social benefits should be delivered directly to those in need, rather than to autonomous families. Furthermore, because capitalist markets simply cannot meet reproductive needs, we must create social institutions to meet those needs directly and democratically, without relying on economic or status coercion to get them met.

By this, I don't only mean state welfare subsidies. I also mean that we need to broaden family structures beyond the pinched confines of the nuclear family, so that mothers and fathers are not left to carry the burden of childrearing and eldercare alone. A first step is simply to imagine the possibility of different family forms, which most mainstream thinkers seem unable to do. Over and over again op-eds bemoan the decline of the two-parent family, noting the correlation between poverty and single-parent households and then urging marriage promotion as the solution. Liberal commentators typically avoid overt moralizing against unwed mothers, but regretfully note the "simple math" that two parents earn more than one and the vanishing likelihood that the US government will ever enact generous enough social supports sufficient to compensate single parents for the absence of a second parent's income. As Melissa Kearney put it in the *New York Times*, we "should be frank about the advantages of a healthy two-parent home for children and challenge ourselves to come up with ways to promote and support that institution."[13] This is the same tired rhetoric as in the 1996 welfare-ending law, which has now had thirty years to promote and support "that institution" without success. Instead, we should challenge ourselves to come up with ways to promote and support extended forms of family. If two people raising a child are better than one, it is simple math that three or four or more would be even better. And we should not accept as inevitable a social system that fails to equitably support reproductive labor.

Each of us enters adulthood in a state of debt that we can only pay forward. The myth of autonomy encourages us to take the perspective of forgetful and ungrateful grown children, ignoring the reproductive labor that brought us to our competent and independent state. Instead, we must take the perspective of the child who will someday mother and the mother who once was mothered. We must be both recipients of care and givers of it. Anything else is unjust and perverts our human nature as well as our politics. As the philosopher Eva Feder Kittay, herself a care provider for a profoundly disabled child, puts it, we are each some mother's child.[14]

As I note in Chapter 3, true democracy depends on ongoing consent from the governed. That is to say, consent must be continually reproduced. Infants must be reared into autonomous citizens who can participate in democratic processes; the sick, elderly, and disabled must receive care to enhance their autonomy; and those who provide this care must receive fair recompense from society. Each of us must have a sense that whatever sacrifices are asked of us, whether of liberty or labor, the burdens and the payoffs are generally fairly shared. It was abundantly clear during the pandemic, when many withheld their consent even to such minimal forms of mutual care as face masking, that wide swaths of America no longer believe there is any such fairness. No robust movement to demand a fair social order has yet emerged.

Nor did a full-throated movement to protect reproductive liberty emerge in time. Even as the likelihood of *Roe*'s demise loomed, Democratic majorities in Congress failed to enact a national law codifying *Roe*. Then, in 2022, the Supreme Court overturned *Roe* and eliminated recognition of the right to abortion. In the months afterward, while Democrats still controlled both chambers of Congress, they did not bother to repeal the Comstock Act. Unleashed by the Court's decision, a federal judge ruled that mailing abortion pills is illegal under the long-dormant Comstock laws.[15]

As of this writing, twelve states have enacted laws banning abortion, and numerous states and municipalities have enacted laws putting bounties on the head of anyone who provides any form of assistance to an aborting woman—just like legislators in 1604, they are targeting "Ayders Abettors and Counselors."[16][17] Mothers have already been arrested for helping their daughters get abortions.[18] Legislators introduced bills to punish women who get abortions with the death penalty.[19] Already, women are facing increasing risks of death from pregnancy. In Texas, since it enacted its ban on abortion, rates of life-threatening sepsis in miscarrying women have shot up, and maternal death rates rose 56 percent in the ban's first year.[20] Pregnancy itself has been criminalized. Several women have already been arrested for their miscarriages, and in Texas, a woman was jailed for five months for allegedly mishandling the remains of her miscarriage.[21] The Supreme Court's decision set us back not fifty years but five hundred years, to capitalism's dawn, when European states sought to subordinate women to capital's imperatives. Witch-burning is the next step.

There will also be modern innovations. In 2025, the grotesqueries of reproductive coercion and care under capitalism converged, when a hospital forced a brain-dead woman in Georgia to be kept "alive" against her family's wishes, to serve as an incubator for her fetus. Because of the state's abortion ban, doctors told the family they couldn't take her off life support until the fetus was "viable." As of this writing, the fetus was not doing well, unlikely to live long or if born alive to ever be able to see or walk. But there's more: The family has to pay for this torture. It may bankrupt them. Because the woman is medically dead, it is unclear whether insurance will cover the treatment.[22] This is a parable of misogynistic capitalism.

In November 2024, America reached an ominous crossroads and chose the darkest path. Capitalist markets have weakened social reproduction to the point of collapse, and fascist political movements channel the resulting fear and rage into further destruction of social institutions. We must organize to resist and reconstruct, whether by protecting public schools, defending immigrants, pressing for social housing, or insisting on the right of all to healthcare, including abortion. As the wages for housework activists recognized, we must make bold demands as an exercise in raising our own expectations. Movements of resistance are opportunities not only to stop further destruction but to proclaim the positive value of social goods. This is a terrible yet exciting moment of open possibility, when the old is dying and the new cannot yet be born.

Notes

Introduction: Welcome to Motherhood! You're Fired.

1. Premilla Nadasen, *Care: The Highest Stage of Capitalism* (Chicago: Haymarket Books, 2023), 30–38.

Chapter 1: Children as Pets

1. Thomas Sigsworth, "Canada vs. U.S. Maternity Leave," *Lowest rates.ca* (blog), March 3, 2015, www.lowestrates.ca/blog/canada-vs-us-maternity-leave-heres-our-experience-both.
2. Erin E. Y. Jefferson, "Will It Ever Change? Lack of Parental Leave and Its Detrimental Effects on Maternal Well-Being," *Lancet Regional Health Americas*, v.5 100572, August 5, 2023, https://pmc.ncbi.nlm.nih.gov/articles/PMC10423924/. Even Oman, a fellow holdout, recently enacted parental leave. "Maternity and Paternity Benefits Launched in Oman," *ILO News*, July 17, 2024, https://www.ilo.org/resource/news/maternity-and-paternity-benefits-launched-oman-pioneering-social-insurance.
3. "Paid Leave in the U.S.," Kaiser Family Foundation, December 17, 2021, www.kff.org/womens-health-policy/fact-sheet/paid-family-leave-and-sick-days-in-the-u-s/.
4. "The U.S. Ranks Last in Every Measure When It Comes to Family Policy," *She the People* (blog), *Washington Post*, June 23, 2014, www.washingtonpost.com/blogs/she-the-people/wp/2014/06/23/global-view-how-u-s-policies-to-help-working-families-rank-in-the-world/.

5. Rachel LaCorte, "Inslee Signs Bill Guaranteeing Paid Family Leave in Washington," *Seattle Times*, July 6, 2017, www.seattletimes.com/seattle-news/politics/inslee-signs-plan-for-paid-family-leave/.
6. Constance Sommer, "The High-Wire Act of Caregiving and Saving for Retirement," *New York Times*, September 9, 2023, www.nytimes.com/2023/09/09/business/retirement-paid-leave-caregiving.html; see also "State Paid Family Leave Laws Across the U.S.," Bipartisan Policy Center, January 16, 2024, https://bipartisanpolicy.org/explainer/state-paid-family-leave-laws-across-the-u-s/; "Paid Parental Leave for Federal Employees, Summary of Paid Parental Leave," U.S. Dept. of Commerce, Office of Human Resources Management, n.d., www.commerce.gov/hr/paid-parental-leave-federal-employees.
7. Kelsey Bolar, "Ben Carson, Critic of 'Government Dependency,' Picked to Lead Housing Agency," *The Daily Signal*, December 5, 2016, http://dailysignal.com/2016/12/05/ben-carson-critic-of-government-dependency-picked-to-lead-housing-agency/.
8. Jim DeMint, *Saving Freedom: We Can Stop America's Slide into Socialism* (Nashville, TN: Fidelis, 2009).
9. Alma Carten, "The Racist Roots of Welfare Reform," *New Republic*, August 22, 2016, https://newrepublic.com/article/136200/racist-roots-welfare-reform.
10. Jeneen Interlandi, "Why Doesn't America Have Universal Healthcare? The Answer Has Everything to Do with Race," *New York Times Magazine*, August 14, 2019.
11. *Smith v. Commissioner*, 40 B.T.A. 1038 (1939), *aff'd*, 113 F.2d 114 (2d Cir. 1940); discussed in Nancy Folbre, *Greed, Lust, and Gender: A History of Economic Ideas* (Oxford: Oxford UP, 2009), 264.
12. Martha Albertson Fineman, *The Autonomy Myth: A Theory of Dependency* (New York: The New Press, 2004), 35–36.
13. Evan Osnos, "The Greenwich Rebellion," *New Yorker*, May 8, 2020.

14. Ann Crittenden, *The Price of Motherhood: Why the Most Important Job in the World Is Still the Least Valued* (New York: Owl Books, 2000), 72–73, quoting Kari Wærness, "The Invisible Welfare State: Women's Work at Home," *Acta Sociologica* (Oslo), supplement, 21 (1978).
15. Nancy Fraser, *Cannibal Capitalism: How Our System Is Devouring Democracy, Care, and the Planet—and What We Can Do About It* (New York: Verso, 2022).
16. *Smith v. Commissioner*, 40 B.T.A. 1038.
17. Crittenden, *Price of Motherhood*, 77.
18. Constance Sommer, "The High-Wire Act of Caregiving and Saving for Retirement," *New York Times*, September 9, 2023, www.nytimes.com/2023/09/09/business/retirement-paid-leave-caregiving.html.
19. "Hospital Average Length of Stay by State," Definitive Healthcare, October 23, 2024, www.definitivehc.com/resources/healthcare-insights/average-length-of-stay-by-state.
20. Austin Frakt, "The Hidden Financial Incentives Behind Your Shorter Hospital Stay," *New York Times*, January 4, 2016, www.nytimes.com/2016/01/05/upshot/the-hidden-financial-incentives-behind-your-shorter-hospital-stay.html.
21. Margot Sanger-Katz, Alicia Parlapiano, and Josh Katz, "A Huge Threat to the U.S. Budget Has Receded. And No One Is Sure Why," *New York Times*, September 4, 2023, www.nytimes.com/interactive/2023/09/05/upshot/medicare-budget-threat-receded.html.
22. "Policy Basics: Temporary Assistance for Needy Families," Center on Budget and Policy Priorities, updated March 1, 2022, www.cbpp.org/research/family-income-support/policy-basics-an-introduction-to-tanf; "Graphical Overview of State TANF Policies as of July 2020," Administration for Children and Families (acf.gov), January 2022, https://acf.gov/sites/default/files/documents/opre/wrd-2020-databook-companion-piece-feb2022.pdf; "Strengthening TANF at 20: A

National View" (links to specific publications), Center for Law and Social Policy, n.d. (CLASP), www.clasp.org/publication/strengthening-tanf-20-national-view/.

23. Personal Responsibility and Work Opportunity Reconciliation Act of 1996, Pub. L. 104-198, 110 Stat. 2105, codified at 21 U.S.C. § 862 and 8 U.S.C. § 1601, www.ssa.gov/OP_Home/comp2/F104-193.html.

Chapter 2: The More Women, the More Witches

1. Associated Press, "Robertson Letter Attacks Feminists," *New York Times,* August 26, 1992, www.nytimes.com/1992/08/26/us/robertson-letter-attacks-feminists.html.
2. Silvia Federici, *Caliban and the Witch* (New York: Autonomedia, 2014), 165.
3. Federici, *Caliban and the Witch*, 76–77.
4. Federici, *Caliban and the Witch*, 86.
5. Federici, *Caliban and the Witch*, 65.
6. Federici, *Caliban and the Witch*, 80.
7. Federici, *Caliban and the Witch*, 80 n.46.
8. Federici, *Caliban and the Witch*, 85.
9. Josephine Billingham, *Infanticide in Tudor and Stuart England* (Amsterdam: Amsterdam UP, 2019), Appendix 1, www.cambridge.org/core/books/abs/infanticide-in-tudor-and-stuart-england/1624-infanticide-act/27AF9A4B2ED42F3947E5F8EC63580F9E.
10. John M. Riddle, *Eve's Herbs: A History of Contraception and Abortion in the West* (Cambridge: Harvard UP, 1997), 134, citing J.H. Aveling, *English Midwives: Their History and Prospects* (London, 1872), 91.
11. Riddle, *Eve's Herbs;* Riddle, *Contraception and Abortion from the Ancient World to the Renaissance* (Cambridge: Harvard UP, 1992).
12. Carla Spivack, "To Bring Down the Flowers: The Cultural Context of Abortion Law in Early Modern England," 14 *Wm. & Mary J. Women & L.* 107, 122 (2007); Riddle, *Eve's Herbs*, 49.

13. W. Jeffrey Hurst and Deborah J. Hurst, "Rue (*Ruta Graveolens*)," Medicina Antiqua, U College London, www.ucl.ac.uk/~ucgajpd/medicina%20antiqua/sa_rue.html; "Foods to Avoid During Pregnancy," Care Hospitals (blog), July 31, 2023, www.carehospitals.com/blog-detail/foods-to-avoid-during-pregnancy/; Olivia Laing, "A Flowered Planet," Aeon newsletter, March 19, 2013, https://aeon.co/essays/the-tangled-roots-of-healing-and-herbalism; "Columbine Flowers for Sale—Buying and Growing Guide," Trees.com, n.d., www.trees.com/flowers/columbine-flower
14. "Witches in the Dock: 10 of Britain's Most Infamous Witch Trials," History Extra, June 8, 2013, www.historyextra.com/period/tudor/witches-in-the-dock-10-of-britains-most-infamous-witch-trials/; first law establishing the death penalty for killing someone through witchcraft passed in 1563: Ellen Castelow, "Witches in Britain," Historic UK, May 29, 2015, www.historic-uk.com/CultureUK/Witches-in-Britain/.
15. Alan MacFarlane, *Witchcraft in Tudor and Stuart England* (Prospect Heights, IL: Routledge, 1970), 15.
16. Federici, *Caliban and the Witch*, 166.
17. Nathan Dorn, "Sir Matthew Hale and Evidence of Witchcraft," Law Librarians of Congress (blog), Library of Congress, October 30, 2021, https://blogs.loc.gov/law/2021/10/sir-matthew-hale-and-evidence-of-witchcraft/; "A Tryal of Witches, at the Assizes Held at Bury St. Edmonds for the County of Suffolk; on the Tenth day of March, 1664. Before Sir Matthew Hale Kt. Lord Chief Baron of His Majesties Court of Exchequer" (London: William Shrewsbury, 1682), Digital Collection, Cornell U, https://digital.library.cornell.edu/catalog/witchcraft097.
18. MacFarlane, *Witchcraft in Tudor and Stuart England*, 67.
19. "A Tryal of Witches at the Assizes Held at Bury St. Edmonds," https://digital.library.cornell.edu/catalog/witchcraft097.
20. Carol F. Karlsen, *The Devil in the Shape of a Woman* (New York: W.W. Norton, 1998), 53.

21. Anne Llewellyn Barstow, *Witchcraze: A New History of the European Witch Hunts, Our Legacy of Violence Against Women* (New York: Pandora/HarperCollins, 1994), 22–23 (she estimates at least one hundred thousand women were executed as witches); Riddle, *Eve's Herbs*, 110 (he suggests that half a million witches were executed, citing Gunner Heinsohn and Otto Steiger, "The Elimination of Medieval Birth Control and the Witch Trials of Modern Times," *International Journal of Women's Studies* 5 (1982), 193–94).
22. Trier: Barbara Ehrenreich and Deirdre English, *Witches, Midwives, and Nurses: A History of Women Healers* (New York: Feminist Press, 2010, first published 1973), 34; Sweden: Brynn Holland, "Beyond Salem: 6 Lesser-Known Witch Trials," History Channel, February 8, 2017 (updated June 27, 2023), www.history.com/news/beyond-salem-6-lesser-known-witch-trials.
23. MacFarlane, *Witchcraft in Tudor and Stuart England*, 105.
24. Federici, *Caliban and the Witch*, 171; see also "Witches in the Dock," History Extra, June 8, 2013, www.historyextra.com/period/tudor/witches-in-the-dock-10-of-britains-most-infamous-witch-trials/; MacFarlane, *Witchcraft in Tudor and Stuart England*, 61, 76, 186.
25. Malcolm Gaskill, *The Ruin of All Witches: Life and Death in the New World* (New York: Knopf, 2022), 14.
26. "Witch Trials in Early Modern Scotland," Wikipedia, https://en.wikipedia.org/wiki/Witch_trials_in_early_modern_Scotland
27. Federici, *Caliban and the Witch*, 171.
28. McFarlane, *Witchcraft in Tudor and Stuart England*, 30.
29. Kate Lohnes, "How Rye Bread May Have Caused the Salem Witch Trials," Britannica, last updated June 13, 2025, www.britannica.com/story/how-rye-bread-may-have-caused-the-salem-witch-trials.

30. "Themes and Variations in Men's and Women's Roles in Colonial America," Digital History, Topic ID 84, 2021, n.d., www.digitalhistory.uh.edu/topic_display.cfm?tcid=84.
31. Gaskill, *The Ruin of All Witches*, 28.
32. Gaskill, *The Ruin of All Witches*, 52.
33. John M. Murrin, "Coming to Terms with the Salem Witch Trials," *Proceedings of the American Antiquarian Society* 110, no. 2 (2003): 316.
34. "Bury St. Edmunds Witch Trials," Wikipedia, https://en.wikipedia.org/wiki/Bury_St_Edmunds_witch_trials; "A Tryal of Witches, at the Assizes Held at Bury St. Edmonds," https://digital.library.cornell.edu/catalog/witchcraft097.
35. Murrin, "Coming to Terms," 315.
36. Murrin, "Coming to Terms," 316; Gaskill, *The Ruin of All Witches*, 88.
37. Riddle, *Eve's Herbs*, 113.
38. Karlsen, *The Devil in the Shape of a Woman*, 14–17.
39. The specific information on Ulalia and Henry Burt comes from family lore and a book their descendant Henry M. Burt wrote, *The First Century of the History of Springfield: The Official Records from 1636 to 1736*, 2 vols. (Springfield, MA, 1898–99), relied on by Gaskill in *The Ruin of All Witches.*
40. Gaskill, *The Ruin of All Witches*, 24.
41. Gaskill, *The Ruin of All Witches*, 24.
42. Gaskill, *The Ruin of All Witches*, 19.
43. Gaskill, *The Ruin of All Witches*, 8, citing Stephen Innes, *Labor in a New Land: Economy and Society in Seventeenth-Century Springfield* (Princeton, NJ: Princeton UP, 1983).
44. Gaskill, *The Ruin of All Witches*, 203.
45. Gaskill, *The Ruin of All Witches*, 8–9.
46. Gaskill, *The Ruin of All Witches*, 39.
47. Colin Dickey, "How New England Blamed 'Witches' for Its Growing Pains," *Slate*, October 31, 2022, https://slate.com/

news-and-politics/2022/10/malcolm-gaskill-ruin-of-all-witches-hugh-parsons-review.html.

48. Gaskill, *The Ruin of All Witches*, 10.
49. Gaskill, *The Ruin of All Witches*, 167.
50. Dickey, "How New England Blamed 'Witches.'"
51. Gaskill, *The Ruin of All Witches*, 205.
52. Murrin, "Coming to Terms," 316–17.
53. Gaskill, *The Ruin of All Witches*, 23.
54. Stacy Schiff, *The Witches: Suspicion, Betrayal, and Hysteria in 1692 Salem* (New York: Back Bay, 2015), 20–22.
55. Schiff, *The Witches*, xii.
56. John M. Murrin, "The Infernal Conspiracy of Indians and Grandmothers," *Reviews in American History,* v.31 no.4, December 2003, 490.
57. Schiff, *The Witches*, 73.
58. Murrin, "Coming to Terms," 347; Karlsen, *The Devil in the Shape of a Woman*, 255.
59. Stacy Schiff, *The Witches*, 347.
60. Karlsen, *The Devil in the Shape of a Woman*, 12. In Ohio in 2022, for example, state legislators debated a law that would require inspection of transgender student athletes' genitals; see Jane Mayer, "State Legislatures Are Torching Democracy," *New Yorker*, August 6, 2022, www.newyorker.com/magazine/2022/08/15/state-legislatures-are-torching-democracy.
61. Francis Floresca, "'We Are All Drinking Other People's Abortions': Kristi Hamrick Testifies on Chemical Abortion Pill Dangers in Texas," *Students for Life* (blog), May 8, 2025, www.studentsforlifeaction.org/we-are-all-drinking-other-peoples-abortions-kristi-hamrick-testifies-on-chemical-abortion-pill-dangers-in-texas/.
62. Rebecca Shabad, "S.C. Republicans propose bill that could subject women who have abortions to the death penalty," NBC News, March 15, 2023, www.nbcnews.com/politics/

politics-news/sc-republicans-propose-bill-subject-women-abortions-death-penalty-rcna75060.

Chapter 3: Just So Stories

1. Clarence Page, "Thomas's Sister's Life Gives Lie to His Welfare Fable," *Chicago Tribune*, July 24, 1991, last updated August 10, 2021, www.chicagotribune.com/news/ct-xpm-1991-07-24-9103220246-story.html.
2. Carole Pateman, *The Sexual Contract* (Boston: Polity, 1988).
3. Publius (attributed to James Madison or Alexander Hamilton), "Method of Guarding Against the Encroachments of Any One Department of Government by Appealing to the People Through a Convention," Federalist No. 49, originally published in the *New York Packet*, February 5, 1788, https://guides.loc.gov/federalist-papers/text-41-50.
4. Thomas Jefferson, "Letter from Thomas Jefferson to Samuel Kercheval," September 5, 1816, Teaching American History, https://teachingamericanhistory.org/document/letter-to-samuel-kercheval/.
5. Mary Anne Case, "Marriage Licenses," 89 *Minnesota L. Rev.* 1758, 1765 (2005), https://scholarship.law.umn.edu/mlr/696/.

Chapter 4: Family Values

1. Stephanie Coontz, *Marriage, A History: From Obedience to Intimacy or How Love Conquered Marriage* (New York: Viking, 2005), 209.
2. Stephanie Coontz, *The Social Origins of Private Life* (New York: Verso, 1988), 132.
3. "Timeline of Women's Suffrage in the United States," Wikipedia, https://en.wikipedia.org/wiki/Timeline_of_women%27s_suffrage_in_the_United_States.
4. Laura Briggs, *Taking Children: A History of American Terror* (Berkeley: U of California Press, 2000), 21.

5. Briggs, *Taking Children*, 22.
6. Debra Michals ed., "Catharine Beecher," National Women's History Museum, 2015, www.womenshistory.org/education-resources/biographies/catharine-esther-beecher.
7. Coontz, *Social Origins of Private Life*, 212; Charles Burroughs, "An Address on Female Education: Delivered in Portsmouth, New-Hampshire, October 26, 1827." (Creative Media Partners, LLC, 2018), www.google.com/books/edition/_/uIixvgEACAAJ?hl=en&sa=X&ved=2ahUKEwjW2fWQvdKJAxX-HDzQIHcWeE0MQ8fIDegQIEhAK.
8. Alexis de Tocqueville, *Democracy in America*, v. 2 (New York: Vintage Books, 1945), 223–25, quoted in Ann Crittenden, *The Price of Motherhood: Why the Most Important Job in the World Is Still the Least Valued* (New York: Owl Books, 2000), 49.
9. Gregory King and Sir William Petty, cited in Nancy Folbre, *Greed, Lust, and Gender: A History of Economic Ideas* (Oxford: Oxford UP, 2009), 28.
10. Crittenden, *Price of Motherhood*, 59.
11. Crittenden, *Price of Motherhood*, 59.
12. Crittenden, *Price of Motherhood*, 61.
13. "Motherhood Wage Gap for Mothers Overall," National Women's Law Center, July 31, 2024, https://nwlc.org/resource/motherhood-wage-gap-for-mothers-overall/; Kathy Gerchiek, "The Wage Gap Is Wider for Working Mothers," Society for Human Resource Management, October 21, 2019, www.shrm.org/topics-tools/news/benefits-compensation/wage-gap-wider-working-mothers; "New Data Shows Just How Little Single Moms Make Compared to Other Parents," Iowa Starting Line, August 7, 2024, https://iowastartingline.com/2024/08/07/new-data-shows-how-little-single-moms-make.
14. Joan Blades and Kristin Rowe-Finkbeiner, *The Motherhood Manifesto: What America's Moms Want—and What to do About It* (New York: Bold Type Books, 2006), 185.

15. Eileen Boris, "The Power of Motherhood: Black and White Activist Women Redefine the 'Political,' " 2 *Yale J. L & Feminism* 25, 26 (1989); "National Association of Wage Earners," Library of Congress, Calvin Coolidge Papers Articles and Essays, Guide to Organizations, People and Topics in Prosperity and Thrift, www.loc.gov/collections/calvin-coolidge-papers/articles-and-essays/guide-to-people-organizations-and-topics/n-to-r/#dtwage; Dorothy Roberts, "Welfare and the Problem of Black Citizenship," 105 *Yale L. J.* 1563, 1570—71, available at https://scholarship.law.upenn.edu/faculty_scholarship/1283/.
16. "Only a Teacher Teaching Timeline," PBS, n.d., www.pbs.org/onlyateacher/timeline.html.
17. Coontz, *Marriage*, chap. 12; Ann Fessler, *The Girls Who Went Away: The Hidden History of Women Who Surrendered Children for Adoption in the Decades Before* Roe v. Wade (New York: Penguin, 2006), 105.
18. Coontz, *Marriage*, 209.
19. Ann Curry, Interview with Rick Warren, NBC News, aired December 2008, excerpt posted December 19, 2008, by Progress Now Colorado Archives, YouTube, 1 min., 44 sec., www.youtube.com/watch?v=X2ZwhdgiBgc.
20. Richard V. Reeves, "How to Save Marriage in America," *The Atlantic*, February 13, 2014, www.theatlantic.com/business/archive/2014/02/how-to-save-marriage-in-america/283732/.
21. Patrick J. Buchanan, *The Death of the West* (New York: Thomas Dunne Books/St. Martin's Press, 2002), 28.

Chapter 5: The Grandmother Hypothesis

1. I am here paraphrasing Jenny Brown, *Birth Strike: The Hidden Fight Over Women's Work* (Oakland, CA: PM Press, 2019), 81–82.
2. Mwenza Blell, "Grandmother Hypothesis, Grandmother Effect, and Residence Patterns," Wiley Online Library,

https://doi.org/10.1002/9781118924396.wbiea2162; Peter S. Kim, James E. Coxworth, and Kristen Hawkes, "Increased Longevity Evolves from Grandmothering," *Proceedings of the Royal Society B*, October 24, 2012, royalsocietypublishing.org/doi/10.1098/rspb.2012.1751; Haider J. Warraich, "'Grandmother Effect' Helps Explain Human Longevity," *Stat*, February 22, 2019, www.statnews.com/2019/02/22/grandmother-effect-helps-explain-human-longevity/.

3. Simon Chapman, Jenny Patay, and Virpi Lummaa, "Limits to Fitness Benefits of Prolonged Post-reproductive Lifespan in Women," *Current Biology* 29, no. 4 (February 18, 2019): 645–50, www.cell.com/current-biology/fulltext/S0960-9822(19)30008-9.
4. Franklin D. Roosevelt, "Message of the President to Congress, June 8, 1934," quoted at SSA.gov, www.ssa.gov/history/whybook.html.
5. "Where the Line is Drawn: From the Indianapolis News," *New York Times*, February 16, 1936, E8; see also "Social Security Act of 1935," VCU Libraries Social Welfare History Project, https://socialwelfare.library.vcu.edu/social-security/social-security-act-of-1935/.
6. Teresa Ghilarducci, "Republicans' Public Opposition to Social Security and Medicare," *Forbes*, November 2, 2019, www.forbes.com/sites/teresaghilarducci/2018/11/02/republican-public-opposition-to-social-security-and-medicare/.
7. Alfred M. Landon, "I Will Not Promise the Moon," Vital Speeches of the Day, October 15, 1936, 26–27, available at https://historymatters.gmu.edu/d/8128.
8. "Social Security Act," Wikipedia, https://en.wikipedia.org/wiki/Social_Security_Act, citing David M. Kennedy, *Freedom from Fear: The American People in Depression and War, 1929–1945* (Oxford: Oxford UP, 1999), 262–66.
9. "Francis Townsend," Wikipedia, https://en.wikipedia.org/wiki/Francis_Townsend; "Townsend Clubs," Encyclopedia.com,

www.encyclopedia.com/history/encyclopedias-almanacs-transcripts-and-maps/townsend-clubs.

10. "Francis Townsend," Wikipedia.
11. "What Is the Average Monthly Benefit for a Retired Worker?" US Social Security Administration FAQ, Topic KA-01903, n.d. www.ssa.gov/faqs/en/questions/KA-01903.html.
12. Jill Quadagno, *The Color of Welfare: How Racism Undermined the War on Poverty* (New York: Oxford UP, 1994), 7.
13. Dorothy Roberts, "Welfare and the Problem of Black Citizenship," 105 *Yale L. J.* 1563, 1577 (1996), available at https://academic.udayton.edu/race/04needs/welfare01c.htm.
14. Quadagno, *Color of Welfare*, 157
15. Quadagno, *Color of Welfare*, 160.
16. "Maximum Taxable Earnings," Social Security Administration, www.ssa.gov/planners/maxtax.html
17. Quadagno, *Color of Welfare*, 160–62.
18. Codified at 20 CFR §404.211. The technical explanation is here, courtesy Social Security: "Computing Your Average Indexed Monthly Earnings," Social Security Administration, n.d. www.ssa.gov/OP_Home/cfr20/404/404-0211.htm. Many finance sites spell it out in simpler terms: see, e.g., "Is the Social Security Retirement Benefit Calculation Based on the Last Forty Years, Or Overall?," Stack Exchange, Personal Finances and Money, May 19, 2015, https://money.stackexchange.com/questions/48203/is-the-social-security-retirement-benefit-calculation-based-on-the-last-40-quart.

Chapter 6: The Girl Who Wouldn't Go Away

1. A version of this chapter first appeared in the *South Seattle Emerald*, January 12, 2020, https://southseattleemerald.com/2020/01/12/essay-the-girl-who-wouldnt-go-away/.
2. Jo Jones and Paul Placek, "Adoption by the Numbers," National Council for Adoption (February 15, 2007), www.

adoptioncouncil.org/publications/2017/02/adoption-by-the-numbers. The 175,000 figure comes from Penelope L. Maza, "Adoption Trends: 1944–1975," the Adoption History Project, U of Oregon, http://pages.uoregon.edu/adoption/archive/MazaAT.htm.

3. "Adoptions in America Are Declining," *The Economist*, June 24, 2017, www.economist.com/news/united-states/21723876-meanwhile-more-children-need-foster-care-adoptions-america-are-declining.
4. Rickie Solinger, *Wake Up Little Susie: Single Pregnancy and Race Before* Roe v. Wade, (New York: Routledge, 1992), 153.
5. Ann Fessler, *The Girls Who Went Away: The Hidden History of Women Who Surrendered Children for Adoption in the Decades Before* Roe v. Wade (New York: Penguin, 2006), 30, citing Sandra Hofferth, Joan R. Kahn, and Wendy Baldwin, "Premarital Sexual Activity Among U.S. Teenage Women Over the Past Three Decades," *Family Planning Perspectives* 19, no. 2 (March–April 1987): 46–53, table 3.
6. Leslie J. Reagan, *When Abortion Was a Crime: Women, Medicine, and Law in the United States, 1867–1973* (Berkeley: U of California Press, 1997), chap. 7.
7. Solinger, *Wake Up Little Susie*, 104.
8. Stephanie J. Ventura and Christine A. Bachrach, "Nonmarital Childbearing in the United States, 1940–1999," *National Vital Statistics Reports* 48, no. 16 (October 16, 2000), www.cdc.gov/nchs/data/nvsr/nvsr48/nvs48_16.pdf.
9. Solinger, *Wake Up Little Susie*, 16.
10. *Seattle Crittenton Home 1954 Report to the Board of Directors*, June Robinson Collection, Seattle Museum of History and Industry.
11. David Wilma, "Florence Crittenton Home for Unwed Mothers Opens in Dunlap on November 21, 1899," HistoryLink, Essay 3128, posted March 24, 2001, www.historylink.org/File/3128.

12. Wilma, "Florence Crittenton Home."
13. Jane Edwards, Interview of Crittenton Society President Jeannette Pai-Espinosa, *First Mother Forum* (blog), May 31, 2012, www.firstmotherforum.com/2012/05/crittenton-today-serving-marginalized.html.
14. *Seattle Crittenton Home 1963 Report to the Board of Directors,* June Robinson Collection, Seattle Museum of History and Industry.
15. Fessler, *Girls Who Went Away*, 39.
16. Meredith Hall, "Shunned," *Creative Nonfiction*, no. 20 (2003), available at www.creativenonfiction.org/online-reading/shunned.
17. *Seattle Crittenton Home 1946 Report to the Board of Directors,* Maida Miller Collection, Seattle Museum of History and Industry; *Seattle Crittenton Home 1956 Report to the Board of Directors,* June Robinson Collection, Seattle Museum of History and Industry; *Seattle Crittenton Home 1966 Report to the Board of Directors,* June Robinson Collection, Seattle Museum of History and Industry; *Seattle Crittenton Home 1968 Report to the Board of Directors,* June Robinson Collection, Seattle Museum of History and Industry.
18. Solinger, *Wake Up Little Susie*, 27.
19. Fessler, *Girls Who Went Away*, 91.
20. Fessler, *Girls Who Went Away*, 37.
21. Solinger, *Wake Up Little Susie*, 6.
22. Elizabeth Tuttle, "Serving the Unmarried Mother Who Keeps Her Child," *Social Welfare* 43 (October 1962), quoted in Solinger, *Wake Up Little Susie*, 6.
23. Hearing transcripts, *New York Times,* quoted in Solinger, *Wake Up Little Susie,* 45–46.
24. Quoted in Solinger, *Wake Up Little Susie*, 47.
25. Fessler, *Girls Who Went Away*, 110.
26. 1.5 million according to Fessler, *Girls Who Went Away*, 8; 2 million according to "Adoption Statistics," the Adoption

History Project, U of Oregon, n.d., https://darkwing.uoregon.edu/~adoption/topics/adoptionstatistics.htm.

27. Rickie Solinger, *Beggars and Choosers: How the Politics of Choice Shapes Adoption, Abortion, and Welfare in the United States* (New York: Hill and Wang, 2001), 74.

Chapter 7: A Right Unknown

1. *Dobbs v. Jackson Women's Health Organization*, 597 U.S. 215, 142 S.Ct. 2228, 2242 (2022).
2. *Dobbs*, 142 S.Ct. at 2249 n.24.
3. Leslie J. Reagan, *When Abortion Was a Crime* (Berkeley: U of California Press, 1997), 10.
4. *Dobbs,* 142 S.Ct. at 2250.
5. Cassandra Tate, "Abortion Reform in Washington State," HistoryLink essay 5313, February 26, 2003, www.historylink.org/file/5313.
6. "Protecting Abortion Access in Seattle," Seattle City Council, 2022, www.seattle.gov/council/issues/past-issues/protecting-abortion-access.
7. Tate, "Abortion Reform."
8. Reagan, *When Abortion Was a Crime*, 11–12.
9. "Comstock Act," Britannica, www.britannica.com/event/Comstock-Act.
10. Aja Romano, "The Right's Moral Panic Over 'Grooming' Invokes Age-Old Homophobia," *Vox*, April 21, 2022, www.vox.com/culture/23025505/leftist-groomers-homophobia-satanic-panic-explained.
11. Rep. Pat Schroeder, "Comstock Law Still on the Books," Congressional floor speech, US House of Representatives, September 24, 1996, Iowa State U Archives of Women's Political Communication, https://awpc.cattcenter.iastate.edu/2017/03/21/comstock-act-still-on-the-books-sept-24-1996/.
12. Reagan, *When Abortion Was a Crime*, 13.

13. Reagan, *When Abortion Was a Crime*, 170.
14. Barbara Winslow, *Revolutionary Feminists: The Women's Liberation Movement in Seattle* (Durham, NC: Duke UP, 2023), 65–66.
15. Harold Rosen, "Psychiatric Implications of Abortion: A Case Study in Social Hypocrisy," 17 *W. Rsrv. L. Rev.* 435 (1965).
16. Reagan, *When Abortion Was a Crime*, 189.
17. Reagan, *When Abortion Was a Crime*, 234.
18. Felicia Kornbluh, *A Woman's Life Is a Human Life: My Mother, Our Neighbor, and the Journey from Reproductive Rights to Reproductive Justice* (New York: Grove Press, 2023), 66.
19. Winslow, *Revolutionary Feminists*, 53–62.
20. Winslow, *Revolutionary Feminists*, 68–70.
21. Schroeder, "Comstock Law Still on the Books."
22. *Roe v. Wade*, 410 U.S. 113, 152–53 (1973).
23. *Roe v. Wade*, 410 U.S. at 152–53.
24. *Roe v. Wade*, 410 U.S. at 158.
25. *Roe v. Wade*, 410 U.S. at 154.
26. *Roe v. Wade*, 410 U.S. at 154.
27. *Roe v. Wade*, 410 U.S. at 159.
28. *Roe v. Wade*, 410 U.S. at 163–65.
29. *Roe v. Wade*, 410 U.S. at 163.
30. *Roe v. Wade*, 410 U.S. at 164.
31. I believe it was Janet Gallagher who coined this phrase. See Gallagher, "Fetus as Patient," in Nadine Taub and Sherrill Cohen eds., *Reproductive Laws for the 1990s* (Totowa, NJ: Humana Press, 1988), 155.
32. "Last Five Years Account for More Than One-Quarter of All Abortion Restrictions Enacted Since Roe," Guttmacher Foundation, January 2016, www.guttmacher.org/article/2016/01/last-five-years-account-more-one-quarter-all-abortion-restrictions-enacted-roe; *Maher v. Roe*, 423 U.S. 464 (1977).
33. *Buck v. Bell*, 274 U.S. 200 (1927).

34. *Skinner v. Oklahoma*, 316 U.S. 535, 541 (1942).
35. Maya Manian, "The Story of *Madrigal v. Quilligan*: Coerced Sterilization of Mexican-American Women," *U of San Francisco Law Research Paper* No. 2018-04, 2, https://papers.ssrn.com/sol3/papers.cfm?abstract_id=3134892.
36. Manian, "Story of *Madrigal v. Quilligan*," 5–7.
37. *Madrigal v. Quilligan*, Civ. No. 75–2057 (C.D. Cal. June 30, 1978).
38. *Relf v. Weinberger*, 372 F. Supp. 1196 (D.D.C. 1974).
39. Brenna Evans, "The Long Scalpel of the Law: How United States Prisons Continue to Practice Eugenics Through Forced Sterilizations," *Minnesota J. of L. & Inequality* (blog), June 7, 2021, https://lawandinequality.org/2021/06/07/the-long-scalpel-of-the-law-how-united-states-prisons-continue-to-practice-eugenics-through-forced-sterilization/.

Chapter 8: No Fault of Her Own

1. Rickie Solinger, *Pregnancy and Power: A Short History of Reproductive Politics in America* (New York: NYU Press, 2005), 146.
2. In 2018, 41 percent of Medicaid recipients were white, 20 percent were African American, and 30 percent were Hispanic. "50 Important Welfare Statistics for 2023," *Lexington Law*, April 10, 2023, www.lexingtonlaw.com/blog/finance/welfare-statistics.html. Whites have always represented the largest fraction of welfare recipients. See Martin Gilens, "How the Poor Became Black," in Sanford F. Schram, Joe Foss, and Richard C. Fording, eds., *Race and the Politics of Welfare Reform* (Ann Arbor, MI: U of Michigan Press, 2003), www.press.umich.edu/pdf/9780472068319-ch4.pdf. Furthermore, whites are disproportionately aided by antipoverty programs. See Tracie Jan, "The Biggest Beneficiary of the Government Safety Net: Working-Class Whites," *Washington Post*, February 16, 2017, www.washingtonpost.com/news/wonk/wp/2017/02/16/the-biggest-beneficiaries-of-the-government-safety-net-working-class-whites/.

3. Ben Heineman et al., "Poverty Amid Plenty: The American Paradox," Report of the President's Commission on Income Maintenance Programs, November 1969, https://babel.hathitrust.org/cgi/pt?id=uc1.b3894373&seq=3, 5.
4. Martin Malin, *Unemployment Compensation in a Time of Increasing Work-Family Conflicts*, 29 *U. Mich. J. L. Ref.* 131, 152 n.72 (1996) (collecting case references to the phrase and locating the origin of the phrase in a model state statute drafted by the Social Security Board).
5. Mark H. Leff, "Consensus for Reform: The Mothers'-Pension Movement in the Progressive Era," *Social Service Review* 47, no. 3 (1973): 404.
6. Excerpted in Gwendolyn Mink and Rickie Solinger, eds., *Welfare: A Document History of US Policy and Politics* (New York: NYU Press, 2003), 61.
7. Linda Gordon and Felice Batlan, "The Legal History of Aid to Dependent Children Program," Virginia Commonwealth U Libraries Social Welfare History Project, April 2020, https://socialwelfare.library.vcu.edu/public-welfare/aid-to-dependent-children-the-legal-history/.
8. Mink and Solinger, *Welfare*, 55.
9. *Smith v. Commissioner*, 40 B.T.A. 1038 (1939).
10. Rickie Solinger, *Beggars and Choosers: How the Politics of Choice Shapes Adoption, Abortion, and Welfare in the United States* (New York: Hill & Wang, 2001), 141.
11. Solinger, *Beggars and Choosers*, 141 n.9.
12. Solinger, *Beggars and Choosers*, 142.
13. Solinger, *Beggars and Choosers*, 143
14. Solinger, *Beggars and Choosers*, 143 n.15 (citing Gilens, "How the Poor Became Black").
15. Solinger, *Beggars and Choosers*, 140.
16. "Background Material and Data on Programs within the Jurisdiction of the Committee on Ways and Means (Green Book, Section 7), Aid to Families with Dependent Children

and Temporary Assistance for Needy Families (Title IV-A)," Government Printing Office, 1998, www.govinfo.gov/content/pkg/GPO-CPRT-105WPRT37945/html/GPO-CPRT-105WPRT37945-2-7.htm.

17. Judith Shulevitz, "Forgotten Feminisms: Johnnie Tillmon's Battle Against 'the Man,'" *New York Review of Books*, June 26, 2018, www.nybooks.com/daily/2018/06/26/forgotten-feminisms-johnnie-tillmons-battle-against-the-man/.
18. "Wages for Housework," Wikipedia, https://en.wikipedia.org/wiki/Wages_for_housework.
19. Emily Callaci, *Wages for Housework: The Feminist Fight Against Unpaid Work* (New York: Seal Press, 2025), 147.
20. "1977 National Women's Conference," Wikipedia, https://en.wikipedia.org/wiki/1977_National_Women%27s_Conference.
21. Callaci, *Wages for Housework*, 152.
22. "1977 National Women's Conference," Wikipedia.
23. Jill Quadagno, *The Color of Welfare: How Racism Undermined the War on Poverty* (New York: Oxford UP, 1994), 65.
24. Alice George, "The 1968 Kerner Commission Got It Right, But Nobody Listened," *Smithsonian Magazine*, March 1, 2018, www.smithsonianmag.com/smithsonian-institution/1968-kerner-commission-got-it-right-nobody-listened-180968318/; see also Quadagno, *Color of Welfare*, 122.
25. National Advisory Commission on Civil Disorders, *Report of the National Advisory Commission on Civil Disorders* (1968), 126, 129, https://belonging.berkeley.edu/sites/default/files/kerner_commission_full_report.pdf?file=1&force=1.
26. National Advisory Commission on Civil Disorders, *Report*, 12.
27. Lawrence Mishel, Elise Gould, and Josh Bivens, "Wage Stagnation in Nine Charts," Economic Policy Institute, January 6, 2015, www.epi.org/publication/charting-wage-stagnation/. On average, wages stayed stagnant, but this average masks very different experiences for different types of workers.

Middle-income earners' wages grew by 6 percent from 1979 to 2015, low earners' fell by 5 percent, and very high earners' wages grew by 41 percent.

28. Arthur Delaney and Ariel Edwards-Levy, "Americans Are Mistaken About Who Gets Welfare," *HuffPost*, February 5, 2018, www.huffingtonpost.com/entry/americans-welfare-perceptions-survey_us_5a7880cde4b0d3df1d13f60b; see also "States with More Black People Have Less-Generous Welfare Benefits," *Washington Post*, June 6, 2017, www.washingtonpost.com/news/wonk/wp/2017/06/06/states-with-more-black-people-have-less-generous-welfare-benefits-study-says/.
29. Quadagno, *Color of Welfare*, 121–22.
30. Ben W. Heineman et al., *Poverty Amid Plenty: The Report of the President's Commission on Income Maintenance Programs*, November 1969, 5, https://babel.hathitrust.org/cgi/pt?id=uc1.b3894373&seq=3.
31. "Workfare," Wikipedia, https://en.wikipedia.org/wiki/Workfare#cite_note-peck-1.
32. A generally forgotten irony of the civil rights movement is that it significantly benefited poor Southern whites, who had been widely disenfranchised, including by poll taxes.
33. Scott J. Spitzer. "Nixon's New Deal: Welfare Reform for the Silent Majority," *Presidential Studies Quarterly* 42 (3): 455–81, July 19, 2012, https://doi.org/10.1111/j.1741-5705.2012.03989.
34. Director of the Office of Economic Opportunity Frank Carlucci, 1971, quoted in Quadagno, *Color of Welfare*, 125–26.
35. Robert James Lampman, *Nixon's Family Assistance Plan*, vols. 57–69 (Madison: Institute for Research on Poverty, U of Wisconsin, 1969), 19–20.
36. Brian Steensland, *The Failed Welfare Revolution: America's Struggle over Guaranteed Income Policy* (Princeton, NJ: Princeton UP, 2011), 161.
37. Quadagno, *Color of Welfare*, 137–40.

38. Jill Quadagno, "Race, Class, and Gender in the U.S. Welfare State: Nixon's Failed Family Assistance Plan," *American Sociological Review* 55, no. 1 (1990): 17, https://doi.org/10.2307/2095700.
39. Associated Press, "Mrs. Chisholm, Mrs. Abzug Introduce Childcare Bill," *New York Times*, May 18, 1971, www.nytimes.com/1971/05/18/archives/mrs-chisholm-mrs-abzug-introduce-child-care-bill.html.
40. Quoted in Quadagno, *Color of Welfare*, 130.
41. Premilla Nadasen, Jennifer Mittelstadt, Marisa Chappell, eds., *Welfare in the United States: A History with Documents, 1935–1996* (New York: Routledge, 2009).
42. Quadagno, *Color of Welfare*, 129.
43. Nadasen et al., *Welfare in the United States*, 55.
44. Tracie McMillan, "How One Company Is Making Millions Off Trump's War on the Poor," *Mother Jones*, January/February 2017, www.motherjones.com/politics/2018/12/how-one-company-is-making-millions-off-trumps-war-on-the-poor/.
45. Michael Greenstone and Adam Looney, "Women in the Workforce: Is Wage Stagnation Catching Up with Them Too?," Brookings Institution, April 1, 2011, www.brookings.edu/blog/jobs/2011/04/01/women-in-the-workforce-is-wage-stagnation-catching-up-to-them-too/.
46. Juliet M. Brodie and Clare Pastore, eds., *Poverty Law, Policy, and Practice* (Boston: Aspen Publishing, 2020), figure 1.4.
47. Working Mothers Issue Brief, June 2016, Women's Bureau, U.S. Dept. of Labor, www.dol.gov/wb/resources/WB_WorkingMothers_508_FinalJune13.pdf.
48. Solinger, *Beggars and Choosers*, 148.
49. Sam Stein, "'A Racist Narrative': Biden Warned of Welfare Mothers Driving Luxury Cars," *Daily Beast*, August 29, 2019, quoting *Newark Post* article, www.thedailybeast.com/when-joe-biden-worried-about-welfare-mothers-driving-luxury-cars.

50. "The New Covenant: Responsibility and Rebuilding the American Community," Remarks of Gov. Bill Clinton at Georgetown U, October 23, 1991, transcript at www.ibiblio.org/pub/academic/political-science/speeches/clinton.dir/c24.txtp.
51. Mary Farrel, Asaph Glosser, and Karen Gardiner, "Child Support and TANF Interaction: Literature Review, for the Office of the Assistant Secretary for Planning and Evaluation," U.S. Dept. of Health and Human Services, April 10, 2003, https://aspe.hhs.gov/basic-report/child-support-and-tanf-interaction-literature-review-april-2003#3.
52. Elaine Sorensen and Helen Olivery, "Child Support Reforms in PRWORA," Urban Institute, 11 n.1, February 1, 2002, www.urban.org/research/publication/child-support-reforms-prwora.
53. Carolyn Skorneck, "Clinton Says He Will Sign Welfare Overhaul; House Passes It," *Associated Press,* July 31, 1996, cited in https://en.wikipedia.org/wiki/Personal_Responsibility_and_Work_Opportunity_Act; full article: https://web.archive.org/web/20200807202843/; www.apnews.com/f11a3d867b896908c6c598e31fb94ff8.

Chapter 9: Faulty Vessels

1. See, e.g., *In re A.C.,* 573 A.2d 1235 (D.C. Cir. 1990); *Pemberton v. Tallahassee Mem. Regional Med. Ctr., Inc.,* 66 F. Supp.2d 1247 (N.D. Fla. 1999); *In re Madyun* (D.C. Super. Ct. 1986), appended to *In re A.C.,* 573 A.2d at 1260–64.
2. See, e.g., *In re Jamaica Hospital,* 128 Misc.2d 1006, 491 N.Y.S.2d 898 (1985); *Fosmire v. Nicoleau,* 551 N.E. 2d 77, 75 N.Y.2d 218 (1990); *Wons v. Public Health Trust of Dade County,* 500 So.2d 679 (1987).
3. See *Burton v. Florida,* 49 So.3d 263 (Fla.App.1 Dist. 2010); *Taft v. Taft,* 388 Mass. 331, 332, 446 N.E.2d 395, 396 (1983).
4. *Pemberton,* 66 F. Supp.2d 1247. This was not an appeal of the decision (as federal district courts lack appellate jurisdiction

over state court decisions). Rather, Ms. Pemberton filed suit against the hospital alleging violations of her constitutional right to bodily integrity and privacy, due process, professional negligence, and false imprisonment. The court dismissed all her claims. Because of this procedural posture, the decision is doubly disappointing. Surveying appellate court cases and published trial cases downplays the real magnitude of the harm being done to women. Not only do these represent only a fraction of the incidents in which pregnant women are subject to compelled medical care, but even where courts overturn lower court's orders, in most cases the harm to the individual women has already been done. To stop this problem requires not only educating trial judges, but presenting doctors and hospitals with a likelihood that they will face liability for compelled medical care. Ms. Pemberton's suit and that in *Hamilton* cited below are the only ones I've seen that are not just appeals, but suits for damages. The failure of these suits is likely to discourage future suits.

5. The court's decision virtually erased the midwife, seeming to assume that birth without a doctor is the same as, and implicitly as crazy as, an unattended birth.
6. *Pemberton*, 66 F.Supp.2d at 1251–52.
7. *In re Madyun*, appended to *In re A.C.*, 573 A.2d at 1260–64 (cited to at 1252–53 n.23).
8. Hospitals typically apply a protocol that delivery should be accomplished within twenty-four hours of waters breaking. This is based on statistical risk factors and assumptions about how risks should be weighed as well as about the normal length of labor. According to practitioners I've talked to in Seattle, there has been a pattern of conflict between the Somali immigrant community and obstetricians in Seattle because of the dissonance between Somali expectations that first births often take a long time and US medical assumptions about the appropriate length of birth. The result, I understand, is a shift

in medical practice in Seattle toward accepting long labors as a normal variant and away from intervention based solely on the passing of the twenty-four-hour mark.

9. *In re A.C.*, 573 A.2d at 1260.
10. *In re A.C.*, 573 A.2d at 1262.
11. Although my focus here is on pregnant women, the cases involving postpartum women so overlap the pregnancy cases that it is distorting to speak of the former without also addressing the latter.
12. *In Re Jamaica Hospital*, 128 Misc.2d 1006, 491 N.Y.S.2d 898 (1985).
13. *In Re Jamaica Hospital*, 128 Misc. at 1008, 491 N.Y.S.2d at 898.
14. *Fosmire*, 551 N.E.2d at 84. The woman had informed her doctor early in her pregnancy of her religious objection to transfusion. The court did not take note of the question of the duties of a doctor in this situation and whether that ought to alter the medical calculus weighing the risks and benefits of vaginal versus C-section birth. It seems to me that a doctor who does not adjust his caregiving in this situation is highly negligent.
15. *Fosmire*, 551 N.E.2d at 84.
16. In one case, the D.C. Circuit overrode a nonpregnant woman's decision in the interests of her seven-month-old child. *In re President & Directors of Georgetown College, Inc.*, 331 F.2d 1000 (D.C. Cir. 1964).
17. *In re A.C.*, 573 A.2d at 1256 (Belson, J., concurring in part and dissenting in part).
18. For example, see Daniel R. Levy, "The Maternal-Fetal Conflict: The Right of a Woman to Refuse a Cesarean Section Versus the State's Interest in Saving the Life of the Fetus," 108 *West Va. L. Rev.* 97 (2005); *In re A.C.*, 573 A.2d at 1256 (Belson, J., concurring in part and dissenting in part).
19. The single apparent exception I found, *Hamilton v. McAuliffe*, 277 Md. 336, 353 A.2d 634 (1976), is distinguished by its

procedural posture. Nearly a year after a judge granted an order to authorize a blood transfusion of a gunshot victim who had sole custody of his two-year-old son, the man filed a civil rights action asking for a declaratory judgment. The appeals court dismissed the claim as involving no actual controversy (since of course the medical emergency for which he required transfusion was long over and there was no reason Hamilton was likely to need any further transfusion). Thus, I think this exception does not disprove the rule that father's rights to refuse medical care are protected, as mothers' and pregnant women's are not. I think one would find the discrepancy even greater if one looked at orders requested and granted, not just at decisions on appeal.

20. *Burton*, 49 So.3d at 263.
21. *Burton*, 49 So.3d at 264.
22. *Taft*, 388 Mass. at 332.
23. *Taft*, 388 Mass. at 332.
24. *Taft*, 388 Mass. at 334, citing *Doe v. Doe*, 365 Mass. 556, 557, 314 N.E.2d 128 (1974) and *Planned Parenthood of Cent. Mo. v. Danforth,* 428 U.S. 52, 96 S.Ct. 2831 (1976).
25. *Taft*, 388 Mass. at 334–35.
26. *Taft*, 388 Mass. at 334.
27. Wendy Adele Humphrey, "'But I'm Brain Dead and Pregnant': Advance-Directive Pregnancy Exclusions and End-of-Life Wishes," 21 *Wm. & Mary J. Women & L.* 669 (2015), https://scholarship.law.wm.edu/cgi/viewcontent.cgi?article=1410&context=wmjowl.
28. "Pregnancy Exclusions: What Is a Pregnancy Exclusion?" Compassion and Choices, n.d., https://compassionandchoices.org/resource/pregnancy-exclusions/.
29. Judgment, *Muñoz v. John Peter Smith Hosp.*, No. 096-270080-14 (96th Judicial Dist. Court, Tarrant Cnty., Tex. Jan. 24, 2014).
30. *See Jefferson v. Griffin Spalding County Hospital*, 247 Ga. 86, 87 and 90, 274 S.E.2d 457, 458 and 460 (1981).

31. That is, it could both be the case that a woman has no right to intrude in her own body to terminate a pregnancy and that no one else has the right to intrude in her body either.
32. 410 U.S. at 154, 93 S.Ct. at 727 (citing *Jacobson v. Massachusetts*, 197 U.S. 11, 25 S.Ct. 358 (1905); *Buck v. Bell*, 274 U.S. 200, 47 S.Ct. 584 (1927)).
33. One thinks of Socrates's criticism of craftsmen's tendency to think their technical expertise gives them moral expertise.
34. 142 S.Ct. 2228.
35. *Dobbs*, 142 S.Ct. at 2242.
36. *Bowers v. Hardwick*, 78 U.S. 186 (1986).
37. See *Cruzan by Cruzan v. Director, Missouri Dept. of Health*, 497 U.S. 261, 269, 110 S.Ct. 2841 (1990) (citing *Schloendorff v. Society of N.Y. Hospital*, 211 N.Y. 125, 129–30, 105 N.E. 92, 93 (1914)); see also *In re Conroy*, 98 N.J. 321, 336, 486 A.2d 1209, 1222 (1985).
38. *Cruzan*, 497 U.S. at 270, 110 S.Ct. at 2847 (citing *In re Quinlan*, 70 N.J. 10, 355 A.2d 647, cert. denied sub nom *Garger v. New Jersey*, 429 U.S. 922, 97 S.Ct. 319 (1976)); see also *U.S. v. Charters*, 829 F.2d 479, 491 and nn.18–19 (4th Cir. 1987). Notably, the Quinlan decision relied on *Roe*.
39. *Union Pacific R. Co. v. Botsford*, 141 U.S. 250, 251, 11 S.Ct. 1000, 1001 (1891).
40. *McFall v. Shimp*, 10 Pa.D. & C.3d 90, 91 (Allegheny County Ct. 1978).
41. See, e.g., *In re A.C.*, 573 A.2d at 1249.
42. *In re A.C.*, 573 A.2d at 1249 (citing *In re Boyd*, 403 A.2d 744,750 (D.C. 1979)).
43. Janet Gallagher, "Prenatal Invasions & Interventions: What's Wrong with Fetal Rights," 10 *Harv. Women's L. J.* 9, 27–28 (1987).
44. *Strunk v. Strunk*, 445 S.W.2d 145, 147–48 (Ky. 1969) (finding that the parents of a retarded boy could authorize his donation of a kidney to his sibling because the boy had a strong interest in his sibling's survival).

45. *In re Richardson*, 284 So.2d 185, 187 (La. Ct. App. 1973) (holding that a minor cannot be compelled to donate a kidney to his sister).
46. See, e.g., *In re Phillip B.*, 156 Cal. Rptr 48, 51 (Cal. Ct. App. 1976); *In re MCauley*, 565 N.E.2d 411, 412 (Mass. 1991). Courts ordering medical care for children over parents' wishes frequently cite *Prince v. Massachusetts*, 321 U.S. 158 (1944) (holding that a parent may not have her children distribute religious tracts on a highway if it places them in danger).
47. *Burton*, 49 So.3d at 263.
48. *Burton*, 49 So.3d at 264.
49. *Planned Parenthood v. Casey*, 505 U.S. 883 (1992).
50. Judge B. Lynn Winmill, Memorandum Decision and Order, *Almerico v. Denney*, April 6, 2021, U.S. District Court for the District of Idaho (1:18-CV-00239-BLW), 14–15, available at https://compassionandchoices.org/wp-content/uploads/2024/04/2021-04-06-0071-memorandum-decision-and-order-the-motion-for-summary-judgment-filed-by-plaintiffs-docket-no-62-wm.pdf.
51. See, e.g., Levy, "The Maternal-Fetal Conflict," 108 *West Va. L. Rev*. at 107, citing *Harper v. Herman*, 499 N.W.2d 472, 474 (Minn. 1993).
52. See, e.g., *Farwell v. Keaton*, 240 N.W.2d 217 (Mich. 1976); *Rhodes v. Ill. Cent. Gulf R.R.*, 665 N.E.2d 1260 (1996); *Gilger v. Hernandez*, 997 P.2d 305 (Utah 2000).
53. *Farwell*, 240 N.W.2d at 284.
54. See, e.g. *Yu v. New York, N.H. & H.R. Co.*, 145 Conn. 451, 144 A.2d 56 (1958) (common carriers); *Anderson v. Atchison, T. & S.F.R. Co.*, 333 U.S. 821, 68 S.Ct. 854 (1948); *Bessemer Land & Improvement Co. v. Campbell*, 121 Ala. 50, 25 So. 793 (1898); *Carey v. Davis*, 190 Iowa 720, 180 N.W. 889 (1921) (employers to employees); *West v. Spratling*, 204 Ala. 478, 86 So. 32 (1920) (innkeepers to their guests); *Farmer v. State*, 224 Miss. 96, 79 So.2d 528 (1955) (jailer to his prisoner), cited in *Farwell*, 240 N.W. 2d at 291.

55. *Harris v. Pennsylvania R. Co.*, 50 F.2d 866 (4th Cir. 1931) (holding there is a duty of rescue by masters to crewmen). Cited in *Farwell*, 240 N.W. 2d at 291. *See also Hutchinson v. Dickie* (162 F.2d 103 (6th Circ 1947) (finding duty of a yacht owner to his guest).
56. See, e.g., Levy, "The Maternal-Fetal Conflict," 108 *West Va. L. Rev.* at 110.
57. I see a direct analogy with *Burton*—her other children, her "crew," were put in danger by requiring her to rescue her fetus through months of bed rest.
58. See, e.g., *McFall*, 10 Pa.D. & C.3d at 90; *In re Richardson*, 284 So.2d at 187.
59. *McFall*, 10 Pa.D. & C.3d at 92 (emphasis in the original).
60. *Cruzan*, 497 U.S. at 280, 110 S.Ct. at 2852.
61. *St. Mary's Hospital v. Ramsey*, 465 So.2d 666, 668, (Fla. 4th DCA 1985).
62. *Fosmire*, 75 N.Y.2d at 227. See also Am. Jur. § 452, "Death, the right to die, generally."
63. *See Norwood Hospital v. Munoz*, 409 Mass. 116, 125–26, 564 N.E.2d 1017, 1023 (1991) (finding that where the decision-maker choosing to discontinue care is the same one who will die, the state's concern is weakened, because there is no vulnerable life in need of protection from another).
64 Gallagher, "Prenatal Invasions & Interventions," 10 *Harv. Women's L. J.* at 24 (surveying cases).
65. See, e.g., *Winston v. Lee*, 470 U.S. 753, 105 S.Ct. 1611 (1985) (finding surgery on a shooting suspect to remove a bullet that could be used as evidence against him to be an impermissible search and seizure and violation of his bodily integrity); *Rochin v. California*, 342 U. S. 165, 166, 173–74 (1952) (forced stomach pumping); *Stouffer v. Reid*, 413 Md. 491, 993 A.2d 104 (2010) (overturning court order for a prisoner to submit to dialysis, on grounds that the prison's interest in maintaining order did not outweigh the prisoner's right to refuse medical treatment). Most jurisdictions recognize even the right of involuntarily committed

mental patients to refuse treatment, at least in theory, if not always in practice, see *Washington v. Harper*, 494 U. S. 210, 229, 236 (1990) (forced administration of antipsychotic drugs); see also William M. Brooks, "Reevaluating Substantive Due Process as a Source of Protection for Psychiatric Patients to Refuse Drugs," 31 *Ind. L. Rev.* 937 (1998).

66. Gallagher, "Prenatal Invasions & Interventions," 10 *Harv. Women's L. J.* at 29.
67. Gallagher, "Prenatal Invasions & Interventions," 10 *Harv. Women's L. J.* at 25.
68. Gallagher, "Prenatal Invasions & Interventions," 10 *Harv. Women's L. J.* at 25, quoting testimony of Prof. Rhonda Copelon before the House Committee on the Judiciary Subcommittee on Civil and Constitutional Rights, April 3, 1985, 19.
69. See John A. Robertson, "Procreative Liberty and the Control of Conception, Pregnancy, and Childbirth," 69 *Va. L. Rev.* 405, 437 (1983); Levy, "The Maternal-Fetal Conflict," 108 *West Va. L. Rev.* at 110 and 124. See also *In re A.C.*, 573 A.2d at 1256 (Belson, J., concurring in part and dissenting in part) (arguing that because the pregnant woman "has undertaken to bear another human being" she has incurred a duty to her fetus).
70. See, e.g., *In re A.C.*, 573 A.2d at 1256 (Belson, J., concurring in part and dissenting in part) (finding the uniqueness of pregnancy justifies unique impositions on pregnant women's autonomy).

Chapter 10: The Prisoner's Dilemma

1. Michael Burke, "Welfare Reform Twenty Years Later: What Worked, What Didn't," *USA Today*, August 21, 2016, www.usatoday.com/story/news/2016/08/21/welfare-reform-20-years-later/88389666/.
2. Robert A. Moffitt, "From Welfare to Work: What the Evidence Shows," Brookings Institution, January 2, 2022, www.brookings.edu/research/from-welfare-to-work-what-the-evidence-shows/.

3. "Work, Welfare, and Families," 2000, *Living with Welfare Reform: A Survey of Low Income Families in Illinois*. Chicago: Chicago Urban League and UIC Center for Urban Economic Development 25. Cited in Linda Burnham, "Welfare Reform, Family Hardship, and Women of Color," *Annals of the American Academy of Political and Social Science* 577 (2001): 38–48.
4. Tracie McMillan, "How One Company Is Making Millions Off Trump's War on the Poor," *Mother Jones*, January/February, 2017, www.motherjones.com/politics/2018/12/how-one-company-is-making-millions-off-trumps-war-on-the-poor/.
5. Paula Span, "Hospice Is a Profitable Business, but Nonprofits Mostly Do a Better Job," *New York Times*, June 10, 2023, www.nytimes.com/2023/06/10/health/hospice-profits.html; Lily Meyersohn, "Profit-Obsessed Private Equity Is Now Dominating the US Hospice System," *Jacobin*, May 25, 2023, https://jacobin.com/2023/05/private-equity-hospice-care-profit-regulation/.
6. Kimberly Bonvissuto, "Aegis Living Settles Staffing Lawsuit for $16.25 Million Despite 'Fervently Disputed' Allegations," *McKnight's Senior Living*, August 25, 2021, www.mcknightsseniorliving.com/news/aegis-living-settles-staffing-lawsuit-for-16-25-million-despite-fervently-disputed-allegations/.
7. Nancy Folbre, *The Invisible Heart: Economics and Family Values* (New York: New Press, 2001), 111–13.
8. The Child Tax Credit was made fully refundable in 2021 under the American Rescue Act. "Policy Basics: The Child Tax Credit," Center on Budget and Policy Priorities, www.cbpp.org/research/federal-tax/the-child-tax-credit.
9. Elizabeth Warren and Amelia Warren Tyagi, *The Two-Income Trap: Why Middle-Class Parents Are Going Broke* (New York: Basic Books, 2003), 5–6.
10. Warren and Tyagi, *Two-Income Trap*, 59–63.
11. Power of Women Collective, 1975, quoted in Kathi Weeks, *The Problem with Work* (Durham, NC: Duke UP, 2011), 129.

12. Weeks, *Problem with Work*, 135.
13. *Borelli v. Brusseau*, 16 Cal Rptr 2d (Cal. Ct. App. 1993), cited in Joan Williams, *Unbending Gender: Why Family and Work Conflict and What to Do About It* (Oxford: Oxford UP, 2000), 119–20, and Crittenden, *The Price of Motherhood*, 64.
14. *Johnson v. Calvert*, 851 P.2d 776 (Cal. 1993), quoting John Lawrence Hill, "What Does It Mean to Be a Parent: The Claims of Biology as the Basis for Parental Rights," 66 *NYU L. Rev.* 353, 415 (1991), discussed in Jennifer Hendricks, *Essentially a Mother: A Feminist Approach to the Law of Pregnancy and Motherhood* (Oakland: U of California Press, 2023), 134–39.
15. *In re Baby M*, 537 A.2d 1227 (N.J. 1988).
16. Hendricks, *Essentially a Mother*, 139.
17. "Surrogacy Laws: The Best States for Compensated Surrogacy," Creative Family Connections, n.d., https://creativefamilyconnections.com/us-surrogacy-law-map/; compare that map to one not updated since 2021: "U.S. Surrogacy Laws by State," Worldwide Surrogacy Specialists LLC, February 15, 2021, www.worldwidesurrogacy.org/blog/u-s-surrogacy-laws-by-state.
18. *Perry-Rogers v. Fasano*, 17 N.Y.S.2d 19 (App.Div. 2000).
19. See, e.g., "What Is Evo Devo?", Interview with Cliff Tabin, Nova, October 25, 2009, www.pbs.org/wgbh/nova/article/what-evo-devo/; Brian K. Hall, "Evolutionary Developmental Biology (Evo-Devo): Past Present, and Future," *Evolution: Education and Outreach* 5, June 8, 2012, https://evolution-outreach.biomedcentral.com/articles/10.1007/s12052-012-0418-x.
20. Danielle Braff, "Desperately Seeking Surrogates," *New York Times Magazine*, April 2, 2022, www.nytimes.com/2022/04/02/style/surrogate-shortage-us-pandemic.html.
21. Beth Braverman, "How Much Surrogacy Costs and How to Pay for It," *US News and World Report*, May 30, 2023, https://money.usnews.com/money/personal-finance/family-finance/

articles/how-much-surrogacy-costs-and-how-to-pay-for-it.

22. "Military Wives Turn to Surrogacy: Labor of Love or Financial Boost," ABC News, October 14, 2010, https://abcnews.go.com/GMA/Parenting/military-wives-surrogates-carrying-babies-love-money/story?id=11882687; Sally Howard, "The Most Sought-After Surrogates in the World," *The Telegraph*, May 7, 2015, www.telegraph.co.uk/women/mother-tongue/11583541/US-army-wives-the-most-sought-after-surrogates-in-the-world.html.
23. Habiba Nosheen and Hilke Schellmann, "The Most Wanted Surrogates in the World," *Glamour*, October 4, 2010, www.glamour.com/story/the-most-wanted-surrogates-in-the-world.
24. David Dodge, "Meet the Women Who Become Surrogates," *New York Times Magazine*, February 15, 2021, www.nytimes.com/2021/02/15/parenting/fertility/surrogates-new-york.html.
25. Anugrah Kumar, "Military Wives Used as Breeder Stock by Surrogacy Industry," *The Christian Post*, May 2, 2017, www.christianpost.com/news/military-wives-used-as-breeder-stock-by-surrogacy-industry.html.
26. Aishvarya Kavi, "Pete and Chasten Buttigieg Welcome Two Children to Their Family," *New York Times*, September 4, 2021, www.nytimes.com/2021/09/04/us/politics/pete-chasten-buttigieg-children.html; Meredith Deliso, "Pete Buttigieg, Husband, Introduce Their Two New Babies in Family Photo," ABC News, September 4, 2021, https://abcnews.go.com/Politics/pete-buttigieg-husband-introduce-babies-family-photo/story?id=79832236; Chris Cohen, "Pete Buttigieg's Paternity Leave Was Complicated. Here's What He Learned," *GQ*, June 14, 2024; www.gq.com/story/pete-buttigieg-paternity-leave.
27. Personal Responsibility and Work Opportunity Reconciliation Act of 1996, Pub. L. 104-198, 110 Stat. 2105, codified at 21 U.S.C. § 862 and 8 U.S.C. § 1601, www.ssa.gov/OP_Home/comp2/F104-193.html.

28. *Hoffman Plastic Compounds, Inc., v. NLRB*, 535 U.S. 137 (2002).
29. Arlie Russell Hochschild, "Love and Gold," in Barbara Ehrenreich and Arlie Russell Hochschild, eds., *Global Woman: Nannies, Maids, and Sex Workers in the New Economy* (New York: Henry Holt, 2002), 22.

Chapter 11: Orphan Trains and Immigrant Cages

1. John Rothwell, "Protesters Demand Bethany End Contract After Accepting Children Separated at the Border," *The Rapidian*, June 21, 2018, https://therapidian.org/protesters-demand-bethany-christian-services-end-contract-after-accepting-separated-children-us-bord.
2. Amy Littlefield and Tina Vasquez, "Bethany Christian Services Is Fostering Migrant Kids. It Also Has a History of Coercive Adoptions," *Rewire News Group*, June 27, 2018, https://rewire.news/article/2018/06/27/christian-group-fostering-migrant-kids-history-coercive-adoptions/.
3. The Dick and Betsy DeVos Foundation donated $25,000 to Bethany in 2015 and 2016, while the Richard and Helen DeVos Foundation outlined $2.5 million in planned and executed donations to Bethany in its 2016 filing alone. Brian DeVos—a cousin of Betsy DeVos's husband, Dick—was the Senior Vice President for Child and Family Services at Bethany as recently as 2015, and Maria DeVos—who is married to Dick DeVos's brother Doug—has served on the board of Bethany. Littlefield and Vasquez, "Bethany Christian Services Is Fostering Migrant Kids," *Rewire News Group*, June 27, 2018, https://rewirenewsgroup.com/2018/06/27/christian-group-fostering-migrant-kids-history-coercive-adoptions/; "Good Samaritan Announces the Hiring of Its New Executive Director," Good Samaritan, November 2023, https://goodsamottawa.org/news/good-samaritan-announces-the-hiring-of-its-next-executive-director/; "Maria DeVos Joins Spectrum Health Board of Trustees," Spectrum

Health, July 19, 2010, https://newsroom.spectrumhealth.org/maria-devos-joins-spectrum-health-foundation-board/; Dan MacGuill, "Christian Nonprofit Faces Scrutiny Over Government Foster Care Contract for Separated Children," *Snopes*, July 11, 2018, www.snopes.com/news/2018/06/26/bethany-christian-services-family-separation-betsy-devos/.

4. Charles Loring Brace, *The Dangerous Classes of New York and Twenty Years' Work Among Them* (New York: Wynkoop & Hallenbeck, 1872), i–ii, 225–27, 234–35, excerpt at the Adoption History Project, https://pages.uoregon.edu/adoption/archive/BraceDCNY.htm.
5. Kristin F. Johnson, *The Orphan Trains* (Minneapolis: Abdo Publishing, 2012), 99.
6. Johnson, *Orphan Trains*, 97.
7. Kathryn Joyce, *Child Catchers: Rescue, Trafficking, and the New Gospel of Adoption* (New York: Hachette, 2013), 46.
8. Laura Briggs, *Taking Children: A History of American Terror* (Berkeley: U of California Press, 2000), 51.
9. John Sciamanna, "New Indian Child Welfare Regulations Released," Child Welfare League of America, 2016, www.cwla.org/new-indian-child-welfare-regulations-released/.
10. Mary Eschelbach Hansen, "Using Subsidies to Promote the Adoption of Children from Foster Care," *Journal of Family Economic Issues* 28, no. 3 (September 1, 2007): 377–93, https://pmc.ncbi.nlm.nih.gov/articles/PMC2646856/.
11. Morgan B. Ward Doran and Dorothy E. Roberts, "Welfare Reform and Families in the Child Welfare System," 61 *U. Maryland L. Rev.* 386 (2002), https://scholarship.law.upenn.edu/faculty_scholarship/586/?.
12. "Summary of Reforms Made by Public Law 104–193," U.S. House of Representatives Committee on Ways and Means, 104th Congress, November 6, 1996, www.govinfo.gov/content/pkg/CPRT-104WPRT27305/html/CPRT-104WPRT27305.htm.

13. "Adoption Credit," Internal Revenue Service, updated May 29, 2025, https://www.irs.gov/taxtopics/tc607.
14. "Adoption Tax Credit," Wikipedia, https://en.wikipedia.org/wiki/Adoption_tax_credit.
15. Kathryn Joyce, "Orphan Fever: The Evangelical Movement's Adoption Obsession," *Mother Jones*, May/June 2013, www.motherjones.com/politics/2013/04/christian-evangelical-adoption-liberiae.
16. For example, see *Jamie Ivey* (blog), "143 Million Orphans," January 30, 2008, www.jamieivey.com/143-million-orphans/; archived copy of deleted post: https://web.archive.org/web/20221127082915/http://jamieivey.com/143-million-orphans/. There is even an organization with that title: www.foreverfamily.org/.
17. "Baby Kimball Tragedy Spurs Newborn Surrender Legislation," *King County Council News*, March 6, 2018, https://kingcounty.gov/council/news/2018/March/03-06-newborn.aspx.
18. Carol Sanger, "Infant Safe Haven Laws: Legislating in the Culture of Life," 106 *Colum. L. Rev.* 753, 779 (2006), https://scholarship.law.columbia.edu/cgi/viewcontent.cgi?article=1182&context=faculty_scholarship.
19. Brief for American Center for Law & Justice et al. as Amici Curiae Supporting Defendant-Appellant at 2, *Carhart v. Ashcroft*, sub nom. *Carhart v. Gonzales*, 413 F.3d 791 (8th Cir. 2005) (No. 04-3379), quoted in Sanger, "Infant Safe Haven Laws," 106 *Colum. L. Rev.* at 786.
20. Associated Press, "Forty-Three Babies Given Up Under Washington's Safe Haven Law," *Spokesman-Review*, April 10, 2017, www.spokesman.com/stories/2017/apr/10/43-babies-given-up-under-washingtons-safe-haven-la/.
21. Gaby Galvin, "A Split Over Safe Havens," *US News & World Report,* July 10, 2018, www.usnews.com/news/healthiest-communities/articles/2018-07-10/baby-boxes-safe-haven-laws-a-last-resort-to-curb-infant-abandonment.

22. Dana Goldstein, "Drop Box for Babies: Conservatives Promote a Way to Give Up Babies Anonymously," *New York Times*, August 6, 2022, www.nytimes.com/2022/08/06/us/roe-safe-haven-laws-newborns.html.
23. Hannah Howard, "Safe Haven Laws: An Invitation to Life," Charlotte Lozier Institute, December 1, 2021, https://lozierinstitute.org/safe-haven-laws-an-invitation-to-life/.
24. JoNel Aleccia, "This Shoreline Woman Has Adopted Abandoned Babies—Twice—and Look at Them Now," *Seattle Times*, April 2, 2016, www.seattletimes.com/seattle-news/abandoned-as-babies-teens-urge-use-of-safe-haven-sites/.
25. Goldstein, "Drop Box for Babies," www.nytimes.com/2022/08/06/us/roe-safe-haven-laws-newborns.html.
26. Katherine F. Stanger-Hall and David W. Hall, "Abstinence-Only Education and Teen Pregnancy: Why We Need Comprehensive Sex Education in the U.S.," *PLoS One*, Public Library of Science, 6(10):e24658, October 14, 2011, doi: https://journals.plos.org/plosone/article?id=10.1371/journal.pone.0024658.
27. Merritt Tierce, "The Abortion I Didn't Have," *New York Times Magazine*, December 2, 2021, www.nytimes.com/2021/12/02/magazine/abortion-parent-mother-child.html.
28. Katharina Buchholz, "US Abortion Rate Ticks Up After Three-Decade Decline," *Statista*, January 16, 2022, www.statista.com/chart/19490/us-abortion-rate-guttmacher-institute/.
29. UNICEF, "State of the World's Children," 2015, www.unicef.org/media/84891/file/SOWC-2015.pdf
30. Kylie Crossland, "As Policies Tighten, International Adoptions Continue to Decline," *World News Group*, April 1, 2016, https://wng.org/sift/as-policies-tighten-international-adoptions-continue-to-decline-1617252197.
31. Kathryn Joyce, "The Trouble with the Christian Adoption Movement," *New Republic*, January 11, 2016, https://newrepublic.com/article/127311/trouble-christian-adoption-movement.

32. Barbara Demick, "The Chinese Adoptees Who Were Stolen," *New Yorker*, May 23, 2025, www.newyorker.com/news/american-chronicles/the-chinese-adoptees-who-were-stolen.
33. Adeel Hassan, "Oldest Institution of Southern Baptist Convention Reveals Past Ties to Slavery," *New York Times*, December 12, 2018, www.nytimes.com/2018/12/12/us/southern-baptist-slavery.html.
34. Kathryn Joyce, "Hana's Story: An Adoptee's Tragic Fate, and How It Could Happen Again," *Slate*, November 9, 2013, www.slate.com/articles/double_x/doublex/2013/11/hana_williams_the_tragic_death_of_an_ethiopian_adoptee_and_how_it_could.html. This story became the basis for a novel; see David Guterson, *The Final Case* (New York: Knopf, 2022).
35. Brandy Mounts and Loretta Bradley, "Issues Involving International Adoption," *The Family Journal* 28, no. 1 (November 25, 2019), https://journals.sagepub.com/doi/10.1177/1066480719887494.
36. "Discontinuity and Disruption in Adoption and Guardianships," Child Welfare Information Gateway, August 21, 2021, www.childwelfare.gov/resources/discontinuity-and-disruption-adoptions-and-guardianships/.
37. Megan Twohey, "Americans Use the Internet to Abandon Children Adopted from Oversees," *Reuters*, September 9, 2013, www.reuters.com/investigates/adoption/#article/part.
38. The Biden administration's Family Reunification Task Force states there are seven hundred, but the ACLU claims the number is closer to one thousand, see Rebecca Beitsch, "Biden Administration Has Reunited 500 Families Separated Under Trump," *The Hill*, October 7, 2022, https://thehill.com/policy/national-security/3678196-biden-administration-has-reunited-500-families-separated-under-trump/; Aline Barros, "Five Years Later, Work of Reuniting Families Separated at U.S.-Mexico Border Remains Unfinished," *Voice of America*, June 11, 2022, www.voanews.com/a/

five-years-later-work-of-reuniting-families-separated-at-us-mexico-border-remains-unfinished/6610677.html.

39. Abby Budiman and Mark Hugo Lopez, "Amid Decline in International Adoptions to U.S., Boys Outnumber Girls for the First Time," Pew Research Center, October 17, 2017, www.pewresearch.org/short-reads/2017/10/17/amid-decline-in-international-adoptions-to-u-s-boys-outnumber-girls-for-the-first-time/.
40. Katherine Wiles, "International Adoptions Dropped by Nearly Half in 2020. But COVID Only Helped to Accelerate a Years'-Long Decline," *Market Watch*, November 13, 2021, www.marketwatch.com/story/international-adoptions-dropped-by-nearly-half-during-2020-but-covid-19-only-helped-to-accelerate-a-years-long-decline-11636496504.
41. Emily Feng, "China Ends International Adoption. Reactions Range from Shock to Relief," *National Public Radio*, October 17, 2024, www.npr.org/sections/goats-and-soda/2024/10/17/g-s1-28521/china-adoption-international.
42. Abortion in the United States Dashboard, Kaiser Family Foundation, updated June 2, 2025, www.kff.org/womens-health-policy/dashboard/abortion-in-the-u-s-dashboard/.
43. Indian Child Welfare Act, 25 U.S.C. § 1901(3).
44. *Choctaw Indians v. Holyfield*, 490 U.S. 30, 34 (1989) (quoting hearings on S. 1214 before the Subcommittee on Indian Affairs and Public Lands of the House Committee on Interior and Insular Affairs, 95th Cong., 2d Sess., at 193 (1978)).
45. Rebecca Nagle, "The Story of Baby O—and the Case That Could Gut Native Sovereignty," *The Nation*, November 6, 2022, www.thenation.com/article/society/icwa-supreme-court-libretti-custody-case/.
46. Joan Biskupic, "Chief Justice John Roberts Prepares to Take the Stage for Impeachment Trial," CNN, January 7, 2020, updated January 17, 2020, www.cnn.com/2020/01/17/politics/john-roberts-senate-impeachment-trial/index.html.

47. *Haaland v. Brackeen*, 599 U.S. 255, 143 S.Ct. 1609 (2023).
48. *Haaland v. Brackeen*, 143 S.Ct. at 1684.

Conclusion: Crisis and Opportunity

1. Eli Hager, "When Foster Parents Don't Want to Give Back the Baby," *New Yorker*, October 16, 2023, www.newyorker.com/magazine/2023/10/23/foster-family-biological-parents-adoption-intervenors.
2. Anya Kamenetz, "Lessons from Europe, Where Cases Are Rising but Schools Are Open," National Public Radio, November 13, 2020, www.npr.org/2020/11/13/934153674/lessons-from-europe-where-cases-are-rising-but-schools-are-open.
3. Daisuke Wakabayashi and Sheera Frenkel, "Parents Got More Time Off. Then the Backlash Started," *New York Times*, September 5, 2020, www.nytimes.com/2020/09/05/technology/parents-time-off-backlash.html.
4. "Paid Sick Days and Paid Leave Provisions in FFCRA and CARES Act," Center for Law and Social Policy, May 6, 2020, www.clasp.org/publications/fact-sheet/paid-sick-days-and-paid-leave-provisions-ffcra-and-cares-act/.
5. Tami Luhby, "Biden Administration Renews Effort to Get Child Tax Credit to Low-Income Families," CNN, May 11, 2022, www.cnn.com/2022/05/11/politics/child-tax-credit-low-income-families/index.html.
6. Kate Watkins, Rebecca Thiess, and Laura Pontari, "What Happens When States No Longer Have Federal Pandemic Child Care Dollars?" Pew Charitable Trusts, March 21, 2024, www.pewtrusts.org/en/research-and-analysis/articles/2024/03/21/what-happens-when-states-no-longer-have-federal-pandemic-child-care-dollars.
7. Leah Hamilton, Stephen Roll, Mathieu Despard, Elaine Maag, Yung Chun, Laura Brugger, Michal Grinstein-Weiss, "The Impacts of the 2021 Expanded Child Tax Credit on Family

Employment, Nutrition, and Financial Well-Being," Brookings Institution, April 13, 2022, www.brookings.edu/articles/the-impacts-of-the-2021-expanded-child-tax-credit-on-family-employment-nutrition-and-financial-well-being/.

8. Selma James, "Marx and Feminism" (1983), in *Sex, Race, and Class: The Perspective of Winning: A Selection of Writings, 1952–2011* (Oakland, CA: PM Press, 2012), 147–60.
9. James, "Marx and Feminism," 152.
10. Kathi Weeks, *The Problem with Work* (Durham, NC: Duke UP, 2011).
11. John Csiszar, "Elon Musk Says Basic Income Is Inevitable: Here's Why He Thinks That's a Bad Thing," *Nasdaq*, March 27, 2025, www.nasdaq.com/articles/elon-musk-says-universal-income-inevitable-why-he-thinks-thats-bad-thing.
12. Skyler Caruso, "Every Woman Elon Musk Has Children With—and How They Feel About Their Blended Family," *People*, April 1, 2025, https://people.com/all-about-elon-musk-mothers-of-children-blended-family-8668121.
13. Melissa Kearney, "The Explosive Rise of Single-Parent Families Is Not a Good Thing," *New York Times*, September 17, 2023, www.nytimes.com/2023/09/17/opinion/single-parent-families-income-inequality-college.html.
14. Eva Feder Kittay, *Love's Labor* (New York: Routledge, 1999), 23.
15. Judge Matthew J. Kacsmaryk, Memorandum Opinion and Order, *Alliance for Hippocratic Medicine v. U.S. Food and Drug Administration*, April 7, 2023, US District Court for the Northern District of Texas, Amarillo Division (2:22-CV-223-Z), https://fingfx.thomsonreuters.com/gfx/legaldocs/myvmojgodvr/ND%20Texas%20Abortion%20Pill%20Ruling%202023-04-07.pdf.
16. Abortion in the United States Dashboard, Kaiser Family Foundation, updated September 2, 2025, www.kff.org/womens-health-policy/dashboard/abortion-in-the-u-s-dashboard/.

17. Erin Coulehan, "Abortion 'Bounty' Laws in States Like Texas and Oklahoma: How They Work," *Teen Vogue*, July 7, 2022, www.teenvogue.com/story/abortion-bounty-laws.
18. Associated Press, "Louisiana Woman Pleads Not Guilty After Allegedly Giving Abortion Pills to Her Teen," CBS News, March 12, 2025, www.cbsnews.com/news/louisiana-woman-pleads-not-guilty-abortion-case-pills-doctor-teen/; Margery A. Beck, "Nebraska Mother Sentenced to Two Years in Prison for Giving Abortion Pills to Pregnant Daughter," Associated Press, September 22, 2023, https://apnews.com/article/abortion-charges-nebraska-sentence-36b3dcaadd6b-705ca2315bc95b99bdc1.
19. Rebecca Shabad, "SC Republicans Propose Bill That Would Subject Women Who Have Abortions to the Death Penalty," NBC News, March 15, 2023, www.nbcnews.com/politics/politics-news/sc-republicans-propose-bill-subject-women-abortions-death-penalty-rcna75060.
20. Lizzie Presser, Andrea Suozzo, Sophie Chou and Kavitha Surana, "Texas Banned Abortion. Then Sepsis Rates Soared," *ProPublica*, February 20, 2025, www.propublica.org/article/texas-abortion-ban-sepsis-maternal-mortality-analysis; "Mothers Living in Abortion Ban States at Significantly Higher Risk of Death During Pregnancy and Childbirth," Gender Equity Policy Institute, April 2025, https://thegepi.org/maternal-mortality-abortion-bans/.
21. Jessica Valenti, "Breaking: Police & Nurses Conspired to Fabricate Evidence Against Brittany Watts, Suit Says," Abortion Every Day, January 14, 2025, https://jessica.substack.com/p/breaking-police-and-nurses-conspired; "Criminalizing Pregnancy," Abortion Every Day, January 9, 2025, https://jessica.substack.com/p/catholic-hospital-refuses-to-provide; "Texas Jailed a Miscarriage Patient for Five Months, " Abortion Every Day, May 20, 2025, https://jessica.substack.com/p/texas-jailed-a-miscarriage-patient.

22. Cody Alcorn, "Family Says Woman Declared Brain Dead but Pregnancy Continues Under State Law," 11 Alive, May 13, 2025, www.11alive.com/article/news/local/family-claims-atlanta-nurse-declared-brain-dead-kept-alive-pregnancy/85-eac5257d-a329-4dd7-b80f-5c0ecd30225a; as regards insurance coverage, see Wendy Adele Humphrey, "'But I'm Brain Dead and Pregnant': Advance-Directive Pregnancy Exclusions and End-of-Life Wishes," 21 *Wm. & Mary J. Women* & L. 669, 674 n.23 (2015), https://scholarship.law.wm.edu/cgi/viewcontent.cgi?article=1410&context=wmjowl.

Acknowledgments

While writing this book, I was prone to the self-pitying delusion that I was laboring alone and unnoticed—the autonomy myth, internalized. At crucial moments, numerous people shattered that delusion and gave me essential support. Sharon Crowley provided meticulous and insightful editing (any errors in the book are entirely mine). Bob Anderton, bike lawyer, secured the excellent settlement for my crash injuries that financed a sabbatical, enabling me to finish and publish this book. The good work of the staff of She Writes Press brought this book to the light of day. Anne Depue, thank you for believing in this book and striving mightily to get it published—and never firing me. I am indebted to Martha Albertson Fineman, whose book *The Autonomy Myth* provided the crucial conceptual starting point for this book.

Without numerous childcare workers I could not have raised my children, gone to paid work in their early years, or snatched moments to begin writing this book. First and foremost, Terza Satow (of blessed memory), talented childcare worker and dear friend, provided skilled care to my children in our home. Over the years, as a childcare center worker and later nanny, Terza cared for hundreds of children with dedication and creativity. Despite the infusions of care she provided to the world, when she became sick and needed healthcare, she lost her house and her livelihood. But her work lives on, in the numerous flourishing humans she helped raise. I am grateful, too, to the immigrant childcare workers of the Refugee Women's Alliance and El Centro de la Raza, bringing skill from all over the world to the great work of reproducing our corner of it.

And, of course, I am so grateful for Jonathan, a dedicated and skilled care worker, without whose unceasing support and belief this book would not exist.

Author Bio

Carolyn McConnell is a lawyer and an activist dedicated to resisting attacks on public services. She has published extensively on reproductive rights, feminism, and women's history and holds graduate degrees in philosophy from Johns Hopkins University and nonfiction writing from the University of Iowa. She lives in Seattle, Washington.

Author photo © Natalya McConnell

Looking for your next great read?

We can help!

Visit www.shewritespress.com/next-read or scan the QR code below for a list of our recommended titles.

She Writes Press is an award-winning independent publishing company founded to serve women writers everywhere.